ALSO BY SYLVIA BROWNE

THE SECRET HISTORY OF PSYCHICS

How to Separate Fact
From Fiction—and Tap Into Your
Own Psychic Abilities

SYLVIA BROWNE

with Lindsay Harrison

A FIRESIDE BOOK
Published by Simon & Schuster

NEW YORK   LONDON   TORONTO   SYDNEY

Fireside
A Division of Simon & Schuster, Inc.
1230 Avenue of the Americas
New York, NY 10020

First Fireside trade paperback edition May 2010

For information about special discounts for bulk purchases,
please contact Simon & Schuster Special Sales
at 1-866-506-1949 or business@simonandschuster.com.

The Simon & Schuster Speakers Bureau can bring authors
to your live event. For more information or to book
an event contact the Simon & Schuster Speakers Bureau
at 1-866-248-3049 or visit our website
at www.simonspeakers.com.

Designed by Ruth Lee-Mui

Manufactured in the United States of America

5   7   9   10   8   6   4

The Library of Congress cataloged the hardcover edition as follows:
Browne, Sylvia.
The truth about psychics / by Sylvia Browne with Lindsay Harrison.
p. cm.
"A Fireside Book."
1. Parapsychology. 2. Psychics. 3. Occultism. 4. Spirituality.
I. Harrison, Lindsay. II. Title
BF1031.B77 2009
133.8—dc22
2009015967

ISBN 978-1-4391-4972-0
ISBN 978-1-4391-5050-4 (pbk)
ISBN 978-1-4391-5565-3 (ebook)

Originally published as *The Truth About Psychics* in 2009 by Fireside.

From Sylvia:

*For Michael—at long last,
the love of my life.*

From Lindsay:

For Mom, as always and for always.

CONTENTS

INTRODUCTION

Difficult times cause all of us to reevaluate our lives, and open our eyes and hearts to new ways of seeing the world around us. Never before in my more than half a century as a spiritual psychic have so many clients come to me asking for my help. Every day, I see people struggling with tough questions and situations, as their normal issues are only exacerbated by the unfortunate events unfolding in the larger world around us.

Some are reeling from devastating losses—of loved ones, of marriages, of jobs, of homes, of financial security, of their basic sense of physical and emotional well-being.

Others are struggling with feelings of depression, anger, betrayal, hollowness, loneliness, emptiness, fear of an impending undefined threat of darkness.

Still others find themselves going through the necessary motions of their lives, fresh out of enthusiasm, unable to remember the last time they laughed and really meant it, or believed in something that actually mattered.

Difficult times can bring out the worst in some people. Unscrupulous corporate giants making multi-million-dollar bonuses amid company layoffs. Mortgage lenders pushing bad loans onto unsuspecting home buyers. And even some purported psychics who seek to profit off the bad luck and gullibility of those in need.

But at the same time, I've been heartened to see the generosity that many in the world have offered to our brothers and sisters who are suffering. There are those who open their homes and hearts to a family member who has lost a job, and people who rally around a friend who is hurting. Whether you realize it or not, when you reach out to someone in need to offer a helping hand—even in a small way—you're reconnecting to the larger spiritual world.

What so many of us are yearning for is a reconnection with our own God-centered spirituality, where you'll find truth, and comfort, and peace, and faith, and joy, and clarity, and genuine hope, and very real answers to very real day-to-day problems.

These people who come to me are on a search as old as humankind, a search I took myself, a search I finally learned doesn't lead "out there somewhere" but instead leads "in here," deep inside each of us where our own spirits wait for us to discover them, explore, and just listen—because they hold wisdom greater than our conscious minds can dream of. They hold our sanctity and our eternity for safekeeping until we go Home again. They hold the certainty that not only will things be okay soon, they're okay *now*, our conscious minds just can't fathom the bigger picture that gives us the context we need to understand the "why" of what's happening to us.

Within this book you'll find the road map of my journey to the divine peace of spirituality, and the many journeys that paved the way for the rest of us. My prayer is that somewhere in these pages you'll rediscover the spark of the sacred light inside you—the spark you were born with, your birthright from your Creator—so that tomorrow, and the day after that, and every day for the rest of this lifetime on earth you'll live with the confidence that God, His Angels, and the infinite spirit world are beside and inside you, just waiting for you to open your arms to them.

—Sylvia C. Browne

PART I
A SPIRITUAL ODYSSEY

1

MY OWN ODYSSEY BEGINS

I can't imagine my life as a psychic without a lifetime equally devoted to God and spirituality.

But then, I can't imagine any life on this rough earth without the comfort, healing, purpose, and joy to be found in God's arms and in spirituality, where His infinite mysteries and answers lie waiting.

I was lucky (although I would never have used that word when I was a child). I never had to wonder whether the spirit world existed. I knew it did. I saw it, I heard it, and I sensed it all around me, whether I wanted to or not. Without my brilliantly psychic and deeply spiritual grandmother Ada Coil there to explain what was happening and build a bridge between my unique reality and the sanctity of where it came from, I'm sure I would have lost my sanity. (There are those who would argue that the debate about my sanity rages on, but I stopped listening to *them* decades ago.) Grandma Ada educated me about the gifts I was born with and helped me appreciate them instead of fearing them. She also taught me never to stop questioning, learning, studying, and exploring every aspect of spirituality that keeps our genetic connection to God thriving and relevant.

She inspired the spiritual journey to which I've devoted my life and gave me her clear footsteps to follow as I started, just as this book is my way of giving you mine.

As some of you already know, I'm a third-generation psychic. Among my particular gifts from birth were clairvoyance (the ability to see beings that originate in other dimensions) and clairaudience (the ability to hear voices and sounds that originate in other dimensions). For added flair, I was even born with a caul, or fetal membrane, around my head, which according to ancient legend is the sign of a psychic child. So when the spirit world came to me long before I would ever have thought of seeking it out, I didn't understand it at first, but there was certainly no mistaking it.

I was five years old when I had my first psychic vision. We were at a family dinner when I looked over to see the faces of both my great-grandmothers melting like lava running slowly down their necks, leaving nothing but their skulls behind. The only thing that shocked me even more than this horrifying sight was the fact that no one else seemed to be seeing it but me— either that or they were awfully nonchalant about it. Less than two weeks later, both great-grandmothers died. And with the logic of a child, I was sure that somehow, because I was the only one who'd seen those melting faces, I was responsible for killing them. It was Grandma Ada who explained that I'd done nothing wrong, I'd just been given a visual form of psychic information about their impending deaths.

At around that same time I discovered (or, in my opinion, was inflicted with) the random, involuntary ability to view the insides of people who had serious medical conditions, as if I were looking at an X-ray. A neighbor or family friend or door-to-door salesman would stop by and all I would see was a blocked colon or a diseased gallbladder floating around the room.

I turned to Grandma Ada again, asking how I could go about getting rid of this supposed "gift" so that I wouldn't have to spend the rest of my life surrounded by melting faces and ravaged organs. She patiently pointed out that God gave me this gift, and gave it to me for a reason, so refusing it wasn't an option. I could, though, ask Him in my prayers not to show me anything I wasn't old enough or emotionally equipped to handle. I did that, and my prayers were answered. The visions didn't go away, but they were never again as graphic and terrifying.

In fact, on a couple of occasions I was grateful for them when they helped to make Grandma Ada very happy. One night she was terribly upset after unsuccessfully searching the house for a steel strongbox filled with important papers she needed. (Like all psychics, she was psychic about everyone but herself. If you lose your keys, I'll tell you exactly where they are. If I lose mine, I'm as stumped as you are.) We were in her bedroom when she explained what the problem was, and at that moment a petite white-haired woman materialized, whom I recognized to be Grandma Ada's mother, and pointed to the back of a massive bureau. I reported this to Grandma Ada, frankly proud to be seeing a spirit she didn't see for a change, and it jarred her memory of slipping the strongbox behind that bureau months earlier where no one (including her, obviously) would think to look for it.

On another evening we were all gathered in the living room when I saw a man's form take shape behind Grandma Ada's left shoulder. I was sitting on the floor beside her and whispered, "Grandma, who is that man behind you?"

My parents had long since learned to ignore this kind of thing, so they just glanced over, saw nothing, rolled their eyes, and went back to their reading while Grandma Ada asked, "What does he look like?"

I described him—tall, reddish hair, round wire-rimmed glasses. Then I added, "There's a string around his neck, and it has a horn on it that he uses to listen to people's chests."

I'd never seen quite so much joy on her face as she instantly recognized it as her Uncle Jim, a doctor who'd died in a flu epidemic twenty-four years earlier. She was thrilled that he was there with her, and I was thrilled that I'd facilitated a reunion that made someone I adored so happy. And between those two spirit encounters with loved ones she missed so much, I started thinking maybe this psychic thing wasn't so bad after all.

I began seeing spirits as clearly as I saw everyone else. They especially filled my bedroom at night, which frightened me, so Grandma Ada gave me a flashlight. (To this day I can't sleep in a completely dark room. I'm not frightened anymore—it's just annoying, like trying to lie down and relax in the middle of a convention.) I also began "knowing things" without having a clue how or why I knew them.

I announced my grandfather's death to my family several minutes before my father rushed in to break the news.

I answered the door before anyone knocked and knew who was going to be standing there before I opened it.

One afternoon I pulled my father out of a movie theater in a panic screaming, "Sharon can't breathe!" We arrived home to discover that my little sister had collapsed with double pneumonia, and the doctors said later that Daddy had reached the emergency room with Sharon with only moments to spare.

A little classmate of mine came to show me the crepe paper witch costume she planned to wear for Halloween trick-or-treating that night. The instant she stepped in the door, I "saw" her costume bursting into flames. Within minutes, while she was prancing around the room perfecting her menacing witch moves, she whirled too close to the wall heating grate and, identical to my vision, her costume ignited. I'm convinced that "seeing" this before it actually happened allowed me to help rather than panic, as I immediately threw her to the ground and rolled her up in an area rug before she even had time to scream. She left the house, completely unharmed, to go find a replacement for her ruined costume.

I "saw" my friend Joan violently slamming her head against the dashboard of a blue car, and it was such a clear, horrible vision that I told her about it and begged her not to get in any blue cars for a while. Within weeks she found herself climbing into the passenger seat of a blue car to run errands with a family friend, then remembered my warning and stayed home instead. A few hours later the brakes failed and the blue car was wrapped around a telephone pole. The family friend and the driver's side suffered minor damage, but the passenger seat where Joan would have been sitting was destroyed.

Of course, I was a child, with what I prefer to look back on as "guileless candor," so not all of my psychic efforts were humanitarian. I remember showing off by telling my mother where my daddy really was when she thought he was at work, for example, and describing with uncanny accuracy the lovely blond woman he was visiting. (If you'd known my mother, you wouldn't have blamed my daddy any more than I did. As I've often said, my theory about why he never left her is that he didn't want to have to kiss her goodbye.)

And then one night when I was eight years old, my life changed, and it would never be the same again.

I was in my bedroom, under strict orders to go to sleep, so I was wide awake, playing with my flashlight, shining it idly around the room. Suddenly, with no warning, the light began to grow and intensify until all I could see was a white-gold glow. And from its core I heard a woman's voice, clear and distinct despite a rapid, unearthly, high-speed chirpiness. "I come from God, Sylvia," she said. "Don't be afraid."

Looking back, I guess I could have found reassurance in the "I come from God" part, or been fascinated that after eight years of being clairvoyant, I could now officially add clairaudience to my list of psychic skills. Instead, I flew out of my bedroom in sheer terror and ran to find Grandma Ada, who was cleaning vegetables in the kitchen. She stroked my hair to comfort me, calmly explained that it was "just" my Spirit Guide, and went back to her carrot peeling.

My Spirit Guide has been a daily presence and a vital part of my life since that night in 1946. She spent her one lifetime on earth as an Aztec Incan and was killed by a spear in 1520 during the Spanish invasion of Colombia. Her real name is Iena, which I apparently didn't care for, since I've never called her anything but Francine.

For those of you who don't understand exactly what a Spirit Guide (or "control") is, it's very much worth explaining, because I promise, you have one too, whether you're consciously aware of it or not. A Spirit Guide is someone who, when we choose to come back to earth again from the Other Side, agrees to be our constant companion and helpmate while we're away from Home. They know what we hope to accomplish during our time here, and it's their divine assignment to encourage, support, and advise us along the way without ever interfering with our decisions or depriving us of our free will. The simple truth is, we're all here for the further education and growth of our spirits, which we can't do without making mistakes and learning from them. Our Spirit Guides would defeat the whole purpose of our trips away from Home if they shielded us from the lessons we mapped out for ourselves in the first place.

So now I had these legions of spirits visiting me, Francine chirping away in my ear, and Grandma Ada reassuring me that there was no reason to be frightened of any of it, that it simply proved that we don't die at all when our lives on earth are over, we go right on living, real as ever, because God promised when He created us that each of us is eternal, which means we always were and we always will be. In the meantime, I was attending Catholic school (part of my Catholic, Lutheran, Episcopalian, Jewish upbringing) and got in serious trouble with one of the nuns one day when she was telling the class about how our spirits survive death. I helpfully chimed in that I knew that was true, because I saw them and talked to them all the time. She essentially called me a liar. I reported this when I got home. Grandma Ada marched down to the school, and the nun never called me a liar again, although the seeds were planted for my reputation as a troublemaker.

By now, though, I was thoroughly confused. We were supposed to believe that our spirits survive death, but it was ridiculous to believe we could see them and communicate with them. What possible sense did that make? And I didn't just believe we could, I *knew* we could. I'd been doing it for years. The suggestion that I was imagining my encounters with the spirit world was as jarring to me as someone suggesting that I was imagining my parents, and I needed to understand what the truth was and where exactly these spirits came from. I wasn't particularly interested in spirituality at the age of ten—"Cincinnati" would have been enough of an answer for me if that's where spirits lived when they weren't dropping in at my house.

So Grandma Ada and Francine started telling me about this breathtakingly beautiful place called the Other Side, our real Home, where we all come from for our brief trips to this "boot camp" called earth and where we all return to our busy lives in the perfection of God's pure, all-encompassing love. It sounded enchanting, if maybe a little too good to be true. I didn't have the attention span to pay much more attention to it than that at the time, but it sounded a lot more logical to me than what the nuns at school had been telling me. And it turned out to be the core of my relentless passion not too many years later for learning everything there was to know about the spiritual world.

When I was eighteen, Grandma Ada went Home. It was the first great loss in my life, the first time I experienced the bottomless ache of grief. She left with such peace, without a doubt in her soul about where she was going, and thanks to what she and Francine had taught me I knew I wasn't grieving for her. I was grieving for me, for the unimaginable void she had left behind in my heart.

Two days after she passed away, I was in my bedroom going through the motions of getting dressed when the feeling crept over me that I wasn't alone. I glanced past my reflection in the mirror and then turned around to look behind me, but no one was there. I'd turned back to the mirror again when I could have sworn I felt a brief warm breath on the back of my neck. I dismissed it as that word Grandma Ada told me a million times should be eliminated from the English language: my *imagination*.

At that instant two things happened less than a second apart: there was a deafening crack, like a bolt of lightning inside the room, and clear as a bell I heard Grandma Ada's voice say, "Sylvia!" And then, nothing, except for that intense silence that thickens the air in the wake of an electrical storm.

My heart was pounding as I raced out of the room and literally ran into my daddy, who was running up the stairs as fast as I was running down them.

"Sylvia, what happened? What was that horrible cracking noise? It sounded like the roof collapsed. Are you all right? You're white as a sheet."

I was still trembling as I described the previous couple of minutes. Not much surprised him anymore, and he just smiled and held me and said, "You know, your grandmother told you she was going to send you a sign to let you know that she made it Home safely. I guess she kept her promise. But that loud crack scared the hell out of me. What was it?"

I had no idea, but I was determined to find out, because I knew it was a sound, and a moment, from somewhere other than earth, connected to Grandma Ada, and I wanted to know everything about it.

That deafening crack, it turned out, is called a "rapport." It's the spirit world's version of a sonic boom. Occasionally, when a spirit pierces the invisible veil between the high-frequency dimension of the Other Side and our significantly lower frequency here on earth, it creates exactly the same shock waves in the atmosphere that any other object creates when it travels faster than the speed of sound. Those shock waves cause sudden, intense buildups and releases of atmospheric pressure, and it's the release of that pressure that causes sonic booms—and rapports.

According to a lot of experts, including Francine, it's not all that uncommon for rapports to accompany spirit visits. They've been reported countless times by psychics, mediums, "non-psychics," and non-believers for many millennia. I've been on the receiving end of thousands upon thousands of spirit visits, but the only rapport I've ever experienced was the one that accompanied Grandma Ada to my bedroom all those decades ago to tell me she'd made it safely Home. I don't doubt for a moment that she just wanted to give me a sign I couldn't possibly miss.

By this time my childhood aversion to too much information had evolved into a passion for learning everything there was to know about anything that captured my curiosity, toward my determination to become a teacher. (This followed a brief obsession with becoming a nun. I'm sure the Catholic Church is as relieved as I am that I came to my senses.) I headed to St. Theresa's College in my hometown of Kansas City, where I majored in education and literature with a minor in theology.

I'd also become fascinated with the working of the human mind, for obvious reasons that definitely included ten years of Francine's constant chirping, knowing things it was "impossible" for me to know, and living among visiting spirits that no one else saw but me. I signed up for a hypnosis class at the University of Kansas City as well as a course in abnormal psychology. And that abnormal psychology textbook, listing symptom after symptom of the truly disturbed mind, shook me to my core, because as far as I was concerned the majority of those symptoms described me so perfectly that my class photo might as well have been printed beside them. The more I studied, the more obvious it became: I was clearly crazy, and certainly too crazy to be allowed anywhere near children, let alone teach them. This much celebrated multi-generational psychic legacy I'd been taught to cherish was probably a euphemism for three hundred years of hereditary insanity. Seeing spirits? Also known as "hallucinating," common in various forms of dementia, right? As for my supposed "Spirit Guide," Francine, could it be more sadly apparent that she wasn't real, that she was just some imaginary alternate personality who didn't exist beyond my own deranged mind?

Once I was completely convinced of my self-diagnosis, I took two immediate steps: I made an appointment with Dr. John Renick, a psychiatrist who'd become one of my favorite, most trusted teachers, and I officially said goodbye to this alter ego I'd been calling Francine for all these years. She took it with her usual unemotional patience, but she did ask me to allow her one demonstration before I permanently wrote her off as a voice in my head that was just more proof of my mental illness: for the first time since I had met her when I was eight, she offered to materialize.

The idea terrified me, but I accepted the challenge—at least when nothing happened, when she never appeared, it would prove once and for all that she didn't really exist. I gathered my parents and my sister for moral support and ignored as best I could their excitement at the prospect of seeing this Francine person I'd been blathering about for so long. It was nighttime, and we could hear rain against the window. I dimmed the lights at Francine's request to protect her eyes on her first trip to this dimension since the early 1500s, she claimed. Then we settled in to wait. It didn't take long.

Slowly and silently the folds of a soft blue dress began to take form in the rocking chair beside me. Next came the shape of a hand with slender, graceful fingers, resting in the lap of the dress.

Daddy blurted out in what little voice he was able to manage, "Don't anyone talk, so we won't influence one another about what we're seeing!" There was no danger of that. My mother and sister were too much in awe to speak anyway.

An arm with light mocha skin extended above the hand, and a long braid of black hair took shape, resting against the arm.

That was all I could handle. My family kept right on gaping, completely overwhelmed, while I turned away and never glanced back. She was tall and very thin, they told me later, with huge dark eyes and high cheekbones, almost Egyptian-looking and placidly beautiful. When they compared notes after Francine had disappeared, it was clear that they'd all seen exactly the same spirit, right down to the last detail.

Dr. Renick was surprised at my reaction when I told him about the whole experience at our first therapy session the next day. He thought I should be ecstatic that my family and I had witnessed proof that Francine was real. And if she was real, I was sane, which should have been cause for celebration. "So why did you turn away from her?"

I'd been awake all night asking myself that same question, but hearing it from this kind, brilliant, compassionate man made me cry. "Because I have to live in this world. I hear and see so much that normal people don't. I want to be normal, Dr. Renick. I want to be a teacher. I don't want to be some goofy, airy-fairy weirdo."

He gave me the greatest smile and replied, "What a perfectly sane thing to say." I finally smiled back.

To this day I have the piece of paper with his written diagnosis: "Normal, but has paranormal abilities?" Even with the question mark, I treasured it, and I never questioned my gifts or my sanity again.

Now that I'd accepted beyond all doubt that Francine was indeed a very real separate entity from the spirit world who was apparently going to be with me for the rest of my life, I started trying to negotiate some kind of compromise about her voice—if maybe she could find some slower, easier to understand, lower-octave, less annoying way to communicate? She reminded me that she had no control over the sound distortion between her dimension and mine. But there was one alternative: if I was willing to trance, she could channel her voice through me, using my vocal cords. I wouldn't have any awareness of what she said while I was channeling her, but I could tape her and listen afterwards as often as I wanted.

So logical, and so out of the question as far as I was concerned. I wanted no part of trancing, let alone handing over control of any part of my body to my Spirit Guide or anyone else. She assured me that trancing was risk-free, it would never happen without my permission, and whenever I chose I could break the trance and take control again. In fact, how about if she tried it sometime when and if the opportunity presented itself, just so I could see what it was like?

I don't remember exactly what my response was, but I probably said something like, "Yeah, right," forgetting as I occasionally did how literally Francine interprets everything. (Ask her, for example, "Can you tell me what you look like?" and she'll reply, "Yes." The end. Technically, it's an accurate answer. But if it's not what you had in mind, you need to reword that to, "Please tell me what you look like.")

Two days later I was in hypnosis class with my oldest friend Mary Margaret. I remember Dr. Royal "counting down" the roomful of students. The next thing I remember was regaining consciousness. It wasn't pretty. I happen to be double-jointed, so I was completely doubled over in my chair with the top of my head touching the floor. For a moment or two I thought that was the reason everyone in the room was gaping at me, including Dr. Royal. But as I sat up and tried unsuccessfully to hide my embarrassment, I started catching excited comments around me—"Never heard anything like that . . ." and, "Where did all that information come from?" and, "Was that for real?," and the one that particularly alerted me, "It was like you were someone else."

Hopelessly confused, I turned to Mary Margaret, who'd known me since kindergarten. She leaned over and whispered, "Francine was here. Talking through you."

I listened, stunned and mortified, as my classmates described the previous half hour. It seemed that while I was "gone," Francine introduced herself to the class and began telling them all about the Other Side, the facts about reincarnation, how and why we acquire our Spirit Guides, and God knows what else (so to speak). There was no doubt in anyone's mind that someone other than me was speaking—apparently, with the exception of my voice itself, the speech patterns, the terminology, the rhythms, and everything else that came out of my mouth bore no resemblance to me at all. Oh, and by the way, everyone loved her and hoped she'd come back soon.

I confronted Francine that night, furious, demanding to know how she could betray me like that. She patiently pointed out that she had said she'd be watching for an opportunity to channel through me. And since I'd voluntarily allowed the hypnotic trance that enabled her to accomplish it, she'd technically kept her promise not to come in against my will. The one point I couldn't argue no matter how hard I tried: I woke up from channeling her with no harm done (if you don't count abject humiliation). In fact, Francine was clearly able to share a lot of fascinating information with a roomful of people who'd had the experience of meeting, "in person," a full-fledged resident of the Other Side and would probably never look at life and death in the same way again.

In other words, the potential value of channeling Francine was undeniable, and I agreed to it with a few non-negotiable conditions: never again would she surprise me as she had during hypnosis class; she would never tell anything but the truth while speaking through me; she would never use my voice to cause harm to me or anyone else; and I would only channel her for the highest possible humanitarian purposes, to benefit as many people as possible with messages of comfort and clarity about the Other Side and our intensely personal relationship with a God who created and unconditionally loves each one of us. Fifty-three years later, she's never breached that sacred contract between us.

I graduated from college at nineteen, ready to progress toward my teaching career, and my husband and baby son Paul and I moved to Northern California. (As I always say, I'm not one bit psychic about myself, and I've got the ex-husbands to prove it.) That's where I started doing psychic readings and trancing Francine for lecture groups to pay for my tuition at San Francisco University as I studied for my master's degree.

My creative writing instructor at SFU was a wonderful man named Bob Williams, who accelerated my spiritual journey more dramatically than either of us knew at the time.

For starters, he and I had shared a mutual interest in metaphysics and the paranormal, which we discussed exhaustively. So imagine my shock when one day in class he announced that I was going to demonstrate my ability to give accurate psychic readings to anyone who cared to volunteer. Of my fifty classmates, fifty volunteered. I apparently demonstrated well, since those fifty told fifty more, and so on and so on, and I quickly acquired a full schedule of clients.

But of far more significance was the day Bob took me to

a tiny, wonderful bookstore and began showing me a wealth of books on the paranormal and the amazing history of spirituality—everything from psychic healer Edgar Cayce and Theosophist/physical medium Madame Helena Blavatsky to the Aborigines and the Incas to the Buddhists and the Baha'i and Tarot cards to phrenology. He told me my assignment was to read them all. In many cases, I already had—I'd minored in theology, after all, and I'd become an insatiable reader in general.

"So read them again, and whatever you haven't read, start now," he said. "And then, do something about it."

"Like what?" I asked him.

"Study. Teach. Explore. Write. Exceed your own grasp. Start a research center to share the wealth of the spiritual world that you might never have found without your gifts. Think of the difference you can make for more people than you can imagine." I'm sure he could read the doubt and insecurity in my silence, because he put his hands on my shoulders and looked right into my eyes when he added, "I believe in you. Just do it. I'll help you."

Sadly, he had to keep that promise from the Other Side. Two weeks later, he left for a long anticipated trip to Australia. I begged him not to go—I "knew" he wouldn't make it back alive. He assured me he'd be careful, but he came home in a pine box. I've missed him, loved him, and thanked him ever since.

Between the shock of losing Bob and the non-stop busyness of my life as a wife, mother, student, and working psychic, I thought I'd forgotten about our conversation in the bookstore until one night not long after Bob's death when a small group of us went to a lecture given by a well-known psychic. No one in that audience was more enthusiastic and receptive than I was when we walked in and sat down. And no one in that audience was more furious and offended than I was as the lecture progressed. I was having enough trouble politely sitting still for the duration that my friends threatened to strap me to my chair. But at dinner afterwards, I exploded.

"All those people showed up tonight looking for some kind of spiritual nourishment, some way to connect to these beautiful unseen forces around them where they can find all the hope and comfort and joy they'll ever need, or just a new perspective on life and death and eternity that might enlighten them or elevate them or at least pique their curiosity and make them think. But instead, all they got was a bunch of trivia, clichés, half-truths, and outright lies. How dare that so-called psychic waste an opportunity like that, let alone those people's time and money?"

When I'd finally finished spinning out about it, the friend sitting next to me simply smiled and said, "Okay, so what are you going to do about it?"

Suddenly my afternoon at the bookstore with Bob Williams came flooding back to me, and my anger gave way to gratitude when I realized I hadn't forgotten that conversation and Bob's challenge to me at all, because in that instant at dinner I knew exactly what I was going to do about it.

Within months I'd founded and registered the Nirvana Foundation for Psychic Research, a non-profit organization with two primary purposes: to teach psychic development; and to explore and prove the survival of the spirit after death.

That was in 1974, and looking back I know that both professionally and personally, my real spiritual odyssey started then. I've spent every day learning and researching and testing and being tested and looking for the same answers to the same questions you have, the same questions humankind has been asking since God breathed eternal life into us. The specifics of what brought me to the threshold of this odyssey might differ from yours, but we share the identical goals: to spend our time here with as much depth, purpose, and peace of mind as we can; to leave this earth better than we found it; to find that truth that resonates so deep inside us that we never feel afraid again; and to know with absolute certainty that we're never alone, we're never as helpless or hopeless as we sometimes feel, and that there really is no such thing as death.

NIRVANA FOUNDATION FOR
PSYCHIC RESEARCH

2

SPIRITUALISM AND DEATH: THE SEARCH FOR ANSWERS BEGINS

Spiritualism is the belief that the soul or spirit is the true essence of every living being, that spirits survive the death of physical bodies, and that the spirits of the dead can make contact with the living. Before you can determine what's real or what's false in the spiritual realm, you need to understand the many different spiritual traditions (particularly those in the ancient world), since so many of them influence the ideas we still carry about spirituality today.

This intimate relationship between spiritualism and death throughout the history of humankind on this earth is fascinating to trace, reflected as it is in the ways in which different civilizations have dealt with death itself. Each culture has found its own ways of expressing and acting on its sense of a relationship with life and with the afterlife and how the Creator intended that relationship to be honored by the living.

Obviously even the earliest humans faced the reality of death, in the animals they hunted for food and in the humans within their own tribes. They learned that the physical body of the dead quickly decayed, reduced to nothing but bones, which led to the first ceremonies and rituals dealing with the fact of

death and what might lie beyond it. They also learned, because
they were hunters, gatherers, and sometimes the hunted, that
their very survival was intricately dependent on nature. The sun
brought warmth and light to see by; the rain gave them water to
drink and made things grow; volcanoes and lightning gave them
fire for cooking and warmth; animals gave them food and hides
to protect them from the elements; the seasons told them when
to move to more hospitable climates and when to plant and
harvest their crops.

It's no surprise, then, that the first religions centered
around nature. They developed their gods and their forms of
worship based on their own "trinity": those things in nature
that provided for humankind; those things in nature that were
dangerous to humankind; and those things in nature that
could not be understood, and were therefore mysteries. Death
was one of those mysteries, something to be feared initially
because life seemed to cease when death occurred. The earliest religious ceremonies were designed to ensure that the living would continue to live and be safe when their bodies no
longer existed, and those ceremonies understandably evolved
into worship of the ancestors whose lives and safety they ritu-
alistically protected.

Scientists and anthropologists agree that ancient humans
had much more highly developed sensory perceptions than
we do. They relied on their advanced senses for every facet of
survival. And those advanced senses also allowed them to feel,
hear, see, and communicate with the spirits of the dead easily
and clearly, especially with no preconditioned beliefs telling
them that spirit communication was either inappropriate or just
plain impossible. It's no coincidence that every ancient religion
included ancestor worship, with ceremonies to honor and ven-
erate the dead—humankind routinely turned to their deceased
ancestors for all kinds of help and advice and considered themselves reverentially indebted to all who had come before them.

Remnants of these earliest religious beliefs are still practiced in parts of Africa. Although the influences of Christianity and Islam have altered a number of the customs relating to the dead throughout certain parts of the continent, many countries south of the Sahara have maintained the basic ideology of pagan spiritualism. They embrace the concept that death doesn't end life, that life simply moves on to continue in another place. "Life" and "death" are not opposites, or mutually exclusive, they're both a part of the process of human existence. This existence involves the increase or decrease of "life power" or "vital force," with different levels of existence occurring in life and in death, and it's this life power/vital force that influences all of humankind's existence. According to Placide Tempels, an African religious scholar, every misfortune that Africans endure is considered "a diminution of vital force" to them. In other words, when illness or death happens to an African, it's because an outside agent (a person, place, thing, or circumstance) contains a greater life force, weakening the African involved, and therefore causing the illness or death.

These same Africans believe that death doesn't mean the end of life or the loss of the personality of any person who's died, it only changes the condition of their existence. This condition takes the form of becoming an "ancestor," which is one who has died but continues to communicate with his or her family and "live" in the community or tribe. The goal in these tribes is to become an ancestor after death, which will deepen the relationship with creation and establish communication between the visible and invisible worlds. Particular care is taken to ensure that everyone who dies is given the proper ceremonies and funeral to become an ancestor. If each detail isn't followed precisely, the dead can wander through the tribe as a ghost and, not having earned the status of ancestor, become a danger to the living. In fact, many scholars believe that the death rituals and ceremonies in these pagan African cultures have more to do with protecting the living from the misguided dead than with ensuring the dead safe passage from this world to the next.

For the most part, these tribes' customs regarding the dead are both simple and motivated by an underlying logic. The custom of removing a dead body through a hole in the wall of a house instead of a doorway, for example, might look hilariously primitive, and/or foolishly impractical at first glance. But by immediately filling and patching the hole after the deceased has been removed, this custom is designed to make it as difficult as possible for the dead person to remember the way back to the living. Another custom is to remove a dead body feet first, symbolically pointing away from its former residence. Other ways of disguising the path from the dead to the living include taking a zigzag path to the grave, or leaving thorns along the way, or creating a wall or other barrier at the burial site.

On the other hand, if it's believed that the deceased will become an ancestor who can be helpful to the living from the spirit world, great care will be taken to remain accessible to the deceased and make it easy for the spirit of the deceased to find its way home, to the point of burying the body beneath or very close to the house.

The simplicity of African pagan beliefs fascinates me, because many of them embrace great universal truths with logical, deductive reasoning. For example, I love their recognition of the difference between the physical, buried body and the whole, intact person who lives on, unlike in Western culture, which so often implies that the spirit is the "part" of the person that survives death, as if the spirit isn't a fully actualized entity all by itself.

And then, of course, to the north of the ancient sub-Saharan African cultures was a highly sophisticated civilization that had its own more complicated views of death and the afterlife, every bit as fascinating and every bit as affirming in its refusal to believe that life ends when the body stops functioning.

THE ANCIENT EGYPTIANS

Belief in the afterlife was a fundamental part of the ancient Egyptian civilization, a fact testified to by over three thousand years of its recorded history. The Egyptians considered preservation of the body to be essential to a successful journey to the soul's eternal destination and invested in the most effective mummification procedures and tombs they could afford. The loved ones of the deceased traditionally filled tombs with the deceased's favorite belongings and nourishment to ensure a happy, healthy transition to the next world.

"The Egyptian Book of the Dead" and other ancient Egyptian writings describe a complex series of events that takes place when the soul passes on, based on the mythology of their religious beliefs.

The Lord of the Universe was called Atum, or Ra. With the goddess Opet he began the divine lineage that included the winged Isis, the goddess of nature, revered as the ideal mother; Osiris, the god of the afterlife, who was Isis's brother and husband; Nephthys, the goddess who symbolized the soul's transition from this life to the next; and her brother/husband Seth, the god of chaos.

Seth, obsessively jealous of his brother Osiris, lured him into a coffin, which he sealed and threw into the Nile River. The grieving Isis searched far and wide for her husband's coffin, finally found it in Phoenicia, and returned with it to Egypt, where Seth seized Osiris's body and dismembered it, scattering the body parts. Isis gathered them up and, with the help of her own legendary magic and the jackal god Anubis, joined them into one body again, and the first mummy was created.

Osiris and Isis's son Horus was born after Osiris's death, and Isis kept her son hidden from Seth. When Horus became a man he attacked Seth to avenge his father's death, and in the process Horus lost one of his eyes. Horus and Seth were both healed by Thoth, the god of wisdom and Scribe of the Dead, and then tried by a tribunal of gods, who found Seth guilty and ordered him to return Horus's eye. Horus lovingly presented Osiris with the eye, at which moment Osiris came to life again.

Osiris, the first of the gods to experience resurrection after death and mummification, settled in Amenthe, the underworld, to become the god of the dead. And so the belief in eternal life beyond the grave of the underworld for the properly mummified deceased was born.

"The Book of the Dead" was traditionally left in the tomb of the deceased to give the soul a guide on its journey to Amenthe and protect it from the dangers that lurked along the way, including demons and monsters that waited with nets to capture it. Snakes threatened the soul as it crossed vast plains, and a boatman was in charge of safely rowing the soul across the water that had to be navigated en route to the afterlife that waited in Amenthe.

The dangerous trip to Amenthe was only the beginning of the challenges the soul had to face to earn its way into a truly blessed eternity. A monster fiercely guarded the gate to Amenthe, ready to rip out the heart of the sinful and undeserving before they entered. Once the soul made it past the monster at the gate, it walked through a series of opulent buildings until it arrived at a panel of judges to whom it was required to make a preliminary Declaration of Innocence, listing its finest, most worthy qualities throughout the lifetime it had just completed.

The soul was then presented to the mighty Osiris and his council in the Hall of the Two Truths. The council—Horus, Thoth, and Anubis—presided over the ritual called the Weighing of the Heart, in which the soul's conscience was placed on a balance scale and weighed against a feather, the symbol of Maat, the goddess of truth. The results were recorded by Thoth as the Scribe of the Dead, and ultimately presented to Osiris, who pronounced the soul's verdict and sentence from his imperial throne.

If the Weighing of the Heart revealed a conscience as light as the feather, the Declaration of Innocence was accepted as sincere, and the soul was rewarded with an eternal life in Amenthe among the gods and its worthy loved ones. There it worked joyfully in the Field of the Sun, planting and harvesting thriving crops for the infinite nourishment of all the blessed souls in paradise.

On the other hand, if the conscience failed the test of the Weighing of the Heart by proving to be heavier than its Declaration of Innocence implied, Osiris might choose from a variety of sentences for the condemned soul. It might be devoured by the monster at the Amenthe gate who thrived on sinful hearts. It might be banished back to earth, reincarnated as one of the lowest of animal species. It might be sent for torture in an abyss filled with fire and demons. It might be sent to the world of Pooh, the god of penitent souls, who ruled in the skies where violent storms could ravage the soul until it genuinely atoned its sins. And in the end, a soul in heartfelt repentance could be given the "probation" of another human incarnation for an opportunity to achieve absolution and finally earn its way into the bliss of Amenthe.

THE ANCIENT GREEKS

The ancient Greeks certainly believed in an afterlife as well, with a journey for the soul of the deceased as challenging as the ancient Egyptians' and a mythology every bit as colorful.

One day the beautiful Persephone, whose mother Demeter was the goddess of bountiful harvests, was abducted by Hades, ruler of the land of the dead, and taken away in his chariot to reign as his queen. Hades' kingdom was an underground world, entered through caves known only to the gods and the dead.

It was the Fates who chose the exact moment of death, according to this mythology, and they would send the Dogs of Hades to seize the already dying person, inflict the mortal blow, and then deliver the soul to the Land of Shadows, where it would exist as a "shade" as it began its journey toward the afterlife. The shade crossed a desolate area filled with black poplar trees called the Grove of Persephone and arrived at the gate that formed the entrance of the Kingdom of Hades. Guarding the gate was Cerberus, a vicious three-headed dog who could be appeased by honey cakes, allowing the shade to enter.

Once inside the gate, the shade was confronted by five underground rivers: the Phlegethon, the Styx, the Cocytus, the Lethe, and the Acheron. To proceed with its journey, the shade was required to cross the Acheron with the help of Charon, the boatman. Charon required a coin called an *obol* for his services, without which the shade would be turned away to wander the shoreline with no hope of rescue. (This explains why the deceased were traditionally buried with a supply of honey cakes, and an *obol* in their mouths.)

Those shades who successfully crossed the river Acheron faced a council of deities: Hades himself, who happened to be the brother of Zeus, the king of the gods; and Aeacus, Minos, and Rhadamanthus, all of whom were Zeus' sons. It was the duty of the council to judge the lifetime the soul had just completed and bestow on it the afterlife it had earned.

The most ordinary of shades, who contributed little or nothing to the world in which it lived and was deemed to warrant neither reward nor punishment, was sent to a joyless, sunless area of Hades to wander forever without purpose.

Those souls who committed mortally offensive crimes during their lives on earth were banished to the underground prison of Tartarus on the river Phlegethon. Tartarus, surrounded by a massive wall, housed the worst of the worst, including those who declared war on Zeus; Tantalus, who murdered his own son and offered him to the gods to eat; and Sisyphus, who delighted in the multiple homicides he had committed, seduced his niece, stole his brother's throne, and betrayed many of Zeus's secrets. (Sisyphus remains legendary to this day for his particular punishment in Tartarus, doomed for eternity to pushing a boulder up a steep hill, watching it roll to the bottom, and pushing it up the hill again. If you've ever heard a pointless, repetitive task referred to as "sisyphean," now you know where the reference comes from.)

Souls who had committed crimes involving mitigating circumstances were sentenced to one year in Tartarus and then sent on to the shores of the Acherusian Lake to be reunited with and ask for forgiveness from those against whom the crimes were committed. If that forgiveness was given, those souls could be returned to earth for another incarnation.

The greatest reward the shade could receive, reserved for only the purest, most generous, and reverent of souls, was an eternity in the Elysian Fields, a magnificent land in Hades at the end of the world, full of sunshine and vast, lush meadows, where all the greatest pleasures of earth were available to the few souls who'd earned their place in paradise.

The brilliant Greek philosopher Plato (c. 428–347 B.C.) wrote in the *Republic* of a variation on that mythical view of the afterlife. In his description, the soul traveled to a place where a council of judges presided over four entrances, two of which led down into the earth and two of which led up into the sky. The blessed, deserving souls were sent to the sky, while the wicked ones were banished into the earth, and they each stayed in their respective destinations, to be rewarded or punished for a thousand years.

At the end of those thousand years, all but the very worst of souls reunited to share their experiences. The worst were doomed to an eternity in Tartarus. All the rest made their way after seven days to a place where a complicated power structure facilitated their transition to their next lifetime, with each soul designing the specifics of its next incarnation.

ANCIENT ROME

There were several views on the afterlife in ancient Rome, both as to whether or not there was an afterlife at all and as to what it might be like if there were.

One view included the belief that an incarnation on earth amounted to a period of mandatory service to the world that the spirit had to perform before it would be liberated from its mortal body and released into the joyful, immortal infinity of the universe.

Another view held that, whatever the afterlife was like, the dead somehow survived the death of the body powerfully enough that they could still dramatically affect the world of the living. In case they were right, those who held that view were very generous with offerings and respectful, praise-filled ceremonies at the burial site. Caskets were weighted down or secured to the ground, and for added security against whatever wandering the dead might be inspired to undertake, bodies were often decapitated and/or dismembered before they were buried or cremated.

There was also a ritual dictating that for the nine days after the interment of the deceased, the family house was thought to be cursed, or polluted (also called a state of *funesta*). During those nine days, the doors of the house would be covered with yew or cypress branches to announce that the residents were in mourning and possibly cursed, after which the house was scrubbed from top to bottom to cleanse it of the ghost that might have returned. Specific days were set aside to commemorate the deceased, though, in case they reincarnated, saw that they weren't being mourned properly, and sought revenge on their disrespectful family.

And then there was the mythology, similar to the ancient Greeks' and embraced by many, which began with the soul's travel to the underworld when the body died. The gods appointed escorts for the soul to the banks of the river Styx, where the boatman Charon met it to transport it safely across. Like the Greeks, many Romans placed a gold coin in the mouths of the deceased as payment to Charon, although sometimes more elaborate gifts, including jewelry, were left with the body for more favorable treatment by the ferryman when the time came to cross the Styx.

Once across the river, the soul was confronted by the three-headed dog Cerberus, which was owned by Pluto, the god of the underworld. In Roman mythology, Cerberus only became vicious when it faced those who had committed serious offenses or those who were trying to escape back to the surface of the earth.

Next came the soul's presentation of its lifetime to the three judges, Minos, Rhadamanthos, and Aeacus, after which the soul would drink water from the river Lethe so that it would forget the life it had just left behind.

Depending on the good or bad deeds during its life as decided by the three judges, the soul would be sent to one of three places: the paradise of the Elysian Fields, where the best, most honorable, and most heroic would spend their eternity; the Plain of Asphodel, where the soul became a shade, or pale version of its former self; and Tartarus, reserved for the worst and most evil, where each soul was punished until it genuinely atoned. A reprieve from Tartarus could also come from Persephone, the queen of the underworld, who had the power to free the soul to travel across the Styx and back to life again. It was also possible for Pluto to deny a soul entry to the underworld entirely, which caused it to wander between life and death in Limbo for the rest of eternity.

THE AZTECS

The Aztec civilization had a fascinating outlook on death and the afterlife, believing that for the most part the eternal destination of the soul was less dependent on how one lived than on how one died. No matter what the good or bad deeds performed during a lifetime, a noble death was honored with far more reverence than a relatively uneventful one, and the fate of the soul was determined accordingly.

After funeral rites that included a baptism and other rituals to ease the soul's difficult journey ahead, the body was either buried or cremated along with a dog sacrificed to guide the spirit to its destination in the underworld. Cremated bodies were covered with paper and then wrapped in cloth, while interred bodies were buried with images of gods.

The soul first set out on the Underworld Way, a path of mountains, lurking serpents, and fierce beasts, deserts, and winds that felt as if they were filled with sharp blades. Once the four-year journey along the Underworld Way was behind it, the soul would arrive in the presence of Mictlantecutli, the god of the dead, a skeletal, blood-covered figure, and the goddess of the underworld, Mictlancihuatl. It was Mictlantecutli who determined the soul's appropriate fate.

Those whose bodies died in battle as warriors, or in sacrifice, were considered heroes, and their souls were sent to a paradise ruled by Tonatiuh, the sun god. They had the honor of following the sun to its apex and then being released to drink nectar from endless fields of flowers.

The setting sun was the realm of women who died in childbirth, considered to be as courageous and selfless as the male warriors whose lives were lost in combat. The souls of these female warriors were given the sacred task of taking the setting sun to the netherworld.

The afterworld of Tlalocan was another paradise, presided over by Tlaloc, the god of rain and water. It was reserved for souls who died by lightning, drowning, diseases that originated in marshes, or any other water- or storm-related deaths, and it was a land of great beauty, abundance, and wealth. The bodies of these particular souls were traditionally buried rather than cremated.

Finally there was Mictlan, the destination of most souls, those whose deaths were the result of old age and/or illnesses not related to water, childbirth, or combat. Mictlan was an arid, joyless, sunless place, gray and ashen, with no exits to provide even a glimmer of hope.

THE INCAS

The Incas had a less depressing view of the afterlife, with considerably more interaction with the deceased. They had their deities, of course. Viracocha was the divine creator. Inti was the god of the sun. Illapa was the weather god, and god of thunder. Mamacocha was the goddess of the sea, Mamaquilla was the moon goddess, and Pachamama the goddess of the earth. But Incan religion revolved around the protective, caretaking souls of their ancestors.

Incas commonly honored their deceased nobility and other important members of society with mummification, and the mummies were traditionally buried with some of their most cherished objects and provisions they would need on their journey into the afterlife. During high holidays and the most important of ceremonies, the mummies would be removed from the shrines and palaces where they were preserved in state, dressed in finery, and became revered participants in parades and other celebrations, always treated as if they were still perfectly alive. Mummies were commonly seen at dinner tables, meetings, and family visits, where they were consulted for any and all messages they might have to offer from the gods. Since the Incas believed that their ancestors continued to strongly affect many aspects of their lives, they worshipped and diligently tended to their mummies, even continuing to maintain whatever property they had owned during their lifetime and bringing them sacrifices.

Essential to the Incan civilization was the *huaca*, which was any person, place, or thing that possessed supernatural power, and there was no more sacred *huaca* than the shrines and bodies of deceased rulers, which were thought of as tangible links between humankind and the deities.

Not all Incans could afford mummification, but the poor were every bit as respectful of their dead as the wealthy. The bodies of deceased peasants were dressed in their finest clothing and placed, usually in a seated position, in a nearby cave or appropriate rock formation.

The Incans were so highly moral that there were no prisons. What crime existed was strongly discouraged by such typical punishments as being hung upside down and left to starve, having the hands or feet cut off, or being chained to a wall until the offender died of exposure or dehydration.

There were just enough criminals and evil spirits for the Incans to conceive of an eternity especially for the wicked—a cold, damp, barren underworld where their diet consisted exclusively of stones.

The revered spirits of the virtuous, though, were honored by joining the sun in heaven, thriving eternally in its warmth as they watched over and protected the living.

NATIVE AMERICANS

The Native American civilization, thought to have begun on the North American continent more than ten thousand years ago, is made up of many tribes with their own specific rituals and beliefs. But it's safe to say that the vast majority of them share a deep sense of connection with nature and the spirit world, and a reverent respect for the spirit world's essential, abiding influence on the physical world. Most believe that the souls of the deceased leave their bodies behind to become part of that spirit world, ruled by one Great Spirit whose divine hand created the infinite universe, Mother Earth, and all the guardians, signs, and blessings for which humankind owes eternal and continual thanks. They were keenly aware of a fact that our "more highly civilized" societies tend to forget: we rely on the earth for our very existence, and we can only thrive if we see to it that our planet thrives first.

The Cherokee, for example, believe in giving thanks each morning to the Creator, to Mother Earth, to Father Sky, to all their relatives and ancestors, and to the four directions: the East, guardian of the healing and nourishment that grows from the earth; the South, guardian of the wind, sky, and air; the West, guardian of life-giving water; and the North, guardian of fire. They believe that all things are connected, that all things have purpose, and that all things contain the spark of life that links them to the divine. They believe that there is no death, just an eternal cycle bestowed by the Great Spirit who created us. Some souls, when they leave their bodies, are selected to stay in the earthly dimension as ghosts who can be seen when they're needed. Others return to the heavens to take their place among the stars from which they came as Starseeds to be born into the human race to bring light and knowledge to the earth.

The Iroquois also worship an omnipotent Great Spirit, with

spirits called "Invisible Agents" to carry out His power and will to the physical world through their assigned forces and elements, such as the sun, the rain, the wind, fire, the rivers, and the generosity of the earth. They believe in a separate entity, the brother of the Great Spirit, who is Evil and controls inferior souls in the spirit and material worlds. The Iroquois feel that humankind is too insignificant in the infinite works of the Creator to try to either comprehend Him or affect His all-knowing plan. But they regularly worship Him and anticipate an afterlife in which obedience to Him will be eternally rewarded, while submission to Evil will be eternally punished.

The Lakota believe that the spirit survives the death of the body and passes on to the Shadow World, where it becomes a more powerful being. They believe that the physical and spiritual realms are intimately connected, and that when critical help is needed they can rely on their ancestors to provide it, summoning them through ceremonial rites.

They also believe that there are spirits who can return to earth to cause trouble and harm to the living. Those spirits originate in mortals who died with feelings of anger, resentment, and general discontent, and they're capable of creating those same feelings among those they leave behind.

The Sioux belief in an afterlife was beautifully expressed by Many Horses, a nineteenth-century Oglala Sioux medicine man:

> *There are but two ways for us. One leads to hunger and death,*
> *   the other leads to where the poor white man lives.*
> *Beyond is the happy hunting ground*
> *Where the white man cannot go.*

According to traditional Sioux beliefs, everything in nature has a spirit—from the trees to the mountains to the rivers to the sun, the moon, and the stars—so that there is no separation between life and the afterlife. When the body dies, the spirit moves on to the Happy Hunting Ground, which resembles an idealized version of their lives here, with perfect weather and game animals that never run away from the hunter.

The Navajo, on the other hand, are traditionally frightened of the whole idea of death and the dead, although they honor many gods and supernatural powers. They bury their dead as quickly as possible and speak of them rarely if at all, and there is no generally accepted belief in rewards or punishments dependent on how one's life was lived.

They believe that long before time began, there were Holy People, who were supernatural, who dwelled in a series of underworlds until each was destroyed. They finally arrived in this world, where they created First Man and First Woman, who are the ancestors of all of what they call the Earth Surface People. Once the Holy People had endowed the Earth Surface People with survival skills and knowledge, they passed on to worlds beyond, where they maintain perpetual interest in the Earth Surface People's lives. Remaining in harmony with the Holy People and all other supernatural forces, who can do harm if they're displeased, is essential to the Navajo, and most of their ritual ceremonies are devoted to pleasing the gods and powers who are so intricately involved in their fortunes.

THE ABORIGINES

It's thought that the Australian Aborigines have been on this planet for more than fifty thousand years. They're nomadic, traveling and living in clans, hunting and gathering, surviving on and giving thanks for what the earth provides, passing down their culture, traditions, and exquisite spirituality orally to their descendants.

The Aborigines cherish nature, their elders, and their ancestors, and they're genetically intent on maintaining a perfect balance between the physical and the spiritual every day of their lives. They believe in God, but they don't separate themselves from Him by conceiving of Him as living in the heavens, above the clouds and the sky. Instead, they believe He lives in all of nature on earth, in every blade of grass, in every waterfall, in every animal and tree and mountain and stream and breath of wind. And at the core of their beliefs is an essence called the Dreaming.

The Aborigines' Dreaming is their past, present, and future. It's their laws, their guide for society, their wisdom, their authority, their ceremonies and rituals, their creation and their destiny. The Dreaming is a continuous consciousness and responsibility, as relevant today as it was when the spirit ancestors moved through barren, unsanctified land and gave it its beauty.

There was the Rainbow Serpent, for example, whose massive body slithered across the earth and formed rivers and valleys.

There was Bila, the Sun Woman, whose fire lit the world, and Kudna and Muda, two lizardlike creatures who destroyed her. And then, terrified of the darkness they'd created by killing Bila, they tried to bring back the light by hurling boomerangs into the sky in every direction. Kudna's boomerang spun off and vanished into the eastern sky, and a ball of fire appeared, which slowly crossed the sky and disappeared again in the west—the birth of day and night.

It's on such beautiful stories and spirits of the Dreaming, or Dreamtime, that the Aborigines build their lives and their inherent certainty that it is humankind's privilege to share this earth with such sacred creations. Their reverent regard of the earth as their Mother is so deeply ingrained that the moment a child is born, the mother traditionally buries the afterbirth in the land, forever connecting the baby to that place on this divine planet.

When a loved one dies in the Aboriginal culture, there is enormous anguish at the earthly loss and a return of the body to their Mother Country if they died elsewhere. Rather than being buried in a grave or cremated, the body is placed in a shallow burial site, or among trees or thickly grown fields, so that it can be offered back to the sanctity of nature. The belongings of the deceased are immediately destroyed, and the name of the deceased is never spoken again, nor can it be used again by anyone else in the community—not as a gesture of trying to forget that person but out of deepest respect for them and for those left behind to grieve.

The soul of the deceased immediately returns to the spirit world, still blessed with all the wisdom and knowledge taught to him or her throughout their life on earth so that their souls can guide, and support, teach, and become part of the cherished spirit ancestry of the ancient Aborigine civilization.

All of these ancient spiritual traditions have come to inform and influence the beliefs of many of today's religions (like Buddhism, Judaism, Islam, and Christianity). In the next chapter, we'll learn a little more about some of these other religions, and how some of them have spurred practices (such as faith healing) that can be a magnet for both great good and great harm.

3

THE GREAT RELIGIONS AND SPIRITUALISM

Theology—the study of religion and the nature of religious truth—has been a passion of mine since my teens. I minored in theology in college, I continue studying it to this day, and I still have miles to go before I would even remotely declare myself an expert. It's that infinite and that fascinating a subject. And it's no surprise, considering my lifelong interaction with the spirit world, that I'm particularly interested in every religion's uniquely beautiful ideology about the afterlife, about exactly what happens to our spirits when our bodies die. The specifics may vary from one religion to the next, but the virtually universal belief that the essence of who we are absolutely survives death is a testament to how we on earth cherish our Creator's promise that we are all, in fact, eternal.

BUDDHISM

Twenty-five hundred years ago, in northern India, Queen Maha Maya, the wife of King Suddhodana, had a dream in which a majestic white elephant wrapped itself around her and entered the right side of her body. The Brahmin wise men she consulted interpreted the dream as a prophecy that the queen would give birth to a magnificent prince who, if he remained within the palace, would become a great ruler, but if he abandoned his royal lineage he would become an Awakened One, or Buddha.

A son was born to the queen and king, and they named him Siddhartha, or "all wishes fulfilled." Seven days after the birth of the prince, Queen Maha Maya died, and the boy was lovingly raised by the queen's sister, who later married King Suddhodana. Siddhartha was a gifted student and athlete, strong, handsome, intensely curious and kind. The king, remembering the prophecy of the wise men, created an exquisite life of privilege for Prince Siddhartha within the high guarded walls he had built around the palace, desperately wanting his son to fulfill his destiny as a great ruler and heir to the throne. Strict orders were given that Prince Siddhartha's isolated perfection was never to be violated—he was never to be exposed to the seriously ill, the elderly, the dying, and especially not to any of the holy men who wandered throughout northern India spreading philosophies that the inquisitive prince might find dangerously irresistible.

Prince Siddhartha married his cousin the beautiful Princess Yasodhara when he was thirteen, and they lived happily within the palace walls for another thirteen years. But finally the prince began to feel that his life was unfulfilled and incomplete, and he became consumed with the idea of discovering what life was like beyond those high walls. He conspired with Channa, his charioteer, to venture out on secret excursions into the streets of the nearby villages, where for the first time he saw the sick, the starving, the dying, and the dead, and it devastated him.

He also learned the prevailing Indian belief that birth and death are simply two parts of a never-ending cycle that could only be escaped by somehow avoiding the trap of perpetual rebirth. The tragic inevitability of birth, deprivation, illness, dying, and death again and again and again became a consuming heartache to the kind young prince. But then, on Siddhartha's final secret excursion, he had an encounter that changed his life. He came across a small, barefoot man with a shaved head, his painfully thin body draped in a simple yellow robe, holding a beggar's bowl. At first the prince mistook the little man for just another desperate, starving indigent. Then he looked at the man's face and was shocked to see the peaceful, radiant dignity he found there. Channa explained to the prince that the transcendant man was actually a monk, a devoutly spiritual wanderer who found fulfillment in a life of simplicity, purity, discipline, and meditation on his path toward delivery from suffering.

Prince Siddhartha, irrevocably transformed, returned to the palace and, in a decision that would one day be known as the Great Renunciation, he said goodbye to his beloved wife and infant son, his father and stepmother, his heritage and his privileged wealth. At the age of twenty-nine, alone for the first time in his life, he set out on a search for the answer to ending the doomed cycle of suffering and rebirth in an effort to make a difference in the sad, afflicted world he so longed to help.

He spent the next six years in brutal deprivation, pain, self-mortification, and punishing discipline, living among zealots who disapproved of allowing themselves even a fleeting moment of comfort. Finally, weak and broken, Siddhartha concluded that a healthy, enlightened mind and spirit couldn't thrive in a body that was exhausted, malnourished, and neglected. He began nourishing himself and sleeping again, rebuilding his physical and emotional health. His companions scornfully abandoned him, cursing his inability to maintain his sacrificial disciplines, and the prince found himself alone again.

On his thirty-fifth birthday, Siddhartha was wandering in a beautiful forest when a woman approached him and held out a bowl of milk rice.

"Venerable sir," she said, "whoever you may be, god or human, please accept this offering. May you attain the good which you seek."

His hunger satisfied, he walked on and came upon a groundskeeper, who offered him a mat of fresh-cut grass to use as a cushion. Siddhartha laid the mat at the foot of a graceful spreading fig tree, which came to be known as the Bodhi Tree, or "Tree of Enlightenment," settled in to contemplate the life and near death he'd experienced in the past six years, and vowed, "Though my skin, my nerves, and my lifeblood go dry, I will not abandon this seat until I have realized Supreme Enlightenment."

As a young child Siddhartha had discovered that by sitting cross-legged, with his eyes closed, and focusing his mind on deeply, rhythmically breathing in and out, he could achieve mental bliss. He remembered that peaceful, private exercise and practiced it again in the shade of the Bodhi Tree.

Waves of doubts, fears, memories, longings, and temptations crashed over him, in a fierce battle with all the good he was seeking, as he sat without moving through a violent thunderstorm. Siddhartha remained in perfect meditative stillness, finally imploring the Mother Earth herself to affirm the worthiness of his journey. He touched the ground with his right hand, and the ground trembled and roared back, "I, Earth, bear you witness."

His deep meditation continued throughout the night, and during it he came to know how the darkness of the mind is born and how it can be destroyed, never to be born again. He banished past, present, and future spiritual ignorance; delusion gave way to perfect clarity; and he ultimately understood "things as they are."

When the sun rose again, it was shining not on Prince Siddhartha but on the great Buddha Sakyamuni, the Enlightened

One, who had formulated the Four Noble Truths that became the foundation of Buddhism:

- Suffering is universal and inevitable.
- Desire is the cause of all suffering.
- There is a path that leads to liberation from suffering.
- That path is the Eightfold Path.

The Eightfold Path consists of a right understanding; a right aim or pupose; right speech; right action; right livelihood; right effort; right mindfulness; and right concentration.

Expanding on his teachings, Buddha gained a widespread following throughout India and was revered among his followers. He reunited with his father, stepmother, wife, and son, and gifted them with enlightenment. He was eighty years old when he died. Teachers who had learned from him and would carry on his message surrounded him as he took his last breath, but he didn't name a successor. Buddhist scripts contain a prophecy of a future Buddha, who will be called *Maitreya*, "the Best of Men." He will come from the *Tutshita*, or heaven, where he currently resides, and his next incarnation will be his last.

According to Buddhist beliefs, the moment the body dies, the soul enters the Bardo state, a forty-nine-day process divided into three stages:

The Chikhai Bardo, which lasts a maximum of four days, begins with a brief, exquisite vision of the "Clear White Light" of the liberating Truth at the exact instant of death, and it's during the essential Chikhai Bardo that the spirit realizes that it's free from its body.

The Chonyid Bardo is the stage in which the spirit enters into a dreamlike state and experiences hallucinations that reflect the mental and karmic conditions that person achieved during his or her lifetime. They encounter lights and colors;

personifications of human emotions in the forms of peaceful and vengeful deities; judgment and punishment; visions of Dharma-Raja, the King of the Dead, holding a scale on which evil deeds are weighed against good deeds; and a jury of gods— all of them thought forms rather than existing beings.

The third and final stage is the Sidpa Bardo, in which the spirit proceeds to the "degradation" of another incarnation if it was unable to move on to Nirvana during the two previous bardos.

And to the Buddhist, Nirvana, the ultimate liberation, literally means "extinction." The highest goal is to escape the cycle that so devastated the young prince Siddhartha: birth, deprivation, illness, dying, and death. Life in a physical body is seen as the source of suffering. But when the soul abandons the false sense of self that revolves around its desires and its base impulses, it becomes truly enlightened and dissolves into the great sacred void, which leaves nothing to reincarnate and therefore nothing to experience further deprivation, illness, dying, and death.

HINDUISM

The ancient religion of Hinduism, thought by many to have begun in about 6000 B.C., has grown from its roots in the Indus Valley of India to become the world's third largest religion, with more than 750 million followers. Unlike most other major religions, its birth wasn't inspired by a single leader or group of leaders, or by any traceable sequence of events. Instead, it seems to have evolved, with sacred texts from around 600 B.C. at its core. Those texts include four volumes called "the Vedas," which contain hymns, incantations, and rituals from ancient India; and "the Upanishads," which expands on the philosophies of an already existing Indian religion called Vedism.

Hinduism worships one God, a divine and supreme entity called "Brahman," who is at one with the universe and transcends it at the same time. Brahman exists as a composite of three separate parts:

- Brahma, the Creator, who perpetually creates new realities;
- Vishnu, or Krishna, the Preserver, who protects and preserves Brahma's creations, traveling to earth in the form of any of his ten possible incarnations to restore eternal order when it's threatened; and
- Shiva, the Destroyer.

Hindus believe in a cyclical creation in which everything comes from nothing and returns to nothing, again and again and again. Brahma creates the universe, Vishnu protects it from extinction, and Shiva destroys it to nothing so that Brahma can begin a new creation cycle again. Each cycle is thought to last a very long time—the current cycle of the universe is thought to have roughly 427,000 years left before it ends so that Brahma can create a new one.

Hindu lives aspire to "the four aims of Hinduism," three of which are geared toward those who are in the world, called the *pravritti*:

- *Dharma*: righteousness in their religious lives
- *Artha*: economic and material prosperity
- *Kama*: finding sensual, sexual, and mental enjoyment

The fourth "aim of Hinduism" is intended for the *nivritti*, or those who renounce this world:

- *Moksa*: those who have become liberated from *samsara*, which is the endlessly repeated cycles of karma

involved in the Hindu interpretation of reincarnation
and eternity.

Hinduism embraces the belief that while our bodies inevitably die, our souls live eternally. When the soul leaves the body, it
simply moves on to another body, which can be that of any living thing, human or otherwise, depending on the karma of the
life lived in the previous body. The soul's karma is the net total
of one's good and bad deeds throughout a lifetime, and karma
in one lifetime determines how you'll live the next—whether
the soul will be reborn at a higher, more successful or privileged
level, or as perhaps a severely disadvantaged person or the most
humble of animals. Eventually, through a lifetime consisting of
the purest acts, thoughts, and commitment to God, the soul
can escape *samsara*, the cycle of reincarnation, and achieve true
enlightenment. The ultimate goal might mean an eternity in the
immediate presence of God's love, or the highest achievement
of all, the dissolving of the soul into the great, unfathomable
oneness of Brahman.

Hinduism and the disciplines of yoga have been intertwined
since Hinduism's ancient inception, and four of those disciplines are thought to provide the path toward ultimate salvation
and enlightenment:

- Jnana yoga: the path of knowledge, in which the mind
  learns to understand the unreal nature of the universe;
- Bhakti yoga: the path of devotion, in which the soul
  achieves enlightenment through a life committed to the
  worship of Brahman;
- Karma yoga: the path of action, which involves a life
  committed to selfless good works; and
- Raja yoga: the "royal road," the use of the many
  techniques of meditative yoga toward ultimate
  salvation.

There are many variations in customs and traditions among the vast number of Hindu sects throughout the world, but they all share a great tolerance for one another and for all religions, embracing the truth that there are countless paths to the one divine, supreme, omnipotent God.

ISLAM

The heart of Islam is total surrender and obedience to one God, called Allah, the all-powerful, all-knowing, all-merciful, supreme, sovereign, and just Creator. Muslims—as followers of Islam are known—believe that since the beginning of time, Allah has sent His prophets and messengers to guide humankind. The last of those prophets was Muhammad. Like all other prophets of Islam, Muhammad was considered to be human, not divinely conceived, and Muslims never refer to him as "Allah." Allah is a name strictly reserved for God, the only truly supreme entity in all of creation who's worthy of being worshipped.

Muhammad Ibn Abdallah was born in Makkah (Mecca) in A.D., 570 in what is now Saudi Arabia. Arabia at that time was a peninsula divided into tribes and cities, all of whom worshipped their own gods and goddesses. In a tradition dating back centuries, they all gathered once a year around the Ka'aba in Mecca, which housed idols from all the Arabian tribes, and called a truce to their battles in a five-day religious celebration called the Hajj.

Muhammad's father died before he was born, and his mother died when he was only six years old. After two years with his grandfather, who also died, his uncle Abu Talib adopted him and raised him as his own. When Muhammad was twelve he traveled with his uncle to Syria, where it is said that a Christan monk named Buhaira proclaimed the boy the last great prophet.

Muhammad became a valued part of Abu Talib's trading caravans and, at twenty-five, married a forty-year-old widow named Khadijah. He continued his life in Mecca as a successful merchant and devoted husband, occasionally leaving the city on foot to fast and pray in the surrounding hills of Hira. One day when he was forty he was on one of his private pilgrimages, in a cave on Mount Hira, when a voice suddenly enveloped him, and he looked up into the darkness to find an Angel standing before him. Muhammad began reciting and memorizing messages dictated to him by the Angel. The first message read:

(Recite): In the name of your Lord who created man from a clot [of blood].

(Recite): Your Lord is Most Noble, who taught by the pen, taught man what he did not know. (Qur'an 96:1–5)

After several more revelations, which Muhammad obediently recited from the Angel's dictation, both the Angel and the voice were gone. And then, suddenly alone and very afraid that the experience was a sign of demon possession, Muhammad hurriedly left the cave and was making his way down the mountain path toward Mecca when he heard the same voice again, saying, "Oh, Muhammad, truly you are the messenger of God. And I am His Angel, Gabriel." A vision of Gabriel appeared in the sky for several moments, filling Muhammad with awe and fear, then disappeared again, and as dawn broke, Muhammad hurried home.

He only spoke to a handful of trusted family members and friends about the experience, still very shaken by it and uncertain of its true source. His wife Khadijah consulted her uncle, Waraca, a Hanefite (Arabs who rejected idol worship) who had become a Christian. Waraca assured her that yes, Muhammad's vision had indeed come from God, and God, through Gabriel, had declared Muhammad a prophet to the Arab tribes and cities. Three years later, Muhammad had another vision that instructed him to "arise and warn" against the worship of false gods and to spread the sacred message that Allah was the one true God.

Muhammad began preaching the message of Allah, and disciples and followers gathered around. As Muhammad and his message became more popular, the city of Mecca became a dangerous place—the growing population of Muslims were resoundingly persecuted by the tribes who much preferred their own gods and goddesses to the idea of Allah. Muhammad and his followers were forced out of Mecca and, in A.D. 622 they settled in Yathrib, later called Medina, which roughly translates to mean "the city of the prophet." The Muslim community grew in size, strength, and devotion in Medina, and finally, in 630, led by Muhammad, they returned to and captured Mecca and declared it the Holy City. All idols were banished from the Ka'aba, and the residents of Mecca converted to Islam.

Muhammad died at the age of sixty-three, two years after his return to Mecca, with messages and revelations continuing to be given to him for the last twenty-three years of his life. His close friend Abu Bakr succeeded him as Caliph, or leader of the Muslims, as the religion and its influence spread rapidly throughout the Arab peninsula, and beyond through North Africa, as well as across Asia, and finally throughout the world.

The holy scripture of Islam is the Qur'an, or Koran, thought to have been the visions of Muhammad dictated by him to scribes who noted them down word for word in Arabic. Muslims believe the Qur'an to be the last of the revelations sent directly from Allah to humankind, and it's only considered sacred in its original Arabic form. Translations, which by definition have been filtered through human minds and interpretations, bear the title *The Meaning of the Koran*.

According to Muhammad and the Qur'an, the spirit, when

it leaves the body after death, faces a day of reckoning in which its actions and intentions are judged according to its own unique potential—how the soul performed or failed to perform to the best of its individual abilities. Those who lived their lives in accordance with the truth and laws of Islam ascend to an eternity in heaven, which is filled with the love of Allah, while those who rejected Islam after being taught its laws fall off the bridge al-Aaraf and descend into the eternal torments of hell.

CHRISTIANITY

> For God so loved the world that He gave His only begotten son, that whosoever believeth in Him should not perish, but have everlasting life.
>
> —*John 3:16*

That Bible verse perhaps sums up the essence of Christianity better than any other. And of course God's "only begotten son" was Jesus Christ, whose birth, life, and death two millennia ago became the foundation of a religion that today is followed by approximately 2 billion faithful around the world.

According to the Gospels, the Angel Gabriel appeared to Mary, a virgin betrothed to Joseph, and delivered the news that she had been chosen to bear the Messiah, the Son of God. Mary and Joseph were forced by an order of Caesar Augustus to leave Nazareth and travel to the land of Joseph's ancestors for a census. Finding no room at the inn or other lodging in Bethlehem, Mary and Joseph settled into a barn, where the virgin Mary gave birth to Jesus. A brilliant star in the eastern sky and the songs of the Angels spread the word to Wise Men and shepherds throughout the land that the King of the Jews had been born.

Jesus grew up and spent his early adulthood in Nazareth. His public ministry began when he was thirty years old. He traveled to the Jordan River to be baptized by John the Baptist, and as he rose from the water, according to Mark 1:10–11, "he saw the heavens torn apart and the Spirit descending like a dove on him. And a voice came from heaven, 'You are my Son, the Beloved, in whom I am well pleased.'"

God then led Jesus into the desert to fast for forty days and forty nights, during which the devil appeared to him, tempting Jesus to prove his divinity by demonstrating his miraculous powers. Three times he was tempted and three times he declined with a quote from the scriptures, and the devil, having failed, departed, whereupon Angels descended to bring nourishment to God's son.

For the next three years Jesus traveled throughout Israel, preaching, teaching, performing miracles and healings, restoring sight to the blind and raising the dead back to life. Traveling with him were his twelve chosen apostles, and Jesus attracted crowds that often numbered in the thousands as he spoke out against anger, revenge, murder, theft, and adultery; advocated love, peace, humility, and compassion; and delivered God's promises of forgiveness for our sins and eternal life.

Among the most exquisite of Jesus' messages came to be known as the Sermon on the Mount, which began with the Beatitudes. Great crowds had followed him from throughout Syria, and from Galilee and Jerusalem, and from beyond the Jordan River.

"Seeing the crowds, he went up on the mountain, and when he sat down his disciples came to him. And he opened his mouth and taught them, saying:

'Blessed are the poor in spirit, for theirs is the kingdom of heaven.

'Blessed are those who mourn, for they shall be comforted.

'Blessed are the meek, for they shall inherit the earth.

'Blessed are those who hunger and thirst for righteousness, for they shall be satisfied.

'Blessed are the merciful, for they shall obtain mercy.

'Blessed are the pure in heart, for they shall see God.

'Blessed are the peacemakers, for they shall be called sons of God.

'Blessed are those who are persecuted for righteousness' sake, for theirs is the kingdom of heaven.

'Blessed are you when men revile you and persecute you and utter all kinds of evil against you falsely on my account. Rejoice and be glad, for your reward is great in heaven, for so men persecuted the prophets who were before you.'" (Matthew 5:1–12)

Jesus' overwhelming popularity, his new interpretations of the Old Testament, and his rumored claim to be the Son of God became a threat to the authorities, and he was arrested and charged with blasphemy and inciting a rebellion against those in power. At the age of thirty-three Jesus was crucified on the order of the Roman prefect Pontius Pilate, with a mocking inscription on top of the cross reading: "Here is Jesus, King of the Jews." As Jesus died, the earth trembled and the sky turned black, and with his last breath he uttered the words, "Father, into thy hands I commend my spirit."

Jesus was buried in a cave, with a boulder at its entrance and armed guards posted beside it to prevent Jesus' followers from stealing his body. On the third day Mary Magdalene, one of his most cherished followers, arrived at the tomb to anoint his body with spices and found the stone rolled away and the guards unconscious. She summoned several of the disciples, and when they went into the tomb they found Jesus' burial robes folded where his body had been.

Alone again inside the tomb, Mary saw two Angels, one at the foot and one at the head of Jesus' burial slab. Then, turning, she saw Jesus, whom she didn't recognize. Believing him to be the gardener, she asked where Jesus' body had been taken. He replied with a simple, "Mary," and she knew it was him and ran to tell the disciples that the Lord was alive and with them.

Jesus appeared to the disciples several times after the crucifixion. At his final appearance before them he promised that he would send power to them from the Holy Spirit when he left, so that they would be his witnesses in Jerusalem, in all of Judea and Samaria and to the ends of the earth. On that promise, Jesus was taken up into the sky before their eyes, where he disappeared into the clouds. And the two Angels standing with them asked, "Why do you stand here looking into the sky? This same Jesus who has been taken from you into heaven will come back in the same way."

It's no surprise, then, that a religion based on this profound life and equally profound death holds a deep, essential belief in the spirit's survival of the death of the body and its eternal life as promised by the Creator. Christians consistently believe that those who obey the laws of God and truly repent their sins will spend that eternity in heaven, living in perfection in spiritual bodies in the presence of Jesus, the saints, and the Angels. Liberal Christians generally believe that hell, where the evil and unrepentant souls are sent, is a concept, a banishment from heaven, while conservative Christians in general think that hell is an actual place, an underground inferno presided over by Satan in an eternity of torment.

CATHOLICISM

The beliefs of the Roman Catholic Church are beautifully expressed in the Apostles' Creed, thought to have been a collaboration of Jesus' twelve disciples, perhaps committed to writing in about the first century A.D.:

I believe in God, the Father Almighty,
the Creator of heaven and earth,
and in Jesus Christ, His only Son, our Lord,
Who was conceived of the Holy Spirit,
born of the Virgin Mary,
suffered under Pontius Pilate,
was crucified, died and was buried.
He descended into hell.
The third day He arose again from the dead.
He ascended into heaven
and sits at the right hand of God the Father Almighty,
whence He shall come to judge the living and the dead.
I believe in the Holy Spirit, the holy catholic [universal] church,
the communion of saints
the forgiveness of sins,
the resurrection of the body,
and life everlasting.
Amen.

The Catholic Church teaches that "the souls of those who have died in the state of grace suffer for a time a purging that prepares them to enter heaven." This place of purging, or "Purgatory," is where the spirit is cleansed of its lesser sins and imperfections in preparation for judgment. Only after this Purgatory can the faithful and devout, who have been baptized in the Church and done good works on earth in Jesus' name, enter the kingdom of heaven.

Hell, an actual place according to Catholic doctrine, is where those who have lived in league with Satan and his angels, or died without repenting their sins to a priest and atoning through whatever means the priest deems appropriate, are punished for all eternity, surrounded by flames which cause pain without ever consuming the body.

JUDAISM

The history of Judaism, the religion and culture of the Jewish people, dates back approximately four thousand years. It rejected the then widespread belief in the powers of many gods and goddesses and instead worshipped one supreme, omnipotent God.

Abraham, whose story is told in the book of Genesis in the Hebrew Bible, is thought to be the first Jew, preaching the word of that one omnipotent God and rewarded by Him with a promise of children who would inherit the land of Israel. Abraham's grandson Jacob, the third biblical patriarch and father of the twelve tribes of Israel, was sent by God to Egypt with his children, where they were enslaved by the Pharaohs. It was Moses, the greatest of all prophets in Judaism, who freed them from their slavery and delivered them to Israel (Canaan), the Promised Land. God then summoned Moses to the top of Mount Sinai and entrusted him with the Torah, which is God's teachings to the Jewish people.

The written Torah, called the Torah Shebiksav, is divided into three parts:

- Torah—the five books presented to Moses by God: Genesis, Exodus, Leviticus, Numbers, and Deuteronomy;
- *Nevi'im*, or Prophets—the messages received from God by the prophets, as written in Joshua, Judges, the two books of Samuel, the two books of Kings, Jeremiah, Ezekiel, Isaiah, and Trey Asar, or the Twelve, which combine the writings of Hosea, Joel, Amos, Obadiah, Jonah, Micah, Nahum, Habakkuk, Zephaniah, Haggai, Zachariah, and Malachi;
- *Kesuvim*, or Writings—written by the prophets with

God's guidance, but not exclusively devoted to
prophecies: Psalms, Proverbs, Job, Song of Songs, Ruth,
Lamentations, Ecclesiastes, Esther, Daniel, Nehemiah,
and the two books of Chronicles.

The primary beliefs of Judaism were first written in the form of
thirteen articles in the eleventh century by the Jewish sage Mai-
monides (Moses ben Maimon):

- *I believe with a true and perfect faith that God is the creator
  (whose name be blessed), governor and maker of all creatures,
  and that he has wrought all things, worketh and shall work
  forever.*
- *I believe with perfect faith that the creator (whose name be
  blessed) is one; that there is no unity like unto his in any way;
  and that he alone was, is and will be our God.*
- *I believe with perfect faith that the creator (whose name be
  blessed) is incorporeal, that he has not any corporeal qualities,
  and that nothing can be compared unto him.*
- *I believe with a perfect faith that the creator (whose name be
  blessed) was the first, and will be the last.*
- *I believe with a perfect faith that the creator (whose name be
  blessed) is to be worshipped and none else.*
- *I believe with perfect faith that all the words of the prophets
  are true.*
- *I believe with perfect faith that the prophecies of Moses our
  master (may he rest in peace) were true; that he was the
  father and chief of all prophets, both of those before him and
  those after him.*
- *I believe with perfect faith that the Law, at present in our
  hands, is the same that was given to our master Moses (peace
  be with him).*
- *I believe with perfect faith that this Law will not be changed,*

and that no other Law will be revealed by the creator (blessed be his name).

- *I believe with a perfect faith that God (whose name be blessed) knows all the deeds of the sons of men and all their thoughts; as it is said: "He who hath formed their hearts altogether, he knoweth all their deeds."*

- *I believe with a perfect faith that God (whose name be blessed) rewards those who keep his commandments, and punishes those who transgress them.*

- *I believe with a perfect faith that the Messiah will come; and although he tarries I wait nevertheless every day for his coming.*

- *I believe with a perfect faith that there will be a resurrection of the dead, at the time it shall please the creator (blessed be his name).*

Judaism tends to concern itself much more with our lives on earth than with the afterlife. The traditional belief is certainly that our lives do not end with the death of our bodies, but specifics of what happens to our spirits after death are largely left to each individual to conclude. There are many Orthodox Jews who believe that souls who live devout lives according to the laws of God ascend to a sacred, perfect place much like heaven, while souls of the unrighteous are either left to an eternity with their own demons or cease to exist entirely. Others believe that souls incarnate many times, while still others believe that souls will be resurrected with the eventual arrival of the messiah.

The messiah will arrive in human form and become the anointed king of Israel, ushering in the seventh millennium of purity and the universal worship of the one true God. His return has been anticipated for many centuries and is taken so seriously that in the walls of Jerusalem a special entrance was built. It's called the Golden Gate, also known as the Gate of

Mercy and the Gate of Eternal Life. Judaism dictates that the messiah will enter Jerusalem through the Golden Gate when he returns. But in 1541 the reigning Ottoman sultan, Suleiman, ordered the gate sealed to block the messiah's entrance, and the Golden Gate remains sealed today.

4

THE PRACTITIONERS

Long before there were psychic hotlines and spiritual gurus and superstars of "New Age" enlightenment, there were those who sought to connect the physical with the divine, the natural with the supernatural, the earthly world with the power of its Creator, not for fame and fortune but purely for the sake of healing and elevating humankind and the sanctity of this planet. It seems that every culture, no matter how primitive, recognized that there's far more to life than what the five senses can perceive, and those with special gifts, powers, and vision stepped forward to lead the search for whatever "more" turned out to be.

THE YOGIS

Any reason for practicing yoga is a good reason. Enhancing flexibility and releasing stress are as noble a purpose for performing yoga as the awakening of spirituality. This is the great gift of yoga—it serves and nourishes us at every level of our being and spontaneously contributes to greater well-being

in all domains of life. Yoga will help you discover gifts within
yourself that have remained unopened since your childhood
gifts of peace, harmony, laughter, and love.

—Drs. Deepak Chopra and David Simon,
The Seven Spiritual Laws of Yoga

I love yoga. I love the relaxation of it. I love the stress relief, the
way it can center me no matter how chaotic my day has been,
and the "thank you!" I can feel throughout my body as I perform
the postures. I love its ability to penetrate all the noise of the
conscious mind and reconnect me with the divine calm of my
soul, to the point where it provided me one night with a spiritual
experience I'll never forget and am looking forward to telling you
about. And, hard as this is to put into words, I love the awareness
that settles over me no matter how brief the session, that I'm
quietly, privately participating in something ancient.

India's huge Indus Valley civilization flourished around 3000
B.C., and stone seals unearthed from that civilization that depict
several yoga postures are the first tangible evidence of this beautiful discipline's existence. The oldest known teachings of yoga
are found in the Vedas, the sacred scriptures of early Hinduism,
and their "Lord's Song," or Bhagavad-Gita, dated anywhere
from the fourth century B.C. to the second century A.D., is the
first known scripture devoted entirely to yoga. As inseparable
from yoga as Hinduism is Buddhism, whose inception (discussed
in chapter 3) began in the sixth century B.C. when Siddhartha's
transformation into Buddha occurred through meditative breathing and postures that were clearly yogic.

In about 150 B.C., an East Indian physician and sage named
Patanjali wrote the *Yoga sutras*, commonly considered to describe
the principles of yoga, embracing both metaphysics and the
concept of a supreme spirit. His Eightfold Path summarized
his approach to the belief that the physical body and the soul
should be separated for the spirit to be cleansed:

1. *Yama*—ethical values
2. *Niyama*—the personal practice of purity, understanding, and learning
3. *Asanas*—physical exercises
4. *Pranayama*—controlled breathing
5. *Pratyahara*—the withdrawal of the senses to prepare for meditation
6. *Dharana*—concentration
7. *Dhyana*—meditation
8. *Samadhi*—ecstasy

The West was first exposed to yoga in the early 1800s, and its teachers, or yogis, who'd been valued for all those millennia in the East as being synonymous with both physical health and an inward rather than outward search for spiritual enlightenment, gained worldwide respect that continues today.

More than a hundred variations of yoga have evolved since its ancient beginnings. Probably the most commonly taught, Hatha yoga, is a combination of physical postures and movements and breathing techniques. Raja yoga, also known as the "royal road," involves exercises and breathing techniques along with meditation and study. My particular favorite is Tantra yoga, which promotes health, concentration, relaxation, deeper meditation, and spiritual growth.

This leads me to the extraordinary experience I mentioned earlier, involving a spiritual concept—and reality, it turns out—called "the silver cord."

The silver cord is a glistening, delicate strand we all possess, attached to our bodies just below the breastbone and seeming to disappear as it leads to the higher dimension of the Other Side. Much like the umbilical cord that nourishes our bodies while we're in the womb, the silver cord keeps our spirits perpetually nourished with the divine during our trips away from Home. It's our unbreakable connection to God's love, His way of making sure that He and we are always touching, no matter how far apart we might sometimes feel from Him.

Ecclesiastes 12:6–7 reads, "Before the silver cord is snapped . . . and the spirit returns to God who gave it." In fact, among world religions and beliefs the concept of the silver cord is fairly common. And several clients have described near-death experiences in which they actually saw their silver cord. Even Francine had assured me it's perfectly real. So it was just my stubborn, habitual skepticism that made me privately think of the silver cord as a sparkling, pretty, well-intentioned and harmless spiritual myth.

Then, when I was fifty years old, I saw my own silver cord, and the myth became a reality.

I was home from a particularly long day's work, lying on the floor of my living room unwinding with a Tantra yoga tape that had led me to such a deep meditation that I actually left my body and was wafting around near the ceiling looking down at myself. I don't happen to love astral travel and have always been grateful that it rarely happens when I'm awake—I know it's natural, I know it couldn't be safer, I know we can return to our bodies the instant we want so there's no danger of our spirits getting stranded in midair. It just makes me feel as if I'm not in control, which I don't enjoy. So, believe me, I would have returned to my body in the blink of an eye the instant I realized I'd left it if I hadn't caught a glimpse of something I'd never seen before and haven't seen since. Leading away from my solar plexus in a glittering trail that disappeared several feet off was a fine silver cord, as delicate as a gossamer thread. It was breathtaking, and it was real, and I felt blessed to have seen it for those few unforgettable seconds.

I've been in deep meditation many times in my life, but I honestly believe it was the combined disciplines of Tantra yoga that made it possible for me to experience such an exquisite moment of convergence between the physical and the spiritual worlds.

THE SHAMANS

Since ancient times, in countless cultures on virtually every continent, shamanism has been a valued link between the physical and spirit worlds. Its practitioners, known as shamans, are highly respected for their unique gifts of healing; teaching; guiding souls safely to their place in the afterlife; summoning help from the spirit world; foreseeing the future; and sending lingering, bothersome ghosts Home where they belong.

Some shamans receive their powers from their genetic lineage. Some experience a divine "calling" and are trained by wise tribal elders. And some are bestowed with their shamanistic powers by a near-death experience, as was the case with the great Native American shaman Black Elk.

Black Elk was born in 1863. At the age of nine, he collapsed into unconsciousness from an illness that caused severe swelling throughout his body. As he lay dying, he heard voices calling to him from the clouds, telling him that he was being summoned by his deceased grandfather.

He was drawn up into the clouds, where he saw a spectacular vision that included horses, a sky filled with lightning, and the center of the earth. He was then told to follow one of the horses, that led him to a rainbow door, behind which he found six ancient elders, who announced that they had gathered to teach him. And with that, each of the elders gave the frightened boy a power.

The first gave Black Elk the power to heal. The second gave him the power of cleansing. The third gave him the power and peace of awakening. The fourth gave him the power of growth.

The fifth gave him the power of supernatural vision. The sixth regressed in age until he became the nine-year-old Black Elk, then returned to his impossibly old age again and gave the boy his own powers, telling him to have courage and use his powers well for the great troubles ahead among Black Elk's people.

Black Elk then found himself standing on the top of a mountain, where he saw and understood the sanctity of all things. He visited the elders again and was then returned to his dying body, where he awoke to find his relieved, overjoyed parents beside him. He'd been comatose for twelve days.

Afraid to tell anyone about his near-death experience for fear they wouldn't believe him, Black Elk spent the next eight years of his life sad, quiet, and withdrawn. But finally he confided in a shaman, who not only believed him but also worked with him to reenact the experience in the form of a ritual. With that reenactment, Black Elk was infused with the powers the elders had given him and became a great healing shaman, heartbroken throughout his life about the one healing he couldn't perform: preventing the destruction of his people by the unstoppable intrusion of industrial civilization.

The holistic healing techniques of shamans vary from one practitioner to the next, but all of them start at the spirit level and "work their way out," whether they're addressing physical health problems or mental/emotional ones. One of the most glaring differences between Western medicine and shamanistic treatments is that Western medicine generally looks to the same cure for each condition that is diagnosed, while shamans view each person, each condition, and each healing as unique. They believe that everything in nature is alive and, as a result, that everything in nature possesses information. Shamans use that information, as well as the spirits of humans and animals around them, to diagnose, to treat, and to heal the soul and any illness that's creating a shadow around it.

As he begins his healing, the shaman shifts his state of

consciousness so that he can examine his patient's spirit through an elevated awareness. He accomplishes his shift of consciousness through astral travel, which he calls the "soul flight," during which he gathers whatever natural information he needs and also seeks out any essential life elements his patient might have unknowingly lost or picked up along the way.

To understand that, it's important to know a few basics about health problems from the shamanistic point of view:

First, illness results from a loss of power, and healing can only take place when that power is restored. That's usually accomplished through a "power animal retrieval." A "power animal" is a spirit protector in animal form whose strength is available to us whenever we need it. To retrieve it, the shaman astrally travels to the patient's power animal and gathers as much restorative strength as the patient needs.

Second, all or part of the soul leaves the body when it needs to protect itself from a serious trauma. From time to time, part of the soul gets trapped outside the body, unsure of how to return. Shamans consider this soul loss to be the cause of bipolarism, schizophrenia, and other mental illnesses, and they typically treat it by performing a soul retrieval to bring back those lost fragments and make the spirit whole again.

And third, our own negativity, or negativity someone feels toward us, is a powerful, physically invasive force, becoming imbedded in the body and causing ulcers, chronic migraines, indigestion, kidney stones, and disabling back and joint pain. Shamans locate and remove the imbedded negative energy in a technique called "shamanic extraction," usually submerging it in water to neutralize it so that it can't return to the body or find its way to another vulnerable soul.

Because of their great reverence for and connection to the spiritual sanctity of all aspects of nature, shamans are being called upon today as they have been since ancient times to heal infertile land, polluted bodies of water, diseased crops, and decimated rain forests, and to perform their specialized rituals for creating shifts in weather patterns to help restore stability to the world's environment. We owe shamanism a debt of gratitude for its countless discoveries in the area of natural healing resources, and for its quiet, ongoing, largely unreported efforts to counteract the tragic abuse of our struggling planet.

WITCHCRAFT

Witchcraft very probably dates back to the Stone Age, and for many thousands of years witches and warlocks (the male counterparts of witches) were valued as village doctors and herbalists. In private they developed their own series of rites for honoring and praying to the nature goddess.

And then, along came the Church. I insist on believing its followers meant well, and God knows they cherish their rites as well, but they sometimes tend to make some rather hysterical assumptions about those who prefer their privacy, especially for an institution whose Bible includes the instruction "Judge not, lest ye be judged." So the Church took an openly contemptuous attitude toward witches and warlocks for their seemingly untraditional, "heathen" practices and celebration of a belief system not consistent with the beliefs of the Church, which was ignorantly misinterpreted to equate witchcraft with Satanism. The inherent privacy among witches and warlocks deepened under the disapproving scrutiny of the Church, which of course made them look even more potentially evil, suspicious, and bizarre.

In reality, at the heart of traditional witchcraft (also called Wicca) in its original form is a worship of nature, a belief that abuse of this planet is a form of sacrilege, and the search for an ecologically balanced and protected Mother Earth, having nothing whatsoever to do with Satanism. I'm sure I'm a little sensitive to the "in league with the devil" accusation, since it's happened to me so often that I stopped listening to it decades ago, when the fact is that you'll never meet anyone more passionately committed to God than I am. Indeed, it's occurred to me more than once that if I'd lived in Salem, Massachusetts, in 1692, doing exactly what I do now, I could easily have been executed along with the rest of the "witches."

The Salem Witch Trials, in case you've never read about them, began with two young girls in search of attention pretending to have fits. These feigned fits were diagnosed as "bewitchment," and the girls were promptly ordered to identify the witches responsible for casting this devil's spell on them so that the witches could be hunted down and killed. What started out as a prank spun out of control as the girls, rather than admit they'd been lying, accused any and every "witch" who sprang to mind, including a four-year-old child. As the insanity of this witch hunt swept through Salem, husbands turned in their wives as witches to punish them for infractions no matter how minor, "positive identifications" were manufactured out of thin air, the mentally ill were coerced into confessions of practicing witchcraft without having a clue what it meant, and the Puritan magistrates looked wildly successful at rounding up virtual throngs of "Satan's disciples."

Luckily, the two girls who started it all finally pushed their luck too far and, in a grand gesture of the highest drama, accused the governor's wife of being a witch, which turned out to be the beginning of the end of the Salem Witch Trials. But by the time it was over, the panic over a prank in which not one crime was ever committed resulted in the arrest of 141 innocent people; one elderly man was crushed under a pile of rocks when he refused to confess to practicing witchcraft; and 19 people were hanged.

So much for wondering why witches and warlocks prefer to keep their rites and practices to themselves.

As for their belief in an afterlife, most witches do believe in some form of our lives continuing after death. They don't believe in an actual heaven or hell but instead believe that our spirits go on by connecting to a new living being. There's a great appreciation for their spiritual bonds to their ancestors and the continuation of their lives through their children and children's children to come.

SPIRITUALIST CAMPS

I come by my interest in spiritualist camps naturally, thanks to my beloved Grandma Ada's brother, Uncle Henry Kaufhold. I still have and treasure some of the letters Uncle Henry wrote to Grandma Ada about his life in the late 1800s when it was both good news and bad news to be a very gifted psychic. The good news was, the spiritualist movement was gaining momentum in the United States, so psychics were no longer in danger of being tarred, feathered, and chased out of town by torch-bearing mobs as they were in earlier witch trial days. The bad news was, the spiritualist movement was gaining momentum in the United States, and fraudulent physical mediums (you'll read about a few of those in chapter 7) were making it difficult for honest, hardworking, legitimate psychics to be trusted enough to build a clientele.

Uncle Henry was born in 1849, a Midwesterner who had every intention of setting up his psychic practice in Springfield, Missouri, and raising a family. But between potential clients' skepticism and his own disgust with the prevalence of frauds he'd personally witnessed among his own ostensible colleagues, he pulled up stakes and headed to the Chesterfield Spiritualist Camp in Chesterfield, Indiana, where he was able to reignite his passion for spiritualism and the humanitarian value of his pursuit of that passion. In fact, after several years at the Chesterfield Camp he studied at a spiritualist college in England

and practiced there for five years before returning to America, settling in Oklahoma with his wife Gertrude and their five children, and happily living out the rest of his life as a successful psychic and healer (who worked strictly on a donation basis, by the way).

Spiritualist camps began in Lake Pleasant, Massachusetts, in 1873 and quickly spread throughout the country. Several of them still exist today, and even though in most cases the tents of Uncle Henry's day have been replaced by more substantial accommodations for crowds that by 1880 sometimes reached twenty thousand, the stated purpose of the camps remains the same: to teach, learn, celebrate, share experiences, attend lectures, and in general deepen the peace, joy, and comfort to be found in a God-centered spiritualist life.

Camps invariably took place in rural settings, with the non-denominational throngs experiencing the atmosphere of social gatherings among like-minded faithful. There were entire temporary communities of tents for vendors, dancing, music, exhibits, and meals. Sailing parties in the rivers were as common as the séances, private readings, and classes in everything from telepathy to channeling to psychokinesis. Speakers gave lectures throughout the day, and in the evening there was typically a huge gathering in an auditorium for band and choir concerts and one or two keynote speakers, who ranged from mediums to ministers to scientists to professors to physicists.

And, as Uncle Henry was quick to point out and applaud in his letters, the pervasive God-centeredness of these amazing gatherings made them fairly risky for any would-be frauds or scam artists. The instant someone caught on that a medium or psychic or anyone else in the camp was there with the intention to deceive the faithful, open-minded crowds, word would spread like wildfire, and the offender would invariably be gone by the end of the day along with his or her "career."

Countless healings for grieving hearts and discouraged souls have taken place at spiritual camps. And there's no doubt that my Uncle Henry experienced a healing as well. He hadn't lost his faith in God or in the eternal survival of the spirit, but he'd lost his faith in the integrity of his life's passion. He found that faith again at the Chesterfield Spiritualist Camp and recommitted himself for the rest of his years to reuniting people with their departed loved ones and with the Creator who makes all things possible.

FAITH HEALERS

There are few more controversial subjects in the already controversial world of spiritualism than the validity or complete nonsense of faith healing. And frankly, there's good reason for all the controversy.

Phony faith healers have been taking advantage of the sick and dying for as long as humankind has included the sick and dying. Some of these frauds are just plain despicable, deliberately fooling as many people as possible while probably preventing them from getting genuine, legitimate medical care, and/or filling their audiences with "plants" who experience miraculous "healings" for physical problems that never existed in the first place. It's my guess/hope that other phony faith healers genuinely believe they're helping while actually only acting as placebos, delaying medical treatment for the faithful and giving illnesses time to get worse.

There are also those who refuse medical treatment altogether, for themselves or loved ones or children, and rely exclusively on their faith in God to heal them no matter what the affliction. If their faith fails them, they either blame themselves for not being faithful enough or they blame God for turning His back on them.

But there are also countless absolutely true and absolutely

beautiful stories of faith healings throughout the world since ancient times. And a majority of licensed physicians and scientists are convinced that faith and prayer can contribute to a patient's healing. So the confusing bottom line seems to be some combination of "Beware!" and "Believe!"

Long before there was such a thing as scientific medicine, people turned to witch doctors, shamans, and medicine men to restore their health. Plants, herbs, and rituals to drive out the demons that were thought to be the cause of physical and mental problems were usually combined with some kind of supernatural powers among these highly revered practitioners. The ancient Romans and ancient Greeks prayed to Asclepius, their god of medicine, to come to the afflicted in their dreams and cure them. In Egypt, couples who had trouble conceiving children traveled to pray at the Temple of Imhotep, whose accomplishments during his lifetime included great medical knowledge and who was sanctified after he died.

Of course, the Bible contains any number of stories of Jesus' faith healings. To cite just a few:

- And at Capernaum there was an official whose son was ill. When he heard that Jesus had come from Judea to Galilee, he went and begged him to come down and heal his son, for he was at the point of death. Jesus therefore said to him, "Unless you see signs and wonders you will not believe." The official said to him, "Sir, come down before my child dies." Jesus said to him, "Go; your son will live." The man believed the word that Jesus spoke to him and went his way. As he was going down, his servants met him and told him that his son was living. So he asked them the hour when he began to mend, and they said to him, "Yesterday at the seventh hour the fever left him." The father knew that was the hour when Jesus had said to him, "Your son will live"; and he himself believed, and all his household. (John 4:46–53)

- And when Jesus entered Peter's house, he saw his mother-in-law lying sick with a fever; he touched her hand, and the fever left her, and she rose and served him. That evening they brought to him many who were possessed with demons, and he cast out the spirits with a word, and healed all who were sick. This was to fulfill what was spoken by the prophet Isaiah, "He took our infirmities and bore our diseases." (Matthew 8:14–17)
- Soon afterward he went to a city called Nain, and his disciples and a great crowd went with him. As he drew near to the gate of the city, behold, a man who had died was being carried out, the only son of his mother, and she was a widow; and a large crowd from the city was with her. And when the Lord saw her, he had compassion on her and said, "Do not weep." And he came and touched the bier, and the bearers stood still. And he said, "Young man, I say to you, arise." And the dead man sat up, and began to speak. And he gave him to his mother. (Luke 7:11–15)

And then there are Christian pilgrimages to such hallowed shrines as Lourdes, a small French town where, in 1858, a fourteen-year-old girl named Marie-Bernade Soubirous was graced with visitations from the Virgin Mary. The pilgrimages to Lourdes began in 1859, and today as many as 5 million believers travel there with the sick and dying every year in search of healings and miracles.

In fact, I feel safe in saying that there's not a religion—Christian or non-Christian—or a culture in this world that doesn't practice some form of faith healing.

I believe in faith healing, to the point where I have a long-established prayer chain, more than 300,000 strong, in which people can call my office to add names of loved ones in need of healing. The list of names is passed along to the fifty ministers of my non-denominational church, *Novus Spiritus*. Each of those fifty ministers passes the list to fifty members of the prayer chain, who pass it along to fifty more, and so on. That same list is also distributed through the cyberministry on my Web site, and every morning at 9:00 a.m. Pacific time, wherever we members of the prayer chain happen to be throughout the world, we offer a prayer for every name on the list:

> *Dear God, in the mind, body or soul, wherever their pain resides, may it be released with Thy help into the healing white light of the Holy Spirit. Amen.*

As much as I believe in faith healing and the miracles of prayer chains, I also believe in the healing and miracles of traditional medicine. I value and admire the medical community more than I can express. I believe God created doctors just as surely as He created the rest of us, and when I get sick, you can count on it that I combine traditional medical help with spiritual help to pull me through.

Last but certainly not least, I believe that healings and miracles are, in the end, intensely personal transactions between their recipients and God. Along with the most thorough, skilled medical attention and the most devout spiritual support available, I believe in something called "exit points," which make healings and miracles much less haphazard and much more understandable.

Before each of us decides to come to earth for another incarnation, while we're still living in the perfection of the Other Side, we write a detailed chart for the lifetime we're about to begin to ascertain that we'll achieve the goals we've set for ourselves. Included in that chart are five exit points: five separate opportunities we design to get safely Home again when we feel that each incarnation has served its purpose.

We don't necessarily wait until the fifth exit point to head back to our lives on the Other Side. We might decide when our first exit point comes along, or our second, or our fourth, that we've accomplished all we need to on this trip, and we don't necessarily space them out evenly when we design them. We might write two exit points to occur in the same year, for example, and then not schedule another one for thirty or forty years.

The most obvious exit points include critical illnesses and surgeries, potentially fatal accidents, and any other events that could result in our death. We design those events, and when they occur, we either choose that exit point and go Home, or we choose to survive and wait for the next one. Other more subtle exit points are those we might not even recognize when they happen: deciding "for no reason" to drive a different route than usual to work or home; "trivial" delays that keep us from leaving the house on time for a commitment; a last-minute change in travel plans "on a hunch"; or canceling an appointment, social or otherwise, just because we suddenly "don't feel like it." Any number of incidents that seem random or meaningless at the time could easily be our spirits remembering an exit point that we wrote into our charts but decided not to take advantage of after all.

Embracing the truth of exit points will liberate you from feeling so responsible when a loved one dies despite our most exhaustive medical and spiritual efforts and our most impassioned prayers. Every one of us came here with five exit points to choose from. And in the end it's no one's choice but our own which one we opt to take.

Please never believe when you lose a loved one that you could or should have done more, or that God ignored your prayers. That simply never happens, *ever*. Instead, remember and respect that, for reasons of their own, your loved one simply said yes to an exit point, designed before they came here. It's neither your fault nor anyone else's, and it will make perfect sense to you when you're reunited with them in the sacred bliss of the Other Side.

PART II

THE TRICKS
OF THE TRADE

5

THE DIVINATION DISCIPLINES

*M*erriam-Webster's *Collegiate Dictionary* defines divination as "the art or practice that seeks to foresee or foretell future events or discover hidden knowledge usually by the interpretation of omens or by the aid of supernatural powers." But in warmer, simpler terms, divination is humankind's effort, through paranormal means, to search everywhere to uncover the answers we're sure God has left here for us.

And when I say "everywhere," I'm not exaggerating. I feel safe in saying that at some point or other since we've existed on this planet, every culture of every country of every continent has devised more divination disciplines in search of God's divine answers than it would be possible to study in depth in a lifetime. To give you just a glimpse of the forms those searches have taken:

- *Alchemy*—an ancient divining practice in which an elusive stone or substance known as the "philosopher's stone" transformed common base metals into gold
- *Aleuromancy*—divination through the use of fortune cookies

- *Astragyromancy*—divination through the rolling of special dice whose facets contain letters and numbers
- *Botanomancy*—divination through studying varying patterns of burning twigs, leaves, and branches
- *Capnomancy*—divination through the varying patterns in rising smoke
- *Caraunoscopy*—divination through the signs found in thunder and lightning storms
- *Daphnomancy*—divination through listening to messages in the crackling of specially selected branches tossed onto an open fire
- *Gyromancy*—a tedious divining process, distantly related to the Ouija board, in which the client walks around a lettered circle to the point of dizziness, and prophecies are spelled out from the letters on which the dizzy client begins to stumble
- *Ichthyomancy*—divination through the movements of live fish
- *Molybdomancy*—divination through the sputters and hisses of molten lead when it's poured into water
- *Myomancy*—divination through the behavior of mice and rats
- *Oneiromancy*—divination through dream interpretation
- *Ophiomancy*—divination through the movements and behavior of serpents
- *Rhapsodomancy*—divination through randomly opening a sacred book or book of poetry and selecting a passage found there
- *Spodomancy*—divination through the images in the cinders of a freshly extinguished fire

That list only scratches the surface of the disciplines developed through many millennia, which I'm sure were at least created in earnest and are still pursued by their share of well-meaning practitioners. Some of them are real. Some of them are unproven. The disciplines I'll be exploring in this chapter are simply those I've personally studied on some level or other, practice myself in some cases, and encourage you to experiment with when and if you find yourself particularly intrigued. Maybe most surprising of all, I don't doubt that some of these divination disciplines are already a part of your life; you just weren't sure exactly what to call them or how to put them to their most practical, effective use until now.

ASTROLOGY

I have to admit, I smile to myself when I hear someone dismiss astrology as "just another one of those hippie New Age fads." The truth is, astrology dates back to the mid-1600s B.C. and was studied and practiced in a variety of ancient cultures including Egypt, Babylon, Greece, and Rome. Now, that's a fad with serious longevity.

Astrology, of course, is the study of mathematically calculated interactions among the stars and planets and their impact on humankind. And its inception is based on the most understandable logic. God didn't create anything haphazard in this universe. Every detail was designed with perfect wisdom and deliberation. So it makes perfect sense that we're constantly searching His creation for any keys that might break His code and enable us to read and interpret His plans for the future of the world, and for us. And what more obvious place to search than the magnificent, unfathomable cosmos, filled with mysteries and unanswered questions? Why wouldn't it at least occur to us to look to the eternal infinity in which we have the honor of being included and think that maybe He's written messages there?

Astrology is an equal opportunity messenger that's been

consulted for all these millennia by everyone from the most common among us to pharaohs, emperors, kings, presidents, and first ladies. It has something new to say every day if we insist on watching that closely. Its most effective intention is to suggest, not dictate, the options and obstacles in our paths and our most advantageous responses to them.

There are thousands of books on astrology, and it's hard to find a magazine on the newsstand that doesn't devote a page to your horoscope, so it's very probably not news to you that the astrology chart, also known as the zodiac, is made up of twelve sun/natal signs, each with its own ruling planet and each designated by a specific segment of the calendar. The sun signs are:

Aries—ruled by Mars—born between March 21 and
    April 19
Taurus—ruled by Venus—born between April 20 and
    May 20
Gemini—ruled by Mercury—born between May 21
    and June 21
Cancer—ruled by the Moon—born between June 22
    and July 22
Leo—ruled by the Sun—born between July 23 and
    August 22
Virgo—ruled by Mercury—born between August 23
    and September 22
Libra—ruled by Venus—born between September 23
    and October 23
Scorpio—ruled by Pluto—born between October 24
    and November 21
Sagittarius—ruled by Jupiter—born between November
    22 and December 21
Capricorn—ruled by Saturn—born between December
    22 and January 19

Aquarius—ruled by Uranus—born between January 20
and February 18
Pisces—ruled by Neptune—born between February 19
and March 20

Every sign is generally associated with its own set of character/
personality traits, tendencies, and habits. But of course there's
far more to astrology than an analysis of our sun signs. In fact,
the sun signs are only the broad strokes of the cosmic influences
that are factored in to compose the totality of our astrological
charts, and of our unique identities. Here are the three most
significant influences, described *very* simply:

- Our sun sign, defined by the position of the Sun at the
moment of our birth, which is our inner self, the "real
us," our most basic outlook on life.
- Our ascendant, or rising sign—defined by whichever
astrological sign is rising above the horizon at the
moment of our birth—which is our core essence, the
"spine" of our character.
- Our moon sign, defined by the position of the Moon at
the moment of our birth, which is like the sum total of
our personality and our emotional structure.

Again, while we tend to categorize ourselves and one another by
our sun signs, it's important to recognize that our ascendants and
our moon signs deeply influence our characters and personalities
as well. If you're someone who regularly reads your horoscope,
you might glance at the forecasts for your rising sign and your
moon sign after a look at what's coming up for your sun sign, because there might be relevant messages for you in those as well.

Still just scratching the surface on the subject of astrology, I
promise you—the signs of the zodiac are also divided into categories according to the four basic earth elements:

- The air signs, with a tendency toward intellect, are Libra, Gemini, and Aquarius.
- The water signs, with a tendency toward emotions, are Cancer, Pisces, and Scorpio.
- The earth signs, the practical ones among us, are Capricorn, Virgo, and Taurus.
- The fire signs, characterized by ambition, are Aries, Sagittarius, and Leo.

Each of the sun signs has its own list of general tendencies, which are affected to varying degrees by the ascendants and the moon signs. If you find yourself getting at all offended by these very brief thumbnail sketches, try reading them with an Aries— they tend to have a great sense of humor about themselves, and the rest of us could learn from their example.

- Aries—both impulsive and compulsive; intensely loyal; enjoy a good laugh even when it's at their own expense; tend to keep proving the same point over and over again until they're convinced of your intelligence; mortally offended if you turn your back on them when they're talking to you; dislike change; need their own space; resist authority
- Taurus—when ascendant and moon sign are also Taurus, i.e., a "triple Taurus," I'm sorry, but boring; chronically act confused to get attention; verbalization patterns tend to be either poetic or overly verbose; stubborn; slow to forgive; artistic; care deeply about ecology and neatness; not family-oriented but very protective of loved ones; sentimental about birthdays, anniversaries, and other personal holidays
- Gemini—avid talkers; cautious about forming friendships; self-conscious; very concerned with learning; changeable and multifaceted; fun; easygoing but fickle and difficult to keep grounded

- Cancer—home-loving and protective; frugal; maudlin and martyred; given to excess; great animal lovers; intensely selective; prone to moodiness but fight it admirably; easily hurt; will tell the same story eighty-five times and leave out the punch line eighty-five times
- Leo—great determination; often hide their insecurity with yelling; strong sense of fidelity; heartbroken if hurt but enraged if someone they love is hurt; hate to lie, hate liars more; not fond of hard work but yearn for material wealth; hate to lose; too often let others form their opinion of themselves; more intuitive about events than about people
- Virgo—promiscuous, with usually prim exterior; organized and meticulous; good with people; obsessive about finishing what they start; equally obsessive about making lists; hyper-sensitive; able to be deeply in love with two or three people at once; better supporters than leaders in an organization; dislike change; tend to be permissive, inconsistent parents
- Libra—natural-born mediators; tend to jump from subject to subject when talking; affectionate; magnanimous but paradoxically secretive; bad tempers; resent unsolicited advice; exceptional love of beauty; empathetic, but see illness and self-pity as weakness; despise ingratitude; honest to a fault; equal balance of male and female aspects
- Scorpio—guided by their genitals but very goal-oriented; not prone to verbalize their thoughts; want to change the world; cover all their bases, personally and professionally; take charge, but slow to battle; innately secure; loners; approach life with their own set of truths; natural stamina; great teachers
- Sagittarius—very analytical; love mind-involved issues; in constant need of validation; anxiety-ridden; quick-witted; love to postulate no matter what the subject; need space and freedom but extremely faithful; softhearted but capable of being vindictive; blunt; highly intellectualized

- Capricorn—strongest sign of the zodiac: tend to intellectu-
alize emotion; love obstacles; analytical to a fault; brilliant
retentive memories; won't tolerate phobias in themselves;
great humanitarians; not vindictive; flexible to others' opin-
ions; fastidious about clothing and neatness; comfortable
with set patterns

- Aquarius—natural-born teachers; more comfortable with
groups than with one-on-one relationships; love to dance;
love water and the ocean; extroverted but with an intro-
verted subtext, as if always containing a hidden compart-
ment; slow to anger but explosive when the "fuse" is used
up; romantic; very ingenious; deeply offended by injustice

- Pisces—the most metaphysical sign of the zodiac: thrive
on compliments but are offended by empty flattery; deeply
sensitive to slights and insults and rarely suffer in silence
when offended; need romance, not just sex, in relationships;
avid readers, students, and note-takers; stubborn but flexible if they see they're wrong; great secret-keepers; despise
prejudice and bigotry in any form; quick to defend others
who are being treated unfairly

An interesting bit of trivia, by the way: to celebrate the birth
of Princess Margaret of England on August 21, 1930, the *Sunday Express* in London published her astrological analysis, and
touched off the ongoing proliferation of newspaper and magazine horoscopes.

So, how do you know if you're getting a true astrological
reading or just a regurgitation of a few typical characteristics
from some book? One key is to ask your astrologer if he or
she knows how to read a complete birth chart. The sun signs
listed above only offer part of the picture. If your astrologer
isn't able to understand and discuss the deeper details of your
chart (including the ascendant sign and your rising sign), keep
looking.

NUMEROLOGY

It was the Greek mathematician and philosopher Pythagoras (c. 580–500 B.C.) who said that numbers are "the ruler of forms and ideas and the cause of gods and demons." Based on his massively influential body of work, the ancient system of numerology was built and interpreted by a number of other cultures as a means of unlocking the mysteries of humankind and the universe.

Numerology is a practical expression of the belief that the universe consists of a series of mathematical patterns, and everything within the universe can be expressed in the form of numbers which correspond to universal energies. By assigning each letter of the alphabet to a specific number, and therefore that number's energy or vibration, names, birth dates, birthplaces, street addresses, and other details unique to each of us, can be numerologically interpreted to determine our personalities, our strengths and weaknesses, and our future.

Very simply described, numerology is based on the use of eleven numbers—1 through 9, and the master numbers 11 and 22. All numbers above 9, except the master numbers, are reduced to their numerological equivalents by simply adding their digits until the sum becomes one of numerology's eleven basic numbers. For example, a birth date of 10/19/1938 would be reduced by first adding 10 + 19 + 1938, which equals 1967. Next you would add 1 + 9 + 6 + 7, which equals 23. Finally, add 2 + 3 and you end up with the numerological number 5 for that birth date, the meaning of which we'll discuss in a moment.

The letters of the alphabet each correspond to a number from 1 through 9:

- 1 is assigned to the letters A, J, and S
- 2 is assigned to the letters B, K, and T

- 3 is assigned to the letters C, L, and U
- 4 is assigned to the letters D, M, and V
- 5 is assigned to the letters E, N, and W
- 6 is assigned to the letters F, O, and X
- 7 is assigned to the letters G, P, and Y
- 8 is assigned to the letters H, Q, and Z
- 9 is assigned to the letters I and R

So, finding the numerological value of the name Jane Doe, for example, would involve adding the corresponding numbers of each letter of the name, or:

$$1 \ (J) + 1 \ (A) + 5 \ (N) + 5 \ (E) + 4 \ (D) + 6 \ (O) + 5 \ (E) = 27$$

Reduced to one of the eleven numerology numbers, 27 would be 2 + 7, or 9.

None of which is all that exciting to discover until you know the numerologically assigned meaning of each of the numbers:

- 0—potentially creative; independent; can be scattered and disorganized
- 1—powerful; a leader and innovator; can be stubborn and resentful of authority
- 2—sympathetic; helpful; appreciates structure and routine; excellent confidant; can be insecure and unambitious
- 3—loves being the center of attention; usually more insecure than initially perceived; can be vain and superficial
- 4—practical; steady; honest; excellent at managing money; can be overly cautious and short-tempered
- 5—resourceful; optimistic; funny; makes friends easily; can be opportunistic and irresponsible

- 6—a diplomat and peacemaker; loves beautiful things; can be a chronic worrier
- 7—introspective; philosophical; maintains a mystical outlook on life; can be isolated and secretive
- 8—ambitious; materialistic; power and success more of a priority than family and relationships; can be self-centered and thoughtless
- 9—humanitarian; generous; compassionate; an idealist; can be egocentric and overly sensitive

Very basically, the number to which your full given name adds up numerologically is your destiny in this life, your true purpose for being here.

The number your birth date adds up to numerologically indicates your life path, the qualities at your core that need to be put to their best use in order for you to make the most of your lifetime.

The number that the vowels in your full given name add up to numerologically is key to the deepest desires and the priorities of your soul, the wisest part of your essence that must be acknowledged in order for you to be fulfilled.

The number that the consonants in your full given name add up to numerologically reveals how the outside world perceives you and your personality, the first impression you make on others, and how others might try to influence you.

So, does numerology really work? I'm not a numerologist myself, but I've seen some amazing insights from the practice. The most gifted numerologist I ever met was also psychic and able to very effectively use numerology as a valuable analytical supplement to his abilities rather than a literal, carved-in-stone tool.

On occasion, after an incredibly accurate reading that perhaps did not go quite as the client had planned, this numerologist friend would recommend that the client change their name—start using their maiden name instead of their married name, use their middle name instead of their first name, or otherwise make an adjustment in the name they most often hear, write, and use to introduce themselves. His explanation to his clients, which I always found to be a wonderful description of the potential of basic numerology, was: "Remember that there's no name you hear or say more often than your own. Now, think of the numbers in your name as corresponding to the keys on a piano. Those keys played together form a chord. And if that chord is discordant to your ear, or to the soundtrack of the life you aspire to, it's time to revise the chord to something that resonates as beauty in both your ear and your soul."

PALMISTRY

Palmistry, also called chiromancy, is the ancient practice of reading a person's past, present, future, health, and character by interpreting the unique topography of the palms of the hands. It's thought to have had its origins in India several thousand years before Christ and is known to have been popular in the time of Julius Caesar in ancient Rome and studied by Aristotle in ancient Greece. It also spread from India to China and Japan in about 3000 B.C., where Arabic merchants learned the skill and traveled with it to Europe. In the Middle Ages the Catholic Church denounced palmistry and all other forms of divination to be "the devil's work," so its pursuit was driven underground for the most part until the 1800s, when it became part of medical studies as a form of diagnosis. By the end of the nineteenth century palmistry had spread from Europe to America, and the modern interpretation of hand reading and analysis took shape.

The basics go like this:

The dominant hand, the hand you write with, reveals your life's path, while the other hand indicates your ultimate destiny.

At the base of the fingers and the thumb are raised mountains of flesh, called "mounts." Each mount is named after a celestial body, and each represents its own set of attributes, with the size of the mount indicating how strongly or weakly that attribute manifests itself.

- Jupiter, the mount beneath the index finger, indicates respect and pride.
- Saturn, beneath the second finger, indicates relationships.
- The Sun, beneath the ring finger, indicates creative talent.
- Mercury, beneath the little finger, indicates resourcefulness.
- Upper Mars, beneath Mercury, indicates courage.
- The Moon, beneath Upper Mars, indicates imagination.
- Venus, at the base of the thumb, indicates love relationships.
- Lower Mars, above Venus, indicates apathy.

Each finger also has its own celestial name and assigned attributes, with the length and shape of the finger dictating the quantity and quality of those attributes.

The Jupiter or index finger represents leadership and self-confidence.

The Saturn or second finger represents destiny.

The Apollo or ring finger represents health and metaphysical consciousness.

The Mercury or little finger represents communication skills.

The thumb, Venus, represents mental and emotional flexibility.

There is also significance in the lines of the palm, four of which are considered to be the most fundamental.

The Heart Line is the top prominent line across the palm of your dominant hand, and it suggests the balance between the mind and the emotions, the importance of love relationships, and the general approach to those relationships. A solid Heart Line, for example, denotes someone who takes fidelity and commitment seriously. A faint Heart Line warns of a flirtatious nature and a fear of commitment. A broken Heart Line indicates a heartbreak of lasting significance in the person's life.

Beneath the Heart Line is the Head Line, which designates the intellect, its priorities and its capacities. If the Head Line is long and not deep or distinct, the intellect will lean toward the creative, the metaphysical, and the abstract, enhanced by a vivid and active imagination. If it's short and thick, the mind will be primarily concerned with physical, practical, logical matters. A broken Head Line means a tendency toward a limited attention span and difficulty in completing projects and plans.

The Life Line starts above the Venus mount at the base of the thumb and ends at the wrist. Don't panic if you just took a look at your own Life Line and discovered that it's short and not clearly defined. That doesn't mean your lifetime will be abbreviated or have no particular purpose. In palmistry, it much more often means that you haven't started taking the fullest possible advantage of your life yet. A thick, clearly defined Life Line indicates a willingness to bravely open yourself to a wide variety of experiences. And a Life Line characterized by a series of shorter lines is interpreted to mean that you've had a widely varied life in which you've probably started over a few times.

The Fate Line can be found running from the second or Saturn finger to the wrist, and its prominence or faintness is a sign of how high or low a career and goals are situated on your priority list.

The other lines on the hand have their own significance as well, as do the intersections of the lines with each other, the sections of each finger, and the distances between the fingers. And then there's the common belief that the markings on the palm change over the years, so that one person's palm readings could change dramatically as time goes by. All of which makes it no surprise that countless volumes have been written about palmistry since its inception many, many millennia ago, and the debates about its validity continue.

PHRENOLOGY

In the early 1790s a German physician named Franz Joseph Gall devised a form of divination in which shapes, bumps, indentations, and other unique characteristics of the human skull were analyzed for the purpose of uncovering a person's intellectual, emotional, and moral skills, or lack of them. Gall called his system "organology," but a couple of decades later Dr. Thomas Forster, an English enthusiast of the system, coined the term "phrenology," from the Greek *phren*, meaning "mind," and *logos*, meaning "study."

Gall's theory was that since the brain is the organ that houses the mind, and the mind contains a wide array of distinct abilities and tendencies (called "faculties"), then each of those faculties must have its own designated "organ" within the brain. The size of each organ dictates the strength or weakness of the abilities within it, and the unique shape of the brain is caused by the varying sizes of these distinct organs as they develop. As the skull forms around the brain, it reflects the size of these organs and becomes an external, tangible indicator of the strengths and weaknesses of the faculties contained in the mind inside it when interpreted by a trained, qualified phrenologist.

According to Gall, there are forty-two faculties, each with its own designated organ. The left and right halves of the brain contain twenty-one faculties apiece and are mirror images of each other. The twenty-one basic faculties are:

- acquisitiveness (a need to acquire and save; greed)
- affection (selfless love)
- amativeness (sexual impulses and desires)
- approbativeness (vanity; need for adulation)
- benevolence (kindness, philanthropy, altruism)
- causality (logical thinking; understanding various theories and philosophies)
- cautiousness (fear, shyness, reluctance to take action)
- comparison (discernment; the ability to reason and think comparatively)
- conscientiousness (sense of morality, justice, duty, conscience)
- constructiveness (initiative, creativity, originality)
- destructiveness (forcefulness; dynamic energy)
- eventuality (insistence on gathering and retaining information)
- firmness (persistence, stamina, determination)
- human nature (intuitive sense of character)
- ideality (striving for perfection)
- individuality (practicality, objectivity, realism)
- locality (grasp of and memory for geographical locations)
- secretiveness (discretion, an urge to conceal)
- self-esteem (self-love, dignity)
- spirituality (embraces spiritual concepts and values)
- veneration (highest values, pursuits, and aspirations)

In phrenology, the prominence or depression in the skull corresponding to each of the faculties determines the degree to which the faculties exist and have a positive or negative influence.

For example, let's say that toward the bottom of your skull, behind your ear, you had a slight indentation. That location corresponds to the organ that contains the faculty of amativeness, or sexual desire. A phrenologist would very possibly interpret that particular indentation as a sign of sexual indifference, or maybe just a tendency to be unaffectionate. But a pronounced bump or protrusion in that same location could indicate promiscuity or a potential sexual addiction. Obviously, there's a lot of subjectivity involved in judging what's slight and what's pronounced when it comes to the size of indentations and bumps, but the accuracy of those judgments is part of what separates the amateurs from the experts in the field of phrenology.

Phrenology enjoyed widespread popularity throughout continental Europe, Great Britain, and America in the early to mid 1800s. (Of course, virtually nothing was known about the brain in the 1800s, so phrenology had the advantage of being as good a guess as any.) The Fowler family—two brothers, a sister, and her husband—were probably the most successful American phrenologists, starting a lucrative reading practice in the 1830s in New York that grew by 1880 into an industry of lecture circuits, societies, a publishing company, and the manufacture of phrenologically divided skull models. The Fowlers had their own theories on phrenology that involved anywhere from thirty-five to forty faculties (the number seemed to vary over the years) and organs.

Phrenology techniques, much like the fees for a reading, were purely a matter of preference among phrenologists. Some declared that accuracy could only be achieved by examining their clients' skulls with the palms of their hands. Others insisted that nothing but the fingertips provided the sensitivity required for true phrenological expertise. Still others examined skulls with a studied combination of their palms and their fingertips, sometimes brandishing scientific-looking measuring devices, especially calipers, for added flair and profit.

By the late 1960s the majority of phrenology societies and publications ceased to exist, although there are a few avid practitioners still insisting that it's a valid system of divination. And to give credit where it's due, Dr. Gall's premise of "organology" in the late 1700s and those who continued to develop it as it evolved into phrenology proved to be right about the fact that specific areas of the brain are dedicated to specific mental, physical, and emotional functions. But the reasons for the skepticism against it are obvious:

For one thing, it's a biological and scientific fact that our skulls are not perfect replicas of the surface of our brains. Protrusions and indentations in the bone structures of our heads aren't necessarily duplicated in the brain, and vice versa, which tends to invalidate the whole premise on which phrenology is based.

For another, phrenology's unreliability tended to quickly catch up with it, despite phrenologists' efforts to explain away the inaccuracies. If a client was known to be a self-absorbed, mean-tempered scrooge, but a phrenology reading revealed a large protrusion of the organ corresponding to the "benevolence" faculty, the phrenologist would typically explain that the brain's other faculties were somehow interfering with the benevolence organ. Any time a "science" has to spend as much effort coming up with excuses for false conclusions as it does coming up with the conclusions themselves, it's bound to squander its credibility sooner or later.

Bottom line: This divination technique is widely discredited, and appropriately so.

PSYCHOMETRY

All living things on earth emanate energy that is powerful enough to be absorbed by all non-living objects around them. Or, to put it another way, every inanimate object around us has absorbed and still contains the sum total of all living energy with which it's come in contact.

Psychometry is the ability to sense and interpret the living energy that's been absorbed by inanimate objects. Those perceptions can come in the form of visions, smells, sounds, emotions, and even specific empathetic physical sensations like pain, heat, and cold. It's a common misperception that because our psychometric responses to these inanimate objects can be so visceral, the objects themselves must be haunted, possessed, or evil. The truth is, that's simply impossible. "Inanimate" means "not alive," and "not alive" by definition means they can't be inhabited by any living thing, from earth or from the spirit world. It is absorbed energy, nothing more and nothing less, that creates the objects' ability to affect us.

A specialist in psychometry who works with law enforcement will typically be handed an object belonging to a missing person. By holding that object and reading the owner's energy it contains, the psychometrist can often perceive images or smells or sounds from where the missing person can be found and even empathetic pain if the person is injured.

Many legitimate, successful psychics and mediums find it helpful during readings to hold some item intimate to their client, or of a deceased loved one the client might be hoping to contact. I don't happen to be one of those psychics, but as long as the information is helpful and can be validated, you'll never hear me dismiss the existence and potential of psychometry.

A client once brought a beautiful antique ring to a reading and asked me to hold it and give her my impressions from it. The instant I closed my hand around it, I was flooded with such clear imagery that I might as well have been thrown into the middle of a saloon on an old western movie set. I saw a dark wooden bar, a brass rail, shelves of glasses beside the large mirror behind the bar, and a pleasant-looking older bartender wearing a vest and sleeve garters drying a shot glass with a bar rag. Neither before nor after have I had such an unmistakable psychometric vision, and I eagerly shared it with my client, frankly expecting her to light up with recognition. Instead, she shrugged and said, "It belonged to my grandmother. That's all I know about it." Which made the value of what I'd "seen" amount to exactly zero, because without validation, none of this means anything.

For the most part, I use psychometry the way you do, in everyday life. I'll be shopping, spot some item that seems to be exactly what I was looking for, pick it up for closer inspection, and find that "for no apparent reason" there's "something about it" that makes me put it back where I found it and keep looking. That's psychometry. I've gone house-hunting or apartment-hunting, walked into a perfectly nice place that fits every one of my requirements, and hurried right back out again because it didn't "feel right" in the pit of my stomach. That's psychometry. I've been given some beautiful pieces of antique furniture and jewelry and couldn't get rid of them fast enough because of how they "felt." No matter how expensive something is, or how much you like the way it looks, or if it's a treasured family heirloom or a potential museum piece, if the energy it has absorbed makes you uncomfortable, remember, it has not possessed or haunted, you're just having a perfectly valid psychometric reaction that's worth paying attention to.

Later in this book I'll be giving you a simple exercise to help you consciously tune in to your own psychometric skills. Psychometry is a subtle, wonderfully useful tool that can help you discard even more of the hidden negative energy in your life, which is, after all, one of the reasons you're here.

REMOTE VIEWING

Remote viewing is one of the most intriguing paranormal skills—so intriguing that in the 1970s the CIA and various branches of the military began studying its potential usefulness, particularly in the areas of defense and intelligence. In 1995, they disbanded the program and published an official report dismissing remote viewing as having no value to the U.S. government. What I've always wondered is, if it really proved to be so valueless, why on earth did it take more than two decades to figure that out? If something just plain doesn't work, why continue exploring it longer than maybe a few months at the most? Or is it possible that maybe the government, in the end, simply couldn't bring itself to officially endorse anything that falls under the umbrella of the term "paranormal"?

Remote viewing is a skill that allows us to perceive and describe details about a specific item or location that we're separated from by time, distance, or a physical barrier. It differs from the related skill of telepathy in that with remote viewing there's no human "sender" or "transmitter" passing along the information and/or images.

Remove viewing allows us, for example, to sit comfortably in our own living room and tour any street in any city in the world and describe the shop window displays, the weather, the smells, and the traffic in detail. We can tune in to a loved one's hospital room to see if they're awake or asleep, who's visiting them at any given moment, what they're being fed for dinner, and what kinds and colors of flowers people have sent. We can even go back in time and eyewitness a formal White House

dinner hosted by John and Jacqueline Kennedy or, for that matter, George and Martha Washington.

One of the luxuries of remote viewing as a paranormal skill
is the ease with which it can be tested, because it boils down to
this: it's either accurate or it's not. If what's being described by
the viewer isn't accurate, the viewing means nothing. (Again,
with that fact in mind, it took the government more than
twenty years to invalidate it?) If I claim to be remote-viewing
the above-mentioned loved one's hospital room and describe
two female visitors and a round white vase of red roses, but
my loved one tells me there was one male visitor instead, who
brought a green vase filled with white roses, my viewing is nothing but noise. But if I go into detail about the ivory Waterford
china and Baccarat goblets at the Kennedy dinner, and the fact
that Jacqueline wore a white beaded Cassini gown and sat next
to Sargent Shriver, who was in full formal white tie and tails,
while his wife Eunice was in blue Chanel with a bow at the
waist, and historical archives confirm that information, I've accomplished a successful remote viewing.

An American researcher named Ingo Swann, who was a
leading expert in this field during the 1960s and 1970s, wrote
that developing the skill of remove viewing can "expand the
parameters of our perceptions." That's a perfect description of
this skill's potential personal and spiritual value. It uniquely
depends on the conscious and subconscious minds working
together and communicating as a team. The subconscious mind
does the actual viewing, but in order to do it effectively, the
conscious mind has to stay out of the way so that the subconscious mind can receive a clear signal from the object or location
it's focusing on. Yet while the subconscious mind is doing its
job, the conscious mind needs to also be involved enough to
accurately express, with no interfering or editing, what the subconscious is receiving.

The last chapter, "How It's Done: Developing Your Own

Spiritual Arsenal," includes a simple exercise to help you experiment with remote viewing. You'll find it to be a wonderful mind-sharpener, and there's no reason to get discouraged if your accuracy leaves a little to be desired at first. Just one or two "hits" are a good starting point to work from, and remote viewing is definitely a skill that improves with practice.

TELEPATHY

Telepathy is the direct, instantaneous passing of information, knowledge, or feelings from one person or entity to another without using the senses of sight, hearing, touch, taste, or smell. It involves a "sender" and a "receiver" silently transferring information, sometimes over great distances, and it can happen deliberately or with no conscious awareness on the part of the sender and/or the receiver that it's happening at all.

Telepathic information is often sent with the intention that the receiver act upon it somehow, so the conscious mind usually becomes aware of it sooner or later, in a variety of forms: words or phrases that pop into the mind for no apparent reason, quick flashes of out-of-context images, exceptionally clear dreams, or a seemingly inexplicable focus on a person we might not have seen or thought about in a long time.

Telepathy is definitely not limited to communication from one human being to another. Residents of the spirit world are very adept at speaking to us telepathically. In fact, many people who've had encounters with deceased loved ones or Angels describe having lengthy "conversations" with them in which neither of them spoke a single word. And if you have the honor of being close to an animal, you experience receiving messages all the time from the most skillful telepathic communicators on earth. Telepathy can actually be transmitted from any energy source (a city, for example, or a country, or any body of consciousness) to any other energy source or sources (from one person to any number of people, whether they know each other or not).

There are plenty of "experts" and skeptics who take the position that telepathy has never actually been proven. I don't quite understand what that means, since it happens all the time, every day, to all of us, whether or not we leap up and yell, "Telepathy alert!" every time we experience it. Volumes have been written about the telepathic communication between identical twins, mothers and their children, close friends, husbands and wives—most configurations of "connected" spirits, for that matter. Does something really need to be proven that just *is*?

My favorite true, documented story of the "unproven" phenomenon of telepathy happened to a news editor for the *Boston Globe* named Victor Samson. One night after work he stopped at a nearby bar to unwind, got a little too unwound, and decided to go back to his office to sleep it off rather than try to make his way home.

He passed out on the sofa and had a violent, graphic dream about a devastating volcanic eruption on an island that in his dream was known as "Pele." Thousands of villagers, with no way to escape, were killed in fiery rivers of molten lava. The dream was so frightening that it woke Mr. Samson up, and he grabbed the closest tablet of paper, which happened to be his reporter's work sheets, and wrote down all the details he could remember. Then, still deeply shaken and wide awake, he headed home for a few more hours of sleep.

First thing the next morning, the *Globe*'s publisher stopped by Mr. Samson's office, spotted the work sheet, and read the heartbreaking story of all those people helplessly trapped by a volcano on their tiny island. With no reason to know that the story was nothing but his news editor's intoxicated dream, the publisher rushed it into print and sent it out on wire services across the country. Mr. Samson was understandably mortified when he arrived at the office later that day to discover that his publisher and his newspaper were facing nationwide embarrassment by printing and distributing this dramatic "news item."

His embarrassment turned to shock when, a few weeks later, a fleet of ships arrived in Boston Harbor with the horrible news that, within the same date and hour of his dream, a volcanic eruption had killed almost forty thousand people on the Indonesian island of Krakatau, which the natives called Pele.

If only they'd had computers for instantaneous communication when this happened in August 1883.

There's a theory among those who've researched telepathy that some of us are senders and some of us are receivers. An overly simplistic explanation would be that if you find yourself thinking of someone and then unexpectedly hear from them, you're probably a sender, while if you tend to know who's calling before you pick up a ringing phone, you're probably a receiver. I don't happen to believe it's necessary for any of us to be categorized or limited to being one or the other. I believe that most of us who are telepathically gifted are capable of being both, and that it's a really worthwhile mental sensitivity exercise to practice as you continue to explore ways to make the unseen a useful, demystified part of your daily life. And you'll find a simple telepathy exercise in the last chapter of this book that you can profit from and enjoy.

INFUSED KNOWLEDGE

Infused knowledge is a fascinating process through which information is directly passed from one mind to another without any of the five physical senses being involved. Unlike other direct mind-to-mind communication, such as telepathy, though, the receiver is given previously unknown information without having any conscious awareness of its source.

I know you've had the experience of going to sleep wrestling with a problem and waking up the next morning knowing how to solve it. The vast majority of the time it's no more mysterious than your mind finally being relaxed and uncluttered enough to be able to think clearly.

But let's say that some night you go to sleep worried about what on earth is wrong with your ailing but undiagnosed Aunt Florence. The next morning you wake up knowing with absolute certainty that your Aunt Florence is suffering from some rare disease you've never heard of but are able to name or describe in detail—and when the appropriate tests are performed, you turn out to be right. It's through infused knowledge that the existence and symptoms of that rare disease came to you, information you were made aware of by a source you can't begin to name or even guess at.

Infused knowledge is one of the simplest, most common ways that the spirit world on the Other Side communicates with our spirit minds here on earth, which are always wide awake and available in our subconscious minds. Our subconscious minds are obviously most accessible when our busy, cluttered, human minds are as far out of the way as possible— while we're asleep, under hypnosis, meditating, or sometimes just extremely tired.

There are also those who, through their own innate gifts, have subconscious minds that are perpetually available to infused knowledge from the Other Side and put those gifts to work for our benefit. Have you ever noticed how often researchers, scientists, inventors, and other great minds on opposite ends of the globe seem to arrive at virtually identical discoveries and breakthroughs almost simultaneously? That's not a coincidence. It's the result of spirits on the Other Side successfully delivering information by infused knowledge to those accessible, appropriate minds on earth who have the wisdom, dedication, expertise, and talent to act on that information and make it a reality.

I have no way to calculate how much of my psychic and prophetic information comes to me through infused knowledge from the spirit world. Yes, absolutely, most often I hear spirit voices thanks to my clairaudience. But when that's not the case, particularly in the areas of medicine and technology, I've been known to race to a dictionary after I'm given a medical diagnosis or future cure, or some technological advancement we have to look forward to, because I'm suddenly being called upon to repeat words I've never heard before and can't begin to spell, let alone explain.

Based on my own experiences with infused knowledge and decades of research on the subject, I've come to two conclusions about it: Its source is invariably God-centered, since it comes from Home, and it's never, *never* negative or potentially harmful in any way; and on those occasions when you're blessed with receiving it, you owe it to its source to pass it along or act on it with speed and impeccable accuracy. Dragging your feet or performing your own editorial work on information you've been given through infused knowledge really does give new meaning to the question, "Who do you think you are?"

KINETIC ENERGY

Kinetic energy is the unintentional, spontaneous, often haphazard manipulation of inanimate objects through no obvious physical means, causing its possessor to become a kind of random, hapless walking force field. The effects can be very dramatic, loud, startling, and annoying—take it from someone who lived through it with a child and a grandchild who were either blessed or cursed with kinetic energy, depending on your point of view. When my granddaughter was very young, she could crash computer hard drives and entire phone systems and cause paper to fly wildly out of idle Xerox machines just by walking through the central workroom at my office. When my son Paul became a teenager, he would involuntarily cause all his shoes to career off the walls and ceiling of his bedroom like rockets every night as he fell asleep. And I think they're both as relieved as I am that they seem to have outgrown it.

There are several theories about what creates kinetic energy, and of course there are just as many skeptics who swear it doesn't exist at all. To this day I wish I'd sent them the bills for all my computer, phone, and Xerox repairs. Some believe that it's simply a powerfully spiking electric emanation from certain people that appears from out of nowhere and then vanishes just as explicably. Others believe, as I do, that it's an innate power that some are born with and others aren't, that ebbs and flows in irregular cycles through the course of a lifetime. Kinetic energy is often at its strongest when the body is going through hormonal changes—particularly during prepubescence or puberty, or in pregnant or menopausal women. And it's not uncommon in very young children, either, as my granddaughter so innocently demonstrated (sometimes accompanied by fits of surprised giggling).

In my personal experience, within my own family and among many clients with kinetic energy, I've seen no indication that it's an inherited phenomenon. My son and my granddaughter are the only two family members in at least three psychically gifted generations who've shown any signs of this particular form of power surge, and those clients who found themselves in possession of kinetic energy weren't aware of that same blessing/curse in any of their relatives.

It's the random, sporadic nature of kinetic energy that's made it so difficult for researchers to study, understand, and arrive at any solid conclusions beyond the basic agreement that yes, there really is such a thing. And then there's the fact that its effects are so often mistaken for other phenomena. I can't tell you how many "hauntings" I've investigated in which people are being subjected to cupboard doors flying open and slamming shut with no one near them, appliances turning themselves off and on at their own whim, TVs wildly changing channels for no reason, and/or phones leaping off their receivers or producing ear-shattering static rather than a dial tone. No doubt about it, all of that chaos can happen during a haunting. But it's far more common for the cause to be simply a family member with kinetic energy who, through no awareness or fault of their own, is creating the atmospheric disturbance. It's not that hard to detect once you're familiar with the possibility—if the phenomena come and go depending on who's in the room, it's a safe bet that kinetic energy, not an attention-seeking ghost, is at the core of what's going on, and it's an equally safe bet that it will pass.

And please understand something equally important. Those who are blessed or cursed with kinetic energy *are not evil. They are not crazy, they are not doomed to a life of weirdness, and they most certainly have not been possessed by the devil or by anyone else.* I don't care what you've picked up through religious dogma or whatever authority, but *there is no such thing as possession.*

If you or someone you know experiences kinetic energy, now that you understand what it is and what it isn't, please help them understand as well; don't punish them for something they're probably more confused by than you are, and be patient. Take it from someone who spent a few months making a morning ritual of gathering her son's shoes from all over his room and simply putting them back in the closet where they belonged, it's only temporary.

PSYCHOKINESIS

Psychokinesis, which is also known as telekinesis, is the ability to move or manipulate objects without applying any physical or other scientifically explainable force. The word originates from the Greek words *psyche*, or "mind," and *kinein*, "to move." Unlike kinetic energy, which is completely random and involuntary, psychokinesis involves deliberate, specific action.

Some of you might remember Uri Geller, the Israeli psychic who was able to bend spoons and other objects purely through the power of his mind, without ever touching them. His televised appearances during the 1970s, all of them live and authentic, provided American audiences with probably the most renowned and unfairly criticized demonstrations of psychokinesis this country has ever seen. But because he was unable to duplicate his skills during strictly controlled lab experiments, many critics were delighted to accuse him of being a fraud who'd tricked nationwide audiences by simply substituting the metal objects involved with flexible or bent ones through sleight of hand.

I only wish Uri Geller's critics' credibility had been called into question just as loudly and publicly, for their inability to prove with absolute certainty that he ever employed a single fraudulent sleight-of-hand trick.

Don't get me wrong—psychokinesis, like every other divination discipline, has been faked millions of times by countless scam artists, and I'll always believe it's a sad fact that an essential part of enhancing spirituality in our lives is learning to distinguish the legitimate from the utterly phony. But toward that end, when it comes to psychokinesis, it's important to note that exhaustive studies have been ongoing for decades by a long, distinguished list of researchers—among them, Dr. J. B. Rhine of Duke University in 1934; the German physicist Helmut Schmidt; several teams of engineers and psychologists at Princeton; experts at the Chinese Academy of Sciences; the physicist John Hasted at the University of London; and any number of biochemists throughout the world. Two of their most important conclusions:

- The validity of the existence of psychokinesis can neither be dismissed nor disproved.
- Harnessing and effectively guiding the power of psychokinesis has enormous biological and humanitarian potential. For example, antibodies have been shown to grow more rapidly in test tubes exposed to the proximity of psychokinetically energized hands than antibodies deprived of that same proximity. And the growth of a variety of molds and fungi has been significantly diminished under the influence of psychokinesis as compared to those not exposed to that influence.

In other words, advocate of skepticism and of demanding proof that I am, I'm just as passionate an advocate of disciplines like psychokinesis and so many others when they've been shown to be of potentially limitless benefit to this planet and to all of us who live here. I sometimes wish we could eliminate the word "paranormal" from the dictionary and instead start classifying all positive, well-intentioned pursuits as simply "valid" or "bogus." With the tired old "scientific vs. paranormal" debate taken off the table and everyone's energy put to more productive use, there's virtually nothing on God's earth we couldn't accomplish.

ASTRAL TRAVEL

Astral travel is the remarkable, and remarkably common, experience in which the spirit temporarily leaves the body for trips ranging anywhere from just a few feet away to the Other Side itself. And it's a skill that comes as naturally to us as breathing, a skill we're born with and that we practice throughout our lives. The reason for this is simple: it's astral travel that brought us here from the Other Side when our spirits entered our bodies, and it's astral travel that will take us Home again when our bodies die.

For those of you who believe that astral travel is just another one of those far-fetched spiritual fantasies, let me promise you that you routinely travel astrally, you just prefer to call it something else. Some of your more graphic daydreams are astral travel. Many of your dreams while you sleep are astral travel—in fact, we routinely take astral trips during sleep on an average of two or three times a week. If you've ever experienced fully anesthetized surgery, physiological unconsciousness, a coma, or a severely debilitating illness that attacks both the body and the mind, I promise your spirit leapt at the opportunity to go busily, joyfully darting from one journey to the next in your "absence."

A client once told me a story that perfectly illustrates an example of instantaneous and unintentional astral travel that she mistook at the time for a daydream. She was in a meeting with several other executives at the major communications company in Houston where she worked. Her mind wandered for a moment, and she let her gaze drift over to the conference room's wall of windows, overlooking the skyline.

An instant later, through no conscious effort on her part, she found herself in the backseat of a Ford Explorer—not in her imagination but as if she were actually physically there, in the most terrifying experience of her life. Just as she "arrived," the Explorer careened wildly off an ice-covered mountain road, crashed down a rocky embankment, and landed upside down in a thick pine forest. She looked up to see her husband behind the wheel of the SUV, his airbag deployed, the left side of his head covered with blood and the driver's window splintered. She then saw her brother in the passenger's seat, his airbag deployed as well, unconscious, his head hanging at such a dramatic angle that she knew his neck was broken, the right side of the Explorer crushed in around him against a tree. Through her shock she vaguely noticed groceries scattered everywhere around her in the backseat. And breaking the horrible silence of the aftermath of this violent, deadly accident was a football game, blaring loud and clear from the radio.

In less than the blink of an eye she was suddenly back in the conference room again. She was so shaken, and the "daydream" had seemed so real, that she immediately excused herself and rushed to her office to call the cabin near Vail, Colorado, where her husband and brother were staying on a week-long skiing vacation. As she was waiting for someone to answer she happened to glance at the clock, which read 3:36 p.m. When no one picked up the phone at the cabin, she tried both her husband's and her brother's cell phones, her heart in her throat when neither phone even rang.

It took her several days to learn all the tragic details from the Vail authorities. Her husband and brother were returning to the cabin from a nearby grocery store when the Explorer hit a patch of black ice on the narrow mountain road, veered out of control, and rolled down the embankment, crashing upside down into a massive pine tree. A driver coming from the opposite direction witnessed the accident and called 911 at 3:24 p.m. Vail (and Houston) time. Her husband died instantly as the result of a skull fracture when his head hit the driver's side window. Her brother died of a broken neck on the way to the hospital. A paramedic at the scene commented later about the eerie effect of a football game still blaring away on the radio in the midst of this fatal destruction, as if nothing at all had happened.

It's worth mentioning, by the way, that this is a perfectly "normal" woman (as often as I use that term I'm still never quite sure what it means), who never considered herself psychic or gifted in paranormal skills, and she couldn't imagine what this bizarre experience was or what had caused it. The answer is that it was an astral travel episode; it can and does happen to everyone, whether or not it's as dramatic as hers. And in this case, happily married as she was, it was her profound spirit connection to her brother that propelled her to his side when she knew he was about to head Home.

Awake or asleep, we routinely astrally travel to meet loved ones, both living and departed, from this life and past lives. We routinely travel the globe revisiting places we've loved, we routinely check up on people we miss or are worried about, and we routinely take trips to the Other Side—that place for which we're Homesick from the moment we leave it until the moment we return.

The astral trips we take while we sleep, and typically mistake for dreams, have several characteristics that set them apart:

- "Dreams" of flying without an airplane or other mechanical means are actually astral trips.
- Astral trips during sleep unfold in a logical sequence of events, just as waking experiences do, rather than in the often random jumble of images, people, and locations that can typify dreams.
- A "dream" you're not only part of but also find that you're watching yourself in is really an astral experience. We've all heard story after story of people looking down from the ceiling at themselves during surgery and being able to accurately describe the doctors, nurses, and conversations while they were "under." The same phenomenon happens during astral trips while sleeping: your spirit and your body have temporarily separated, and there's a certain curious fascination with finding that you're able to observe yourself as an "outsider."

Once we've left our bodies for an astral trip, there are three speeds of travel to choose from. Your spirit already knows that, so this is just to help your conscious mind recognize it when it happens. The slowest speed is the least disorienting—our spirits move at the same pace our bodies do when we're walking. The intermediate speed is fast enough to create the illusion that we're standing still while everything around us is flying past us from front to back. It's often accompanied by the sensation of moving against a strong wind, which isn't wind at all but actually our own forward movement instead. At supernormal speed, our spirits can travel incomprehensible distances faster than our finite minds can imagine, to the point where we might remember our destinations and what we did while we visited, but we have no awareness at all of how we got there or how we got back. If you've ever had an extremely realistic dream of moving through the stars, exploring a distant planet, or touring a newly discovered galaxy halfway across the universe, chances are you've experienced astral travel at supernormal speed.

Some of you believe astral travel is possible but not something that has happened or will happen to you. Others of you believe astral travel is just another one of those myths we paranormal weirdos hope you're gullible enough to fall for. I respectfully leave you to your beliefs, but hope you'll leave your minds open enough that when you have a "dream" that you *know* was more than a dream, or a daydream you *know* was more than a daydream, you'll remember that your spirit is the wisest, most liberated, most joyful part of you, exploring and traveling and learning, having the most beautiful reunions week after week after week, and just waiting for you to be nourished by all that it's bringing back for you.

IMITATIVE MAGIC

Imitative magic is an ancient form of divination practiced among many Native American and African tribes, the Australian

Aborigines, witches, and many more of us, whether or not we realize it. The theory behind it is as uncomplicated as it gets: the practitioner simply acts out the result they're hoping to effect, often but not necessarily in the course of a ceremonial ritual.

For example, to bring rain to drought-stricken land, a native chieftain, to the beat of drums that will attract the attention of the earth's gods and goddesses, might pour an urn of water into a symbolic circle.

To ensure a successful hunt, tribal warriors might act out the hunt in front of their tribe, with the warrior hunters ultimately "slaying" warriors who are wearing the heads of wild animals.

To encourage the growth of crops, witches might ride broomsticks (with which they sweep away evil forces) through newly planted fields, jumping as high as they can to simulate to the crops the act of growing. (And that, by the way, is the origin of the myth of witches flying on broomsticks.)

To inflict pain, revenge, or a curse on an enemy, a Haitian folk tradition dictates the use of voodoo dolls. Sticking a pin into a doll representing the enemy will, according to imitative magic, create a simultaneous pain in the enemy himself.

All of which might make imitative magic sound primitive and even a little quaint, until you realize how deeply ingrained it is in some of our own traditions.

Next time you, your friends and/or your children dress up for Halloween, for example, don't hesitate to pause for a moment and recognize that you're acting out your own form of imitative magic. According to folklore, there are evil demons called ghouls who lurk around graveyards, eating the flesh of corpses and possessing their spirits to prevent them from reaching paradise. On All Hallow's Eve, the souls of the deceased were thought to rise from their graves, which would predictably attract ghouls from miles around. Frightened of the ghouls and not wanting to be mistaken for their potential next meal, villagers began dressing up in their best guess at what ghouls probably looked like, the theory being that imitating what scares us will ward it off or at least inspire it to ignore us.

If you've ever hung lights on a Christmas tree, or lit holiday candles throughout your house, you're carrying on an ancient form of imitative magic whose purpose was to summon back the warmth of the sun to drive away the winter cold.

And then there's a phrase that was drilled into me as a child by my Grandma Ada and that's frequently quoted by the members of at least one very worthwhile organization I can think of: "act as if." Like so many other families, mine was hit very hard by the Depression. My father's income went from comfortable to meager, and I was too young to understand why all the indulgences I was used to had been swept away by a strange new mantra of, "We can't afford it." I think for about thirty seconds I got away with pouting and behaving like a needy, deprived child before Grandma Ada pulled me aside for one of her best stern, no-nonsense lectures.

"That's enough of that," she told me. "Starting right this minute, you're going to act as if you have everything you could possibly want. You're going to act as if everything's just fine. Do that, and I promise you, sooner or later, it will be." Notice, she wasn't trying to convince me that I *had* everything I could possibly want, or that everything *was* fine. She'd never lied to me, and she wasn't about to start then. She was simply telling me to *act as if*. It was a simple, brilliant form of imitative magic that a child could understand and that I still use and endorse to this day. You can ask my family, my staff, and my close friends—through the roughest times of my life, and there have been plenty, unless I'm behind closed doors and can fall apart in private, I insist on acting as if I have the world by the tail. And Grandma Ada was right, it really does work.

So, before we snicker with a little too much sophisticated superiority at the primitives with their bizarre, preposterous imitative magic rituals, we might want to take a look around at how many of those rituals and approaches to life we've adopted ourselves, and how effective the positive ones really are.

AURAS

Your aura is the etheric substance, or life force, that emanates from within you and encompasses your body like a subtle cloak of colors. There are those who think it's comprised of energy, while others use the word "electricity" instead. Whatever word works for you is fine, as long as it helps you envision a power field around you that others sense and respond to whether they're consciously aware of it or not, and some are able to see.

Each aura contains all the colors of the rainbow, starting with three core bands of constant color and intensity at its base. A band of white, radiating from the Holy Spirit within us, is closest to the body. Next is gold, the innate dignity of our divine birthright. The third is purple, glowing proof of our spirits' sacred lineage. These three inseparable core bands are no more than four to five inches thick.

It's the outer band that changes color depending on our physical and emotional health. Red indicates anger. Black is a sign of physical illness. Grief and depression manifest themselves as a murky yellow-green. Green signifies health, while blue is an indication of heightened awareness. And a deeply disturbed mind—a psychopath or sociopath, for example—will have an outer band that's the brown-black color of mud. This outer band is capable of "spiking," creating the same effect as a sunspot flaring up from the surface of the sun, when the cause of its color has a sudden surge of intensity. A spike in a black aura, for example, typically means an onset of complications in an already existing illness, while a spike in a green aura tells you that a person's health has undergone an upswing from good to great.

So, for those of you who are able to see auras—and there are many of you—please remember that any flares of color you're reading are temporary physical or emotional conditions. Look closer to the body and you'll see the white, gold, and purple bands at the aura's base to find that person's true, unchangeable character.

For those who can't see auras, don't doubt for a moment that we all have one and that we can and do make use of them, by projecting them to those around us. We've all been on the giving and receiving ends of those projections, whether we thought of them as auras or not. Someone who's in an angry, violent, self-pitying, or depressed mood can walk into a room and, without giving a single outward indication, plunge that room into thick, dark tension. Someone else in the same situation can make that same room feel peaceful, calm, and safe no matter what else is going on around them. The essential difference is which aura they're projecting.

At our best, regardless of what the outer band of our aura is doing, we project our core, positive aura, and we can make an active decision to do that simply by forming an image. The core bands of white, gold, and purple, when they're combined and projected, form a bright, almost fluorescent glow of dusty mauve edged in gold. Get a picture in your mind of what that looks like as it surrounds your whole body, and make it beautiful. Then extend the image to bathe your surroundings and everyone in them in a golden mauve that's glowing from you as if you'd turned up a dimmer switch to its strongest power. There may not be an immediate conspicuous effect, but I promise you, it will make a difference, even if it's only to you, like the satisfaction of giving a lovely anonymous gift.

And as you practice, don't get discouraged if sometimes it seems as if this doesn't work at all. It's fascinating to me that the negative or dark outer band of an aura has a projection range of about 150–200 feet, while the projected range of the positive core bands averages 30 to 40 feet. If you're skeptical about that, watch what happens the next time a happy, peaceful, loving person arrives at a party, closely followed by an angry or depressed person, and see which one of them has a more dramatic effect on the party guests. If I were a betting woman, I'd put my money on the angry, depressed person every time. It's unfortunate but true, and it's one of the main reasons you'll find a useful list of Tools of Protection starting at page 256 in the last chapter of this book.

Of course, auras aren't limited to us humans. Every living thing on this earth has an aura, because every living thing by definition contains a life force that emanates from within it. This life force we share comes from the same Source, which means that we humans have a divine connection to all living things. And only by treasuring and nurturing the life around us will we truly make it possible for humankind to thrive again.

KIRLIAN PHOTOGRAPHY

In 1939, two Russian scientists, Semyon and Valentina Kirlian, discovered what has come to be known as Kirlian photography—a method of capturing on film the auras, or energy patterns, that surround all living things. It involves passing a high-frequency electrical current through an object while photographing that object either directly or through glass. The result is an image of the object encompassed by a colored aura capable of indicating stress, illness, fear, and other disturbances within the object itself.

Kirlian photography has been a target of skeptics since it became widely known, and in some cases that skepticism has been well deserved. Photographing auras has great potential for countless frauds and scams, and there were more than enough victims of doctored or completely phony Kirlian photography, with any number of very expensive fake diagnoses and cures based on that photographic "proof," to inspire thousands of question marks. While I've never personally taken a Kirlian photograph or examined the equipment involved (as if I would understand it if I did examine it), researcher friends who have extensive experience with it tell me it's one of the easiest forms of photography to manipulate to create almost any result the photographer wants. There are even do-it-yourself Kirlian photography kits available, presumably to explore your aura in the privacy of your own home. You're free to do whatever you choose with your own money, of course, but when it comes to "private" Kirlian photographers and do-it-yourself kits, I promise you'll get exactly as much value for your investment and save yourself a lot of time and energy if you just run your cash through your shredder instead.

Fortunately, for all the con artists who were capitalizing on this well-intentioned discovery, there were just as many legitimate researchers around the world who were conducting well-documented, successful experiments with the vast potential of Kirlian photography and the study of aura images in all areas of the life sciences. Dr. Thelma Moss, the brilliant UCLA neurologist and researcher, led invaluable explorations into the potential of Kirlian photography for a wide array of practical applications. Among the discoveries of Dr. Moss and many other equally qualified researchers:

- One hundred lab rats were easily distinguished from 100 lab rats whose tails were injected with cancerous tissue, simply by the visible difference in the Kirlian photographs of the auras of the cancer-injected tails.
- When a seed with a blue aura begins to sprout, the seed's aura remains blue, while the aura of the sprout photographs as a bright pink. The pink aura follows the tip of the sprout as it continues to grow, but more and

more of the sprout's stem aura becomes the identical blue of the original seed.

- In a large group of patients being screened for cancer, Kirlian photography was able to detect and reveal six more tumors than those previously uncovered by conventional medical testing.
- A visible transfer of energy takes place when a freshly picked leaf is laid beside a leaf picked hours before.
- Fertile plant seeds have conspicuously larger auras than infertile seeds.
- As claimed for many millennia by those who are able to read auras with the naked eye, spikes, or flares, do occur in auras during stressful, traumatic, and fearful situations.
- The aura dramatically increases in size when the subject is intoxicated with drugs or alcohol.
- With practice and concentration, we can willfully diminish or significantly project our auras.

In other words, in the hands of trained, reputable researchers whose lives are committed to discovering cures and other medical and scientific breakthroughs by studying the life force called auras, Kirlian photography is a miraculous tool whose potential even seventy years after its discovery is only in its infancy.

6

THE DIVINATION DEVICES

You may or may not be familiar with the word "scrying"— it's a means of fortune-telling that involves an object for the fortune-teller to focus on or stare into until a vision of sought-after insight and/or the future appears. Since the beginning of time humankind has found any number of objects through which to channel the skill of scrying and to tap into external guides that might offer pathways to healing, wisdom, protection, spiritual depth, and, in the end, the ability to tune in more clearly to messages from the spirit world and from God Himself.

In this chapter I don't pretend to even be scratching the surface of the divination devices that have been used and are still being used as those external guides. I can't imagine how many volumes it would take to fully explore all of them. This is just an overview of a handful of the ones that have caught my attention over the years, for better or worse, that I hope will inspire your curiosity to continue exploring on your own (or, in one case, stop exploring immediately and head straight to a Dumpster).

TEA LEAVES

The divination skill of reading tea leaves, or (usually Turkish) coffee grounds, has been practiced since ancient times, possibly because it involves such historically accessible "props." All that's required is tea made with loose leaves or coffee that leaves grounds in a preferably pure white cup so that there's maximum contrast and no pattern to interfere with the images formed by the leaves or grounds. But there's also the fact that tea has been valued for thousands of years as a homeopathic healing agent.

The process of a tea-leaf or coffee-grounds reading goes like this: the client drinks a cup of tea or coffee, leaving a small amount of liquid and sediment in the bottom of the cup. The client then swirls the contents of the cup slowly, clockwise, three times; places the cup upside down on a saucer for several seconds (some readers recommend seven seconds, others nine) to let the fluids drain out; and sets the cup upright again with the handle facing the reader.

The reader interprets the images left behind in the cup, usually according to some common ground rules and symbolism, although there are certainly readers who apply their own psychic, intuitive variations.

It's commonly thought, for example, to name just a few basics, that the larger the image, the more important the issue it depicts in the client's life; images closer to the bottom of the cup are likely to indicate the past, while images closer to the rim are probably present or future issues or events; and conflicting images imply a struggle with an important decision.

Of course, essential to the reading is the reader's ability to find and intuitively interpret symbols in the tea leaves or coffee grounds, rather than taking them literally. The more psychic the reader the more he or she can use the symbols to act simply as a guide rather than implying that the reading addresses all of the client's concerns.

You can look online to find some of the most common tea leaf pattern meanings. The value of these readings really is entirely dependent on the skills, gifts, and imagination of the reader. I've never given tea leaf reading a try, probably because I literally can't imagine being creative enough to look into a cup of leaves and see a zebra or an ostrich. But I'm not about to be dismissive of a practice that has survived from ancient times until the twenty-first century.

OUIJA BOARDS

The Ouija board, or "talking board," came bounding into popularity in the late 1800s once the spiritualist movement had taken a foothold. As you probably know, a Ouija board is a rectangle of wood, usually about 18 by 12 inches, with the letters of the alphabet in an arch across it, the numbers 1 through 0 beneath the alphabet, the word "yes" in the upper-left-hand corner, the word "no" in the upper-right-hand corner, and the word "goodbye" (or "farewell") centered at the bottom. A triangular planchette with a small pointer in its tip is mounted on little felt-covered casters or "feet" so that it will move smoothly across the wood, theoretically to indicate or spell out answers to the questions asked by the person(s) whose fingertips have been placed lightly on the planchette.

The word "Ouija" has been credited with several different origins, from a combination of the French and German words for "yes" (*oui* and *ja*) to a claim that it's a derivation of the Moroccan city of Oujda. Wherever it originated, the board and the movements of the planchette are generally thought to have two different explanations for their "effectiveness."

One is that the planchette moves to various responses due

to the users guiding it subconsciously, unaware that they're in any way responsible for the movement, causing the Ouija board to give answers that the subconscious mind is directing.

The other is that the planchette is being guided by residents of the spirit world who've seized the opportunity to communicate clearly with this world.

Frankly, I'm not sure it matters which explanation is more accurate. I would guess that both of those possibilities happen from time to time. (And then, of course, there are those who deliberately move the planchette and feign surprise at the results, which isn't even worth discussing.) What does matter very much, in my opinion, is that I find Ouija boards to be potentially dangerous, and the only reason I'll go anywhere near one is to pick it up and carry it straight to the nearest wastebasket where it belongs.

Please don't misunderstand—when I say "dangerous," I don't mean evil. Ouija boards don't have one shred of power on their own. Being very generous, let's say that once in every two hundred uses of a Ouija board, a resident of the spirit world decides to chime in through the movement of the planchette. I don't care how earnestly you might have blessed the board, the planchette, and/or the room you're sitting in, you'll still have no control whatsoever over the identity and motives of that spirit. It could easily be a dark entity who's turned away from God, or a terribly confused and angry ghost for all you know, and in either of those cases, giving it a "voice" through a Ouija board or, even worse, taking orders from it, is a potentially harmful way to spend your time and energy. And if you think you'd be able to tell if a negative spirit who means you harm were communicating with you, ask yourself how many negative, manipulative people you've met in your lifetime who revealed their dark side right up front. Didn't they typically try to gain proximity to you by charming you when you first met them and only show their true colors once you'd started trusting them and emotionally investing in them? Why wouldn't negative spirits behave exactly the same way?

So here's the image I want you to fix firmly in your mind the next time you're tempted to sit down at a Ouija board, even if it's "just for fun": I want you to imagine that you've left your front door unlocked, there's a knock at that door, and instead of yelling, "Who is it?" you yell, "Come on in!" It might be a friend, it might be that nosy neighbor you've been trying to avoid, it might be the world's most obnoxious and relentless door-to-door salesman, or it might be a vicious group of thieving home invaders; but whoever it is, you have no one to thank but yourself for whatever the consequences turn out to be. If you're perfectly comfortable with that image, and with essentially doing exactly the same thing with the spirit world, then enjoy your Ouija board. If you wouldn't dream of doing anything so reckless, careless, and downright insane, run, don't walk, to a trash can and throw that Ouija board away.

TAROT CARDS

Tarot is a means of divination through the use of pictorial, artistic cards, each of them with its own name, image, and significance. There are several theories about the origin of Tarot—some believe it had its roots in ancient Egyptian hieroglyphics, while others feel certain the Tarot decks were created and first used in northern Italy in the 1400s. The symbolism portrayed on the cards has varied over thousands of years, and during the evolution of Tarot reading, because of that varying symbolism, there have been theoretical philosophical links to everything from the Kabbalah to alchemy to Christianity.

Whatever the variations in the artwork from one Tarot deck to another, all decks involve the same basics:

The seventy-eight cards in a traditional Tarot deck are

divided into two categories: the Minor Arcana and the Major Arcana.

The Minor Arcana is made up of fifty-six cards—four "suits" (the Swords, the Wands, the Pentagrams, and the Cups), each containing ace through 10 and four "face cards" (the Page, the Knight, the Queen, and the King), much like a standard deck of playing cards. In general, the Swords are associated with the element of Air, the Wands are associated with Fire, the Pentagrams are associated with Earth, and the Cups are associated with Water. The face cards are associated with the elements as well—the Page with Earth, the Knight with Air, the Queen with Water, and the King with Fire.

There are twenty-two cards in the Major Arcana, each bearing its own symbolism and its own general interpretation:

The Fool—aspiration toward limitless potential
The Magician—manifesting ideas and goals into
    realities
The High Priestess—the balancing force between the
    conscious and subconscious minds
The Empress—the creativity and imagination found in
    the subconscious mind
The Emperor—orderliness, a systematic approach to
    the way thoughts are transformed into realities
The Hierophant (wise teacher)—the inner self,
    intuition
The Lovers—relationships, partners, the blending of
    two things that are sometimes opposite but still
    compatible
The Chariot—the soul and the ability to express it
Strength—control over material forces
The Hermit—elevated wisdom, holding a lantern to
    light the way for others
Wheel of Fortune—true understanding of the inner self

Justice—righting past wrongs

The Hanged Man—an indication that not everything is
as it appears to be

Death—transformation and rebirth

Temperance—perfect balance between such opposites
as positive and negative, male and female,
conscious and subconscious, good and bad

The Devil—foolishness when facing facts and
circumstances

The Tower—sudden jolts of insight and understanding

The Star—gathering and sharing universal knowledge

The Moon—evolution of the soul

The Sun—the fixed, objective, all-embracing nurturer

Judgment—spiritual understanding

The World—the continuing, unending cycle of life

Of course, the key to successful Tarot readings is the interpretation of the cards, which depends not only on each card's meaning but also on the relationship of the cards to each other in what's usually referred to as a "spread." After the deck is shuffled, there are several different patterns, or spreads, in which the cards are arranged by the reader and then interpreted one by one as the cards are turned over.

The astrological spread, for example, is a pattern in which twelve cards are arranged in a circle, signifying the twelve signs of the zodiac. A thirteenth card, placed in the center of the circle, is the "significator," or the card that represents the primary concern of the person receiving the reading.

In the horseshoe spread, seven cards are placed in a semicircle. Reading from left to right, the cards signify the past, the present, prevailing influences, relevant obstacles, hopes or fears, the most successful approach, and the most probable outcome.

The three-card spread simply involves three cards placed side by side, with the first representing the past, the second representing the present, and the third representing the future.

In addition to these and many other spreads that are traditionally used by Tarot readers, there are also various interpretations to the significance of whether or not a card, when it's turned over, is right side up or upside down to the person receiving the reading. Some readers believe that an upside-down card reverses its usual meaning; some believe it indicates a deep underlying issue that needs to be addressed; and some believe it has no significance at all.

I happen to love the skill of Tarot and used it myself very, very early in my career as a kind of "visual aid" in my psychic readings. Once I developed my gifts enough to "get there without a map," I set the cards and all other devices aside. But I feel safe in saying that the more psychic/intuitive the reader, the more effective a Tarot reading will be, because there are so many different interpretations of the cards themselves in their own right and in relation to each other.

CRYSTAL BALLS

The use of crystal balls, like so many other divination practices, dates back thousands of years, and it's not hard to understand why. As you'll learn shortly about the health and healing properties of crystals and gemstones, all natural elements, especially those that are formed over time within the earth, contain and emit powerful life forces that draw us to them. They're also beautiful in their simplicity and symmetry and appealing as the focal objects that crystal ball readings require.

I should add that I've never used a crystal ball, not out of disrespect but because, as a point of personal preference, I've found that traditional divination tools are more of a distraction in my readings than a help. Colleagues who have used crystal balls, though, have discussed them in depth with me over the years and shared a lot of interesting information about them. And so, based on what I understand:

Each crystal ball is considered deeply personal to its owner, never used by or loaned to anyone else. When not in use, it's never put on display but is stored, with its stand, in a safe, dark place covered by a black, non-abrasive cloth to protect it from the sun and artificial light sources. Some believe protection is necessary because these light sources can cloud the crystal over time, while others believe it's because the power of crystal balls is the exclusive domain of the moon—which might explain why crystal balls are almost exclusively used after sundown, and why their regular physical and spiritual cleansing (with water that's been blessed with prayer and a sign of your faith) should take place on the first night of a full moon.

The typical reading takes place in a quiet, darkened room, lit only by a candle that's also been blessed with prayer, and apparently there should never be more than three people gathered in the room where a crystal ball reading is happening.

The ball is placed on its designated stand, and the reader takes a seat facing it. The reader sits quietly, eyes closed, for a brief period of deep, rhythmic breathing to relax the body and mind. Then, eyes open again, the reader focuses on the crystal ball and stares into it. (Some prefer to choose a particular spot on/within the ball to stare at.) It's not uncommon for beginners to experience nothing of interest the first few times, and if that's the case it's a good idea to simply put the ball away after fifteen minutes or so and try again the next evening.

When some combination of the reader and the crystal ball is working correctly, the ball will appear to fill with a smoky mist within several seconds, and through that mist images and/ or entire scenes will emerge. Rarely if ever are these visions meant to be taken literally. Much more typically they'll have symbolic relevance of the issues the reading is meant to address, and their effective interpretation is largely dependent on the intuitive and psychic gifts of the reader. Those issues can be stated before the reading begins or written on a slip of paper that's placed beneath the crystal ball stand. But once the images begin revealing themselves, the reader should do all the talking and interpreting, and the entirety of the reading should be recorded on paper or on tape, since very often the significance of some of the imagery will be more apparent later than it is at the time.

The moment the reading is finished, the crystal ball and its stand should be covered with its cloth again and put back into its dark, designated place until it's needed again.

DIVINING RODS/DOWSING

Dowsing is a form of divination in which, in its most common form, the dowser uses a stick or rod—sometimes forked, sometimes L-shaped—called a dowsing or divining rod. Holding the rod, the dowser walks across an area of land in search of anything from underground water to oil to minerals to buried treasure to booby traps and land mines. If and when the resource or danger is located, the rod is drawn downward, or, if two rods are being used, the rods cross each other. It's been practiced by everyone from ancient Eygptians in 5000 B.C. to Chinese royalty in 2200 B.C. to such biblical figures as Aaron and Hosea to Albert Einstein to British army officers to trained Marines during the Vietnam War.

Of course, there are probably as many skeptics as there are dowsers today, but at least dowsing has found its way into more positive, productive pursuits since its "discovery" all those millennia ago. Ancient dowsers, particularly in Egypt, Syria, and Babylonia, often used their skills to determine the true wishes of the gods, including who might be a candidate for being banished or sacrificed, and to reach verdicts and sentences in trials.

(The use of divining rods in trials wasn't actually outlawed until the early 1700s.) Dowsing enjoyed a more clandestine popularity during the Middle Ages when the rumor spread that dowsing was somehow Satanic. But sometime in the 1400s the Germans, who were completely disinterested in all this talk of the will of the gods, or Satanism, or using rods to decide the outcome of trials, decided to explore the potential of using dowsing rods to search for metals and other underground resources. They were successful enough that the practice caught on around the world, and there are still active dowsing societies in every part of the globe.

The most currently popular divining rods seem to be made of brass, steel, or twigs. Dowsers who prefer brass or steel insist that metal rods are far more sensitive to the magnetic field of their target, and they wrap a non-conductive material around the rod's handle to keep the dowser's own electromagnetic energy from interfering with the signals. But those who prefer twigs argue that only natural divining rods can adequately respond to the natural elements that are usually the objects of the search.

A fascinating variation is "map dowsing," in which the dowser stands over a map of the area in question and, using a pendulum as a dowsing tool, lets the pendulum hone in on the target location. Map dowsing is especially popular among dowsers in search of missing persons.

There are countless explanations for why dowsing works, and/or why it doesn't, but predictably, they all revolve in general around the question of whether or not the dowser is manipulating the movement of the rod. The argument goes like this:

Those who dismiss dowsing as nonsense take the position that of course the dowser is manipulating the movement of the rod, therefore the whole practice is a fraud.

Those who embrace dowsing as legitimate take the position that of course the dowser is manipulating the movement of the rod, therefore the practice is legitimate.

In other words, dowsers insist that it's a combination of their own paranormal and electromagnetic sensitivity to the object of their search, the involuntary hand movements that sensitivity creates, and the resulting amplified movement of the rod that make dowsing worthwhile. Skeptics often insist just as loudly that any involvement on the part of the dowser, either voluntary or involuntary, invalidates the whole idea. And so it continues today, and will undoubtedly continue for as long as dowsers continue to exist—and, by the way, remain successful.

CRYSTALS AND GEMS

Crystals and gemstones really can be of subtle, real help to our physical and emotional well-being. But as with pretty much anything, taking this to extremes, no matter how "in" it is, is just plain silly, as a friend of mine discovered the hard way: At the height of New Age mania, she wore so many crystal necklaces to help ease her chronic neck pain that she actually ended up making it worse from all that added weight. This is why I almost wish (the operative word is "almost") that using and wearing crystals and other significant gemstones would become such an overhyped fad that it would be offputting to mainstream society—but then, many people would not have benefitted from or given it a try.

The effect crystals and gemstones can have on our health has been acknowledged and taken advantage of for thousands of years. The reason behind that fact is that they're formed within the earth over countless millennia, absorbing rich, ancient, potent natural energy, and their atoms are arranged with amazing geometric precision. This means that they also emit potent natural energy with geometric precision in a consistent pattern that's capable of balancing our own often inconsistent energy. And since every natural element on this earth contains a life force, crystals and gemstones are powerful magnetically charged sources of potential healing when they're used properly.

We humans emit a wide variety of colors in our auras, too, and the colors of various crystalline stones have been found to hold specific health and healing benefits on specific chakras. In case you're not familiar with chakras, they're basically the seven energy centers of the life force each of us possesses, our own personal vortexes. In fact, countless physical and emotional health problems manifest themselves in the chakras even before they manifest themselves within the body. The aura surrounding the chakra that rules the potentially affected area of the body will actually appear darker, murkier, duller, and less vital than the rest of the aura, and cleansing, unblocking, and restoring energy to that particular chakra can heal the health problem to which the chakra was reacting. Working with the body's chakras is a practice that began among the Hindus and Buddhists, by the way, long before Christianity and Judaism were born, so please don't dismiss them as too "New Age" to be taken seriously.

So, wearing crystals and other gemstones that are known to target specific chakras can definitely be beneficial. The basic guide goes like this:

Amber—targets the spleen chakra in the center of the
     abdomen; calms nerves
Amethyst—targets both the throat chakra at the base
     of the throat and the brow chakra in the middle of
     the forehead; enhances inner peace and spirituality,
     helps battle addictions
Aquamarine—targets the heart chakra in the center of
     the chest; enhances strength and a feeling of power
     in fearful situations
Citrine—targets the spleen chakra; cleanses the body
     and the aura

Diamond—targets the crown chakra at the top of the head; attracts love, peace, and abundance

Emerald—targets the heart chakra; promotes general healing and the significance of dreams as well as the ability to remember them

Garnet—targets the root chakra between the sex organs and the anus, as well as the heart chakra; enhances imagination and improves energy balance

Gold—targets the solar plexus chakra halfway between the navel and the bottom of the breastbone; purifies, heals, promotes masculine energy

Jade—targets the heart chakra; very calming for the eyes; enhances longevity

Lapis lazuli—targets the brow chakra; stimulates the thyroid; increases perception

Malachite—the "lucky money stone"; targets the heart chakra; also eases asthma

Moonstone—the "lucky love stone"; targets the spleen chakra; also increases emotional balance

Onyx—targets the root chakra; helps healing during grief

Peridot—targets the heart chakra; stimulates emotional growth and new opportunities

Quartz—targets all of the chakras; can be programmed for specific purposes

Ruby—targets the heart chakra; stimulates circulation; can create anger in others by disrupting their energy field

Sapphire—targets the throat and brow chakras; very spiritual and helps achieves goals

Silver—targets all of the chakras; effective energy conductor; promotes feminine energy

Tanzanite—targets the brow chakra; enhances spiritual insights

Turquoise—targets the throat chakra; helpful to the
upper respiratory system

Parenthetically, there's a myth that opals attract bad luck. They
don't. It's that simple. What they do is intensify whatever energy you're already projecting, which makes it a good idea to
avoid them if you're going through grief, or if you experience
chronic depression.

TALISMANS

A talisman is a token, charm, or other small object that's worn,
carried, or kept to help ensure a specific goal—good luck, protection, self-confidence, mental and emotional clarity, strength
through a crisis, healing from grief, and so on.

The belief that an object that's been blessed and infused
with the energy necessary to achieve a designated purpose is
ancient, global, and non-denominational. Every culture, religion, and belief system has embraced some form of "good
luck charm" since the beginning of time. So, even if our logical
minds dismiss the idea of talismans as silly superstitions, our
attraction to them is almost a genetic legacy from thousands of
generations of ancestors.

The Greeks, Egyptians, and Babylonians included a variety
of sacred talismans in their rituals for everything from luring
favorable weather to curing illnesses. Ancient Africans carried
body parts of swift, agile animals to give themselves added
speed and agility. The gorgeous (and true, by the way) legend
of King Arthur would not be complete without his talisman,
Excalibur, the sword he withdrew from a stone that endowed
him with special powers. A case could be made that rosaries and
crucifixes are nothing more and nothing less than age-old Christian talismans. Christian and non-Christian travelers alike carry

St. Christopher medals for added protection, and a medal of St. Michael, considered among other things to be the patron saint of law enforcement officials, has been hidden inside the uniform of many a police officer, no matter how cynical or non-religious. And since not all talismans were adopted for the most noble intentions, there was also a revolting favorite among thieves a century or two ago called the Hand of Glory, the severed right hand of a hanged felon, which was carried to bring good luck and a safe escape to every robbery attempt.

If you choose to embrace a talisman for yourself, it's essential to remember that no object possesses special power— your belief is the only power any talisman will ever have, and its greatest value can be found in perpetually reminding you of your connection to God, the only Source of any real power.

7

THE PIONEERS

When I finally accepted the fact that I was "different," that I saw, heard, and sensed things that other people didn't, I took some comfort in knowing that my beloved Grandma Ada was as "different" as I was. I took even more comfort in learning that a long line of "different" people had come before me, some of whom made wonderful contributions to humankind and some of whom didn't, but all of whom were utterly fascinating to study. Those who fascinated me the most, from the sublime to the ridiculous, are the subjects of this chapter.

Before we start, I want to clarify a few of the terms you'll come across in these pages that might be confusing:

Several of the pioneers you'll be reading about were "mediums." A true, legitimate medium is someone whose psychic gifts include an expanded range of frequency perceptions, so that they're able to communicate with spirits from other dimensions that operate at higher frequency levels than ours on earth.

Some were legitimate "channels," which simply means they could literally absent themselves from their bodies and let a resident of the spirit world—usually their "control," or Spirit Guide—speak through them. There's actually a practical reason for this: spirit voices, coming from their higher frequency to our much lower one, sound like rapid-fire, high-pitched chirping noises that are very difficult to understand, or even tolerate for any length of time. Channels do exactly what the word implies—they provide a clear *channel* for a spirit to transmit through.

You'll also be reading about séances, which started in America in about 1845, in Hydesville, New York, where three sisters named Fox, who were alleged mediums, began holding sessions in which they communicated with the spirit world through a complex code of rapping patterns. These sessions, called "spirit circles," became enormously popular as the spiritualist movement took hold throughout the world, and the term "spirit circle" gave way to the word "séance," from the French word that simply means "sitting." Séances came to be thought of as any gathering where, through a variety of means, spirits communicate to the assembled group through a medium or channel.

With those definitions in mind, then, here is what might be called my own personal "hit parade" of the pioneers of spiritualism, in chronological order to help keep them in some kind of historical context. I don't pretend for a moment that I've included all of them. These are just the ones who, for a variety of reasons, intrigued me the most and I believe will intrigue you, too.

THE FOX SISTERS

The Fox sisters of Hydesville, Wayne County, New York, are often credited with being the primary founders of the spiritualist movement in America. They're also among the most controversial, dubious, and ultimately tragic figures in the history of spiritualism, which makes their "founder" status even more remarkable.

There were three Fox sisters: Leah (1814–1890), Margaret (1833–1893), and Kate (1837–1892). By 1848, Leah had married and moved to Rochester, so she was long gone when, on the night of March 31, Margaret, age fifteen, and Kate, age eleven, decided to play a joke on their superstitious, high-strung mother. They'd discovered that by tying strings to apples and dropping them on the floor and down the stairs, cracking the joints of their toes, and snapping their big toes and second toes together much like snapping their fingers, they could produce a whole array of ghostly noises. Those noises echoed across the wood floors so loudly that night in March that they woke up and terrified Mrs. Fox, who was immediately convinced the house was haunted. Lighting her way with a candle, she searched the house and quickly arrived at the door of her daughters' bedroom.

Kate took immediate advantage of this opportunity to elevate the prank to a whole new level and demanded of the "ghost" in the darkness: "Mr. Splitfoot [a reference to the mythical cloven hooves of the devil], do as I do!" She snapped her fingers, and the "ghost" repeated the sound. Maggie clapped her hands four times, and the "ghost" rapped back four times.

The very effective joke went on until Mrs. Fox was frightened to her core, at which point Kate decided enough was enough. "Tomorrow is April Fool's Day," she reminded her mother. "I'm sure somebody's just playing a trick."

But Mrs. Fox refused to be comforted, thoroughly convinced by now that there was a ghost in her home. She began asking questions of her own—how many children she had, their ages, etc.—and what do you know, the "ghost" rapped out the answers with uncanny accuracy. Mrs. Fox asked the identity of the restless spirit, and the girls manufactured the story of a thirty-one-year-old peddler named Charles Rosma, who'd been murdered five years earlier and buried in the cellar of the Fox family's house.

Mrs. Fox promptly began inviting neighbors to come hear these mysterious rappings. Rather than embarrass themselves and their family by admitting that this was simply a prank that had spun out of control, Margaret and Kate dutifully clicked and rapped their way through a growing number of amazed guests who eventually flooded in from all over the countryside. By late 1848, the media joined in with a widespread pamphlet called *A Report of the Mysterious Noises Heard in the House of John D. Fox in Hydesville, Arcadia, Wayne County.*

As luck and fate would have it, Leah Fox, who was by now the divorced Leah Fox Fish, saw the pamphlet and promptly headed back to Hydesville, not to rescue her poor besieged family from the undead but to become her sisters' manager and cash in on the odd, expanding phenomenon they'd become. Before long Kate, now twelve, and Maggie, sixteen, were performing at a non-stop whirlwind of séances and auditorium displays of their "gifts." Most appearances went smoothly. Others inspired jeers, hisses, and mixed cries of "Frauds!" and "Heretics!" Investigations into the two girls' public hoaxes went nowhere—unable to find any suspicious props hidden in their clothing, the investigators could not come up with any reasonable explanation about how the undeniable sound effects were taking place. The girls were inexplicably accurate at just enough séances that they managed to convince even the most cynical skeptics as their tours and audiences continued to grow. Riding the wave of the phenomenon, and in the process helping perpetuate it, newspapers and magazines quickly discovered that articles about the Fox sisters, and about spirituality in general, were guaranteed moneymakers. Mediums sprang up around the country, undoubtedly taking the position that if the Fox sisters could do it so could they, and the spiritualist movement officially became an American craze.

Margaret took a break from her "gifts" in 1852, when she

fell in love with Elisha Kane, an Arctic explorer from an aristo-
cratic family who didn't approve of Margaret's infamy or her
humble lineage. The couple were never legally married, but
their affair lasted until 1857, when Kane died, leaving Margaret
in virtual poverty and sending her back to Leah and Kate to
resume her life as a medium.

By that time Kate had developed a drinking problem, but
in spite of it she traveled to England, where she performed as
best she could for several British spiritualists before meeting
and marrying a lawyer named Henry Jencken in 1873. She and
Jencken had two sons. Jencken died of a stroke in 1885, and
Kate returned to New York with her children. In 1888 she was
arrested for public drunkenness and loitering, and Leah participated in efforts to get Kate's sons taken away from her, since
Kate was clearly incapable of taking care of them. Margaret,
who'd wandered into alcholism herself by then, was prevented
from taking guardianship of the boys but did get them safely
into the custody of a relative. Kate and Margaret's hatred of
Leah, which had been smoldering for years, became an abyss
from which the sisters never recovered.

Many believe it was that hatred, not to mention an offer
of $1,500, that inspired Margaret, in 1888, to take the stage
at the New York Academy of Music and demonstrate her
ability to create a variety of noises with her knuckles, joints,
and toes that had nothing to do with the spirit world. She
followed the demonstration with a signed confession of her
lifetime of fraud that was published in *New York World*. Kate
was privately "shocked" at Margaret's confession but never
publicly denied it.

In the end . . .

Margaret recanted her confession in 1891 and died at a
friend's home in 1893 without a dime to her name.

Kate died of alcoholism in 1892.

Leah, who had long since rejected her sisters as an embarrassment and married a wealthy businessman, preceded her sisters in death, dying quite comfortable circumstances in 1890.

Oh, and that murdered thirty-one-year-old peddler the young Fox sisters had contrived, whose body they said was buried in the basement of their "haunted" house? In 1904 the basement was excavated, and skeletal remains were unearthed. The remains were never identified.

MADAME HELENA BLAVATSKY

She was complicated, controversial, outspoken, fascinating, and famously imperfect. And no discussion of spiritual pioneers would be complete without her.

Her name was Helena Blavatsky, and she was born in Russia in 1831. Her father was a soldier and her mother a successful author. One of countless mysteries about Helena's life is her frequent claim that her mother died when she was an infant, when in fact she was twelve years old when her mother died. By all accounts Helena was a fairly unhealthy, unstable child, with a tendency to sleepwalk and to collapse into occasional emotionally triggered convulsions.

Helena's mind and temperament were fertile ground for the devoutly superstitious Russian culture into which she was born, and she was mesmerized by the idea that she was surrounded by a wealth of otherworldly beings and powers. She especially loved the story of the green-haired nymphs called *russalkas* who were said to live in the willow trees by the river near her house. One day when she was four years old and on a walk with her nurse, a fourteen-year-old boy began teasing her. Helena let out a loud, angry roar and threatened to have the *russalkas* tickle him to death. The boy ran away from her, disappearing over the riverbank, and wasn't seen again until his drowned, lifeless body washed up on the shore downstream a few weeks later. His death was undoubtedly accidental, but for the rest of her life Helena would occasionally talk about the homicide she committed at the age of four.

Helena's nurses and the rest of the household staff, through some combination of their superstitious culture and discomfort around this very peculiar little girl, concluded that Helena had special powers and was able to control supernatural beings, and they performed secret rituals to honor and protect themselves from that belief. It's no surprise that Helena concluded the hired help was right, she was special and powerful, and she felt completely entitled to control everyone in the household by any means necessary, from highly dramatic tantrums to intimidation to threats and curses.

At the age of seventeen Helena entered into a loveless marriage to General Nikifor Blavatsky, who was more than twice her age. Three months later she left him, literally escaping past the general's bodyguards and vanishing into a vague ten years of travel, the details of which vary widely from one biographer to the next.

Helena's version included two years in Tibet, which seems to be undisputed and is remarkable, considering the fact that admittance to Tibet wasn't easily granted during the nineteenth century, especially to women.

Even more remarkable was a story she told about her travels, an experience her fans marvel at and her critics refuse to believe. Helena claimed that in 1856, while wearing a disguise, she gained entry to a sacred reincarnation ceremony in India by showing the guard a special talisman she'd carried with her since childhood.

The ceremony began with a four-month-old baby being placed on a prayer rug in the center of the assembled group. Then, according to Helena's account, "Under the influence of the venerable lama, the baby rose to its feet and walked up and down the strip of carpet, repeating, 'I am Buddha, I am the old Lama, I am his spirit in a new body.'"

Helena eventually returned to Russia and to General Blavatsky, on the condition that she be required to spend as little time with him as possible. By then a significant cross-section of educated Russian intellectuals had become increasingly fascinated by both the paranormal and Madame Blavatsky, and she began holding séances on their behalf. Her guests were particularly impressed when, during several of the séances, a closed piano in an adjacent room began to play as if a pair of unseen hands was reaching beneath the cover and masterfully performing on the keyboard.

Helena managed to conduct a fairly complicated social life while expanding her renown as a paranormalist. She became romantically involved with an Estonian spiritualist named Nicholas Meyendorff and a married opera singer named Agardi Metrovich while continuing to live with her husband. She gave birth to a son, Yuri, during her involvement with these three men, and none of them claimed paternity. Tragically, Yuri was born with an array of deformities and medical problems and passed away at the age of five. Yuri was the only thing on this earth Helena ever claimed to love more than she loved the occult sciences.

As she grieved the loss of her child, her money began to dwindle and her life as a medium began to show signs of needing broader horizons. Before long Helena started traveling again, to Odessa, to Egypt, and to Paris. It was while she was in Paris that she heard about the growing spiritualist movement in the United States. She saw it as an opportunity for a whole new beginning, and with barely a dime to her name, she set sail on a steamship across the Atlantic and landed in New York City in July 1873.

Her new beginning in America didn't come easily. Helena barely made ends meet by holding séances on Sunday nights and working in sweatshops when jobs were available. But finally, still intent on pursuing her passion for the occult, she found her way to a remote farm in Chittenden, Vermont, in October 1874, for the singular, fateful purpose of meeting Colonel Henry Steel Olcott.

Colonel Olcott, an attorney and former appointee to a three-man committee investigating the assassination of President Lincoln, had been hired by the *New York Daily Graphic* to write a series of research articles on William and Horatio Eddy. The Eddy brothers were conducting séances on their Chittenden farm, and the skeptical but open-minded colonel was there to objectively report and explore.

Helena read the first of Olcott's articles and knew he was someone she wanted and needed to meet. She stayed at the remote Vermont farm for ten days, conducting séances along with the Eddy brothers. Not only was Olcott impressed enough to write several articles about her, but he gratefully accepted her offer to translate them for publication in Russia.

Madame Blavatsky's fame spread as a result of Colonel Olcott's articles, and the two of them ultimately founded the Theosophical Society in 1875. Its purpose was to study spiritualism, the occult sciences, Egyptian mysteries, the Kabbalah, and other similar esoteric fields. It's still alive and well today, with a worldwide membership of approximately 30,000, and has blossomed into a non-denominational, non-dogmatic organization devoted to promoting cultural understanding between Eastern and Western philosophies, religions, and sciences. The emphasis is on peace and individual freedom of thought, rejecting blindly accepted declarations in favor of beliefs based on personal experiences.

The controversies and contradictions about the life and work of Helena Blavatsky will probably never be resolved, and there's no doubt that she may have "pushed the envelope" on more than one occasion when it came to her credibility. In fact, there were those who claimed that she admitted to her share of hoaxes shortly before her death in 1891. One of her most infamous claims was a parade of manifested spirits who appeared during séances and materialized to pose with her for a notoriously incredible photograph in which she's seated in front of three "Ascended Masters": her own "master," El Myora; an ermine-cloaked St. Germain; and her teacher, Kuthumi, through whom she channeled much of her written work, including *The Secret Doctrine*.

On the other hand, there are aspects of her work that couldn't have been faked—most notably, her prophecies and insights that defied existing scientific "fact," many of which were committed to paper in *The Secret Doctrine*, with or without the channeled guidance of her teacher Kuthumi. *The Secret Doctrine* was published in 1888. In it, for example, she wrote that atoms can be divided, that atoms are perpetually in motion and that matter and energy can be converted. In 1897, eight years after her death, Sir Joseph John Thomson discovered the electron; in 1900, Max Planck's work laid the foundation for the quantum theory of physics; and in 1905, Albert Einstein unveiled his theory of relativity, abbreviated as $E = mc^2$. Einstein's niece even reported that her brilliant uncle kept a copy of *The Secret Doctrine* on his desk.

In the end, for all her controversy, complexity, histrionics, and undeniable flaws, it speaks volumes about the life of Madame Helena Blavatsky and her contributions to the world of spiritualism that she and the Theosophical Society she co-founded have retained their impact and their relevance more than a century after her death.

SIR ARTHUR CONAN DOYLE

Arthur Conan Doyle was born in Edinburgh in 1859, one of ten children in a family with Irish Catholic roots. His early education was in Jesuit-run schools, but by the time he reached adulthood as a medical student he was an avowed agnostic. An unlikely beginning for a future active spiritualist, but I guess in the world of spiritualism it's understandable that there's no such thing as a "norm."

It's no surprise that Conan Doyle is best known for creating the legendary detective Sherlock Holmes and featuring him in four brilliant novels and fifty-six short stories.

He also more than earned his place in history as a skilled physician and surgeon, a career that included service in a medical unit in South Africa. As a result of that service, Conan Doyle wrote a political pamphlet, *The War in South Africa: Its Causes and Conduct*, in which he defended England's handling of the Boer War and its aftermath. King Edward VII rewarded that work by conferring a knighthood on Arthur Conan Doyle in 1902, an honor he would have modestly declined if his beloved mother hadn't insisted he accept.

In 1885, he married Louise Hawkins, whom he met when he was treating her brother Jack for terminal cerebral meningitis. Jack's illness and death created an enormous fondness and respect between Conan Doyle and Louise, and their marriage produced two children and was a backdrop for his transition from doctor to renowned, successful author.

In 1893, Louise was diagnosed with tuberculosis, and the family made a series of moves to climates that would make her more comfortable. They fatefully ended up in Hindhead, Surrey, in 1897, where Conan Doyle met and fell in love at first sight with a young woman named Jean Leckie. For almost ten years Arthur Conan Doyle and Jean Leckie carried on a deeply passionate but, by most accounts, purely platonic relationship, true to their mutual oath that Louise was never, ever to be hurt.

Louise died in 1906, and Conan Doyle sank into health problems and depression, undoubtedly from guilt over a decade of keeping secrets and withholding love from a wife who'd devoted her life to him. He and Jean were married a year after Louise's death. They had three children together and were completely committed to each other until Conan Doyle's death from heart disease in 1930.

Clearly one of the most pivotal experiences of Arthur Conan Doyle's life happened in 1881. He'd shown no interest in any belief system throughout his adulthood, but something inspired him to attend a lecture on spiritualism. The evening resonated in him so profoundly that from then on he began attending séances, writing articles for spiritualist publications, and volunteering to be hypnotized at lectures on mesmerism. He credited spiritualism with seeing him through the grief of losing his son Kingsley and his brother Innes in a flu epidemic. He even joined the Society for Psychical Research in 1893—an organization that, among other pursuits, investigated alleged hauntings and other unexplained phenomena.

By 1920, Conan Doyle had become an ardent, popular writer and public speaker on the subjects of spiritualism and the afterlife; and in 1923, with the help of Jean, he started channeling and openly writing about his Spirit Guide, Phineas. In 1926, he wrote a two-volume work entitled *The History of Spiritualism*. As he'd expected, his total devotion to the paranormal cost him some of his credibility among more conservative fans throughout England and the United States, but his convictions were so unequivocal that he paid that price without apologies until the day he died.

Shortly before his death in 1930, Arthur Conan Doyle wrote a letter that spelled out prophecies based on information he'd received from Phineas and from various mediums he'd come to know and respect over his years of intensive research. He predicted severe earthquakes and tidal waves; a three-year period of upheavals, primarily in the eastern Mediterranean basin; the reemergence of the lost continent of Atlantis; great upheavals in the southern Pacific and Japan; and finally, what so many other spiritualists and civilizations before and since have echoed too often to be ignored: "Mankind can be saved by returning to its spiritual values."

ALEXANDRA DAVID-NEEL

One of spirituality's most fascinating and courageous explorers was Alexandra David-Neel, who was born in Paris in 1868. She was an adventurer, writer, lecturer, researcher, and scholar who was committed to experiencing as many spiritual disciplines as her lifetime would allow. Traveling throughout Asia and North Africa, usually on foot, she studied Eastern mysticism, philosophy, mind-over-matter techniques, the teachings of Buddha, the Qur'an, and the practices of Indian swamis. She was the first Western woman in history to enter Lhasa, the capital and "forbidden city" of Tibet, and she spent four years in a cave with a monk learning Tibetan spirituality. Her pursuit of knowledge continued until her death in 1969 at the age of one hundred and one.

One of David-Neel's most extraordinary experiments in the spiritual world was the result of her fascination with the Tibetan concept of *tulpa*. A *tulpa* is a being that originates in the mind and then, through countless hours of intense belief, visualization, and focus, becomes actual physical reality. They're not shared hallucinations based on rumors and legends. They're very real, living entities that exist completely separate from and independent of the thoughts that created them.

As always, Alexandra David-Neel wasn't content to study the phenomenon of *tulpa* by simply reading and talking to the Tibetan masters about them. She wanted to explore firsthand the possibility of creating one herself. And so she began to mentally conceive the figure of a round, happy, friendly little monk, kind of a Friar Tuck character, adding more and more details to him and his persona as he took clearer and clearer shape in her mind. Then, through a series of disciplined visualization techniques, she was able over time to see the monk not just as her own mental image but as a tangible being with a life of his own, as real as the rest of the world around David-Neel that he started inhabiting. The more mental energy she invested in him, the more visible and viable he became, and, to her growing dismay, the less able she was to control him. He began appearing on his own timetable, whether she manifested him or not, and within a few weeks of his creation, people around her who didn't know a thing about her *tulpa* experiment were asking her about the pleasant little monk who seemed to be hanging around with increasing regularity.

What alarmed David-Neel even more, though, was the fact that the longer the *tulpa* existed as an independent being, the more its own will took over, replacing the persona she'd visualized for it. Slowly but surely her round, cheerful monk evolved into a stronger, more muscular figure whose happy demeanor changed, and became dark, brooding, and potentially menacing. David-Neel realized with increasing horror that her control over him was diminishing and that she was solely responsible for having created an entity who was becoming dangerous. This left her with no choice but to take sole responsibility for destroying him, and the only way she could accomplish this would be to absorb him back into her own mind where he'd originated. The *tulpa* was so independent of her by that time that he felt completely entitled to exist, and he put up a fierce fight for his life. It took David-Neel more than a month of the same intense mental discipline that made the *tulpa* a reality to eliminate him, and it was such a debilitating process that her health was almost destroyed before she finally succeeded in reabsorbing the menacing little being she'd brought into the world.

Alexandra David-Neel's brave, risky experiment with the *tulpa* is graphic proof of the power of human thought. For better or worse, we create what we project, and the more energy we invest in what we're projecting, the more capable it is of developing a life of its own, beyond our control or initial intention. There are *tulpa* in existence on this earth right now—most notably, the yeti, or "abominable snowman," of the Himalayas, and Scotland's Loch Ness monster, both of which were created by myth and legend and then given living, breathing physical form by centuries of the masses' fearful belief in their existence. Consistent in all descriptions of these creatures by those who are absolutely convinced they exist is their ability to appear and disappear whenever they choose, identical to Alexandra David-Neel's *tulpa* monk.

Before we dismiss the idea that an actual tangible being can be projected into reality by the power of the mind, it's essential to remind ourselves that everything on earth that was ever created by humankind originated with a single thought. As we look around us at the state of the world and the general condition of life on this planet, we'd do well to remember the work of Alexandra David-Neel and wonder how many *tulpa*, seen and unseen, are among us that our own fear, anger, and negativity have made real.

EUSAPIA PALLADINO

When it comes to physical mediums—mediums who produce physical phenomena such as moving objects or unexplainable noises—there are probably none more controversial than Eusapia Palladino, who was born near Bari in southern Italy in 1854. She was orphaned by the age of eleven and went to live with a family in Naples.

Legend has it that six years later, in 1872, a séance was held in London that was attended by the wife of an Italian psychic investigator named Signor Damiani. At this séance, a spirit named John King appeared and revealed that his beloved daughter had been reincarnated as a very powerful medium. She could be found, he said, at a specified address in Naples. Signor Damiani traveled to that address and found Eusapia Palladino living there.

Eusapia had already claimed that as a child she'd experienced a variety of paranormal phenomena, from illuminated eyes staring at her to invisible hands pulling the covers off her when she was in bed. So she was very receptive to the possibility that she was the reincarnated daughter of a manifested spirit, and she immediately devoted herself to becoming a physical medium. By no coincidence her "control," or Guide, became John King, whom she channeled through trances and who exclusively spoke Italian.

All practitioners of the paranormal were being routinely investigated during the second half of the nineteenth century and the beginning of the twentieth, so Eusapia wasn't particularly singled out for scrutiny at the beginning of her career. But for several reasons, many of which were self-imposed, she became one of the most exhaustively researched, debated, and publicized mediums in history.

Her appearance and behavior definitely contributed to investigators' fascination with her—for better or worse. She was consistently described as unattractive and "rotund," coarse, illiterate, impulsive, and given to wild mood swings that could change from joy to violent anger in the blink of an eye. It also wasn't unheard of for Eusapia to make extremely inappropriate passes at any man who happened to catch her eye while attending one of her séances.

Of far more lasting and controversial intrigue, though, were her special effects. Guests at a Eusapia Palladino séance would invariably be treated to the usual table tilting and musical instruments flying through the air or being played by unseen artists. But for added measure, witnesses, even the most skeptical researchers, found themselves being touched by a phantom human hand that would materialize out of nowhere while both of Eusapia's hands were being held by the guests on either side of her. Eusapia would fully levitate to a horizontal position in a brightly lit room and, with nothing more than a look, draw furniture toward her from across the room, or make it rise several feet off the ground and suspend itself until her gaze released it to the floor again. Sitters would place a bowl of smooth soft clay in a corner and moments later discover the perfect image of a face imprinted in it. Disembodied faces would appear from behind a curtain, float across the table, bow a few times, and then disappear behind the curtain again. Spectacular light shows and added limbs would emerge from Eusapia's body, and her height would occasionally increase by as much as four inches.

Her séances weren't always limited to physical phenomena. She did successfully remember sometimes that the true calling of a medium was to offer reassurance that the spirit survives death, and there were times when she accomplished this beautifully. Dr. Giuseppe Venzano attested to a remarkable event he experienced while studying Eusapia Palladino at a series of séances, which he reported in the *Annals of Psychical Science* in August and September 1907. While Eusapia sat at the table in full view of the sitters, Dr. Venzana became aware of a woman behind him, crying. The woman began gently kissing him, and he saw and felt her face. He asked who she was, and a series of raps spelled out the name of a deceased relative that no one but Dr. Venzana would have known. In a soft voice that everyone at the table could hear, the relative apologized for her part in a feud that had taken place within the Venzana family, giving highly detailed personal information in the process. Dr. Venzana lovingly forgave her, after which, according to his report, "The form then said to me, 'Thank you,' embraced me, kissed me, and disappeared."

One of the first and most outspoken skeptics to investigate

Eusapia Palladino was Professor Cesare Lombroso, the founder of the science of criminology. He attended a séance in Naples and was impressed enough to arrange a series of séances in Milan for Eusapia to conduct in the presence of several renowned scholars and researchers. These séances were a significant part of Professor Lombroso's transformation from skeptic to believer, and in a letter dated June 25, 1891, he wrote: "I am filled with confusion and regret that I combated with so much persistence the possibility of the facts called Spiritualistic."

More scholars and researchers joined the parade of Palladino investigators, including members of the Society for Psychical Research, founded in London in 1882. A majority of them, including some skilled magicians who were recruited to look for signs of tricks, were convinced that she was legitimately gifted. The controversy about her was focused on what also seemed to be a widely accepted fact, summarized by the French astronomer and author Camille Flammarion in his *Mysterious Psychic Forces* (1909):

"One can readily conceive . . . that when [Palladino] is able to perform certain wonders without any expenditure of force and merely by a more or less skillful piece of deception, she prefers the second procedure to the first. . . . Her fixed idea is to produce phenomena, and she produces them, no matter how."

Hereward Carrington, an investigator with the American Society for Psychical Research, describes in *Eusapia Palladino and Her Phenomenon* (also written in 1909) a sitting to which he invited a renowned magician named Howard Thurston. Carrington had come to believe that Eusapia was a gifted, legitimate medium who was simply willing to cheat if she thought she could get away with it, or if she thought her guests were expecting more than she could produce on any given evening. The séance with Howard Thurston illustrated that theory. Shortly after the sitting began, both Carrington and Thurston easily caught Eusapia "levitating" the table with her foot. Carrington called her on it immediately with a wry smile and shake of his head.

"She thereupon smiled also, settled down in her chair, went into a light trance, and soon produced a series of perfectly magnificent genuine levitations, which so convinced Thurston that he came out in the papers the next day with a thousand-dollar challenge to any magician who could produce table levitations under the same conditions. The challenge was never accepted."

W. W. Baggally, a writer who believed in Eusapia's authenticity when he first attended her séances in 1908, decided that maybe her gifts had declined with age, disappointed as he was with the "spurious nature" of the séance he attended in 1910. In his *Report on a Series of Sittings with Eusapia Palladino*, he described the lack of any genuine phenomena at that séance, and Eusapia's excuse of not feeling well that evening. He couldn't resist adding: "She nevertheless accepted her full fee."

Eusapia herself summed up her position on the deceit she admitted to when she explained to a newspaper reporter, "Some people are at the table who expect tricks—in fact, they want them. I am in a trance. Nothing happens. They get impatient. They think of the tricks. Nothing but tricks. They put their minds on the tricks, and I automatically respond. They merely will me to do them. That is all."

Eusapia Palladino died in Rome in 1918 at the age of sixty-one, leaving behind an ongoing issue: if some of her work (or that of any spiritualist, medium, or psychic) is found to be deceptive, does that automatically mean that all of it should be dismissed? As the historian Ivor Gratton-Guinness points out in his *Psychical Research* (1982), "If all scientific work were treated this way, then science would disintegrate rather quickly into a collection of scientists rejecting all evidence except their own."

HARRY HOUDINI

On March 24, 1874, Erik Weisz, the boy who would become
Harry Houdini, was born to Cecilia and Mayer Samuel Weisz
in the Jewish section of Budapest, Hungary. Four years later
the family, which included five children, emigrated to America
to start a new life. Their names were somewhat Americanized
by immigration officials, and soon "Ehrich" and the rest of the
"Weiss" family settled in Appleton, Wisconsin, where Mayer
had a friend who was a successful businessman. With the
friend's help, Mayer, the former Budapest soapmaker, became a
rabbi in Appleton.

It was in Appleton that seven-year-old Ehrich saw and
became enthralled with a tightrope walker who was passing through town with a traveling circus. Ehrich, nicknamed
"Ehrie," which easily morphed into "Harry," was a gifted and
determined athlete. After some very painful, awkward missteps,
he mastered tightrope walking and quickly moved on to other
skills that led to his debut as a trapeze artist, acrobat, and con-
tortionist by the age of nine.

As indelible as Harry Houdini's impact was on the world of
magic, he also made an invaluable contribution to the world
of spiritualism by devoting the last thirteen years of his life to
crusading against fraudulent mediums who were exploiting the
bereaved.

Ironically, Houdini had conducted his own séances in the
late 1800s before his career as a magician took off. He was
understandably brilliant at making tables levitate and musical
instruments play themselves in midair. But when magic began
providing a substantial living, he abandoned his work as a medium.

In 1913, Houdini's beloved mother died. His profound grief

over losing her made him extraordinarily sensitive to anyone who was yearning to contact a departed loved one, and he was outraged at the knowledge that many people were being tricked out of their money by the séance business when they were at their most vulnerable. He'd been there and done it himself, and now he understood the depth of the pain that he himself had taken advantage of when he needed the money. Other magicians had been debunking phony mediums ever since the spiritualist movement had taken a firm hold throughout the world. But who was in a better position to expose the sheer trickery involved in producing "spirit manifestations" than the greatest magician the world had ever seen?

Oddly, Houdini's crusade against fraud among mediums was helped enormously by Sir Arthur Conan Doyle's genuine, heartfelt efforts to convert him to spiritualism. Houdini was a fan of Doyle's wonderful Sherlock Holmes mysteries and wanted to pursue a friendship with him. And Doyle, who'd become an important spiritualist leader, welcomed that friendship and, with the best intentions, arranged sittings for Houdini with some of the most respected mediums of the era. Houdini met with one after another and came to a conclusion that he found unavoidable but Doyle found insulting: not a single medium whose work he'd witnessed had displayed any supernatural powers at all, or produced any effect that he or any other skilled magician couldn't easily duplicate.

The friendship between Harry Houdini and Sir Arthur Conan Doyle was over, and Houdini's campaign against fraudulent spiritualists became his passion. Houdini began attending séances in disguise, accompanied by at least one reporter and one police officer so that arrests could be made and evidence of intentional deceit could be publicized. He gave demonstrations of typical "spiritualist" techniques at churches, police academies, and universities. He invited mediums onstage to demonstrate whatever supernatural powers they possessed. He testified before Congress in support of an anti-fortune-telling bill, arguing that there should be a distinct separation between religion and the "medium business."

One of Houdini's most public battles was inspired by a challenge issued by the magazine *Scientific American*, which offered a prize of $2,500 to any medium who could produce a genuine spirit manifestation in the presence of its hand-selected committee. One of the mediums who competed for the prize was Margery, widely known as "the Boston medium." The first committee members who tested her were impressed with her displays of flashing lights, loud flying bugles, levitating tables, ringing bells, and channeled voices. But after Houdini's séance with her, he declared her a fraud—he'd caught her in any number of well-executed tricks that had fooled the rest of the committee, and Margery was not awarded the *Scientific American* prize money.

Houdini also offered Margery the opportunity to appear onstage with him at Boston's Symphony Hall. He would give $5,000 to her and $5,000 to the charity of her choice if she could produce a spirit manifestation that he couldn't duplicate. When she declined his offer, Houdini treated the Symphony Hall audience to a spectacular recreation of his séance with Margery, and in 1925 he incorporated the how-tos of traditional medium tricks into all of his stage performances. He also published several books on the subject, including *Houdini Exposes the Tricks Used by Boston Medium "Margery"* and *A Magician Among the Spirits*.

It's a fascinating, essential footnote that Houdini was offended by suggestions that his crusade against fraud among spiritualists implied his disbelief in God and the possibility of an afterlife. Prior to his death from peritonitis on Halloween Day in 1926, he promised his wife Bess that if it were possible for the spirits of the deceased to contact the living, he would contact her and use a specific code to verify his identity. Bess attended séances with several mediums who claimed to have received the code, but on the tenth anniversary of Houdini's death she announced that she no longer believed he could come back to her, or to anyone. Her last words on the subject were, "It is finished. Good night, Harry."

EDGAR CAYCE

One of the spiritual leaders who has inspired me most in my decades of study is a man who never intended to be a spiritual leader at all but instead came upon his gifts completely by accident and then devoted his life to putting them to their highest, most generous use. His name was Edgar Cayce, and he was known as "the Sleeping Prophet" because he performed every one of his readings, healings, spiritual and metaphysical dictations, and prophecies in a deep, self-induced, trancelike sleep that he had no memory of when he was awake.

Cayce was a Kentucky farm boy, born in 1877. He wasn't a good student, and his formal education ended with grammar school. He was in his early twenties, earning a modest living as a photographer, when he lost his voice to an undiagnosed illness. After a year of unsuccessful medical treatments, he tried hypnotism on a friend's recommendation.

That single hypnosis session changed Cayce's life and ultimately the lives of thousands of others throughout the country and the world.

Cayce's friend accompanied him to a local hypnotist, where Cayce suggested it would be easiest if he put himself to sleep, which he'd learned to do as a child. Once he was completely "under," the hypnotist and Cayce's friend were witnesses to an extraordinary phenomenon: Edgar Cayce, whose limited education and complete disinterest in reading had provided him with not a shred of knowledge about human anatomy, proceeded to describe and diagnose the exact cause of his throat condition with the precision of a skilled physician studying an X-ray. He then gave the hypnotist a list of physiological hypnotic suggestions to repeat over and over while he was still in his trance, which arteries should open to restore blood and life to specific paralyzed muscles and which vocal cords should relax. The hypnotist followed instructions and so did Cayce, responding to his own commands as they were repeated to him, and he awoke with his full voice restored but no awareness at all of what had happened or how.

Cayce's hypnotist and his friend naturally told anyone and everyone who would listen about this seemingly impossible self-healing they'd witnessed, and before long Edgar Cayce was flooded with requests from people begging for healings for themselves or sick loved ones. His first reaction was to decline, not because of any lack of desire to help but because he felt inadequate—he had no idea how he'd managed to cure himself, and he wasn't about to make promises to strangers in need that he wasn't one bit sure he could keep, especially when their own educated, experienced doctors had failed.

What he couldn't deny, though, was that somehow, while "asleep," he'd succeeded where his own doctors had failed. If he really did possess a gift that would allow him to accurately diagnose and cure the previously incurable, he'd never forgive himself if he didn't at least try.

And so he began to give readings that over his lifetime would total more than fourteen thousand. Clients rarely came to him in person. Instead, they wrote letters, often from many hundreds of miles away. Cayce would lie down on the couch in his office and loosen his tie and shoelaces. His wife Gertrude would give him the information he needed from each letter: the subject's full name and address, and the exact location where he or she would be at the designated time of the reading. Cayce would put himself into a deep trance and, when he was ready, he'd signal the start of the reading with the words, "Yes, we have the body." Gertrude would then ask her husband relevant questions from the letters while Gladys Davis, Cayce's secretary, recorded his diagnoses and instructions in shorthand.

Eventually, thanks to a man named Arthur Lammers, Edgar Cayce's "physical" readings expanded into what he called "life" readings as well. Lammers was a printer Cayce knew from his photography years, and he had a great fascination with the worlds of metaphysics and spiritualism. Rather than wanting a reading from Cayce about health and healing issues, Lammers wanted to ask the "sleeping" Cayce questions about the meaning of life, the nature and perpetuation of the soul, the truth about death and the afterlife, and any other answers Cayce might offer about the vast world of the unseen.

Lammers's was the first of what grew to be more than two thousand of Edgar Cayce's "life" readings, during which Cayce explored his clients' past lives and the infinite subject of metaphysical philosophy. The information Cayce shared while he was "under" was completely foreign to his strict Protestant upbringing, but it was also so inarguable and felt so "true" in his soul that he evolved into a firm believer in reincarnation and in the fact that, in every area that really matters, all the great religions of the world share the same basic principles.

Cayce took no credit for the healing and wisdom that he always said came "through" him, not "from" him. He explained, during trances, that he was simply accessing information from his subjects' subconscious minds and from the Akashic Records, which are the written entirety of God's knowledge, laws, and memories, kept in sacred perfection in the Hall of Records on the Other Side.

Edgar Cayce's modesty extended to his lifestyle as well. He lived simply and refused to get rich from his tireless work. His life on earth ended on January 3, 1945, but more than three hundred books about his work ensure that his contributions to the unseen worlds of metaphysics and spirituality will continue to teach, intrigue, and inspire.

GLADYS OSBORNE LEONARD

One of the most gifted and thoroughly investigated mediums of the spiritualist movement was Gladys Osborne, who was born in Lythom, England, in 1882. One of many reasons I particularly related to her from the moment I started studying her work is that her first paranormal experiences began happening when she was just a child, through no effort at all on her part. In fact, she assumed everyone saw the same thing she did, which she described in her autobiography, *My Life in Two Worlds*:

"Every morning . . . I saw visions of . . . valleys, gentle slopes, lovely trees and banks covered with flowers . . . restful, velvety green grass that covered the . . . valley and the hills. Walking about . . . were people [whose] every movement, gesture and expression suggested in an indefinable and yet positive way a condition of deep happiness, a state of quiet ecstasy."

Whether she was aware of it at the time or not, she was seeing and describing the impossibly beautiful landscape of the meadows and valleys that greet us all on the Other Side when we first emerge from the legendary tunnel. She discovered that her daily visions were unique when she casually mentioned them at breakfast one morning, in the form of a comment about the lovely place "we" were being shown that day. Not only did her parents not have a clue what she was talking about, but her father insisted that she never mention any such nonsense again.

Gladys's family fell on hard times during her teenage years, and she became a singer, dancer, and actress to earn a living. Without a doubt the most significant singing engagement of her career was a performance at a spiritualist church, where one of the mediums sought her out to tell her that she was destined to accomplish "great spiritual work." My Grandma Ada told me the same thing when I was in my teens, and like me, Gladys had no idea at the time what this meant or how to proceed.

She continued her low-paying theatrical career in London and met and married Frederick Leonard, an actor who became a devoted husband and helpmate in Gladys's pursuit of spiritualism throughout her life.

She also met two sisters who were interested in spiritualism, and the three of them started meeting in Gladys's dressing room for an hour every night between performances, gathering around a table for a kind of makeshift séance. It was during their twenty-seventh session that Gladys's Spirit Guide finally revealed herself. The Guide introduced herself as a Hindu girl who'd been married to Gladys's great-great-grandfather and had died in childbirth in 1800 at the age of thirteen. Gladys found her Guide's long, complicated Hindu name too difficult for comfort, so she renamed her Feda. I renamed my Spirit Guide too, not because her given name Iena was difficult to pronounce but because for no apparent reason I just plain didn't like it. I preferred Francine, and that's what I've called her since the night I met her. I'm sure Gladys found with Feda exactly what I've found with Francine—our Spirit Guides don't care what we call them as long as we *do* call them.

Gladys was also as reluctant as I was to "step aside" in trance form so that she could channel her Spirit Guide; but when there's important work to be done, efficiency tends to take over. Gladys began channeling Feda for readings, or "sittings" as they were called in the late 1800s and early 1900s, and over the next fifty years she became one of the most highly regarded mediums of her era.

One of her most significant "sittings" took place in 1915, when Sir Oliver Lodge and his wife came to Gladys in a desperate, highly skeptical attempt to contact their son Raymond, who'd been killed in the First World War. Feda's information was so accurate throughout her series of sessions with the Lodges that they were completely convinced they were communicating with their son and that he'd survived death.

Gladys's fame spread quickly through the publicity surrounding her success with the Lodges, and with the media scrutiny came an interest in investigating and testing her skills, all of which she welcomed, just as I welcomed any number of tests throughout the decades, particularly from Dr. Bill Yabroff, a psychology professor at the University of Santa Clara. In Gladys's case she was thoroughly investigated by a variety of prestigious psychic researchers, none of whom found her to be anything less than completely authentic and sincere in the highest possible humanitarian uses of her paranormal gifts.

Incidentally, one story I heard several times while I was researching Gladys Leonard is that occasionally, while Gladys was channeling her Spirit Guide, Feda would give away Gladys's jewelry to her clients. Believe me, especially now that the man in my life is a very gifted and successful jeweler, I've made it clear to Francine that handing out my jewelry while I'm channeling her is not an option.

Thanks to her reliable authenticity, her integrity, and her utter devotion to mediumship as a means to advance humankind's certainty of God's promise of a joyful afterlife, Gladys Leonard was and is an inspiration, long after her own passing into that afterlife in 1968 at the age of eighty-five.

EILEEN GARRETT

There is only one philosophy that makes sense: Everything that grows gives sustenance and pleasure, to mark time and finally disappear; but its true essence remains.

—*Eileen Garrett*

With the exception of my Grandmother Ada, I don't think there's a psychic trance medium I've admired more and been more inspired by than Eileen Garrett, who balanced a life of tragedy and chronic health problems with a productive, exhaustively explored practice of her paranormal skills.

She was born in 1893 in Meath County, Ireland—a land whose people embrace their ancestral traditions of a genetic connection to nature and a respectful belief in the unseen. Both her parents committed suicide not long after her birth, and she was raised on her aunt and uncle's farm. She briefly attended a Protestant boarding school in Dublin when her uncle passed away, but was suspended for sneaking out during the night to explore her new surroundings, and shortly after arriving home again she was diagnosed with tuberculosis. That and other recurring breathing problems were combined with several heart attacks throughout her life until she died of bone cancer in 1970.

She had three sons and a daughter by her first husband, an architect, Clive Barry. All three boys died during childhood, two from meningitis and one just a few hours after his birth. After her divorce from Clive Barry, she married a soldier who was killed in action in the battle at Ypres during the First World War. Three weeks before the armistice was declared she married another soldier, James Garrett, and averted another potential tragedy. Doctors had told him that amputating his badly injured leg was his only hope for avoiding an onset of gangrene. Eileen "knew" that the operation wasn't necessary, and as his wife, she had the authority to refuse to allow it. The amputation was canceled, and James Garrett's leg healed on its own.

She'd had a conscious awareness of the "unseen" since childhood without finding it that extraordinary, but her first experience with trance channeling happened without any voluntary effort on her part. She was sitting with a small group of women who were hoping to contact deceased loved ones. She found out the details later, since all she remembered was that one minute she and the women were sitting there talking and the next minute they were gently shaking her awake. It seems that while she "slept" she began describing the loved ones the women were searching for, and she also channeled an Asian "control" named Uvani.

Rather than being thrilled by the news of this amazing event, Eileen was frightened at first and even a little repulsed, but she was also curious enough that for the next several decades she actively participated in any number of formal tests by everyone from the Society for Psychical Research in London to various psychology professors and researchers at Duke University, Johns Hopkins University, and the New York Psychiatric Institute. No one was more interested than she was in finding out how and why her considerable paranormal gifts worked, and the barrage of experiments only enhanced her credibility with scholars, her peers, and the general public alike.

Eileen did extensive work at the British College of Psychic Science in London, where she worked on advancing her clairaudience, clairvoyance, and telepathic skills, but she primarily made peace with and pursued her trance work. She also began what would evolve into countless poltergeist investigations, the first of which offered yet another example of her gifts and her integrity.

In 1925 Eileen received a letter from a man who was concerned about his elderly mother. The woman was convinced that there were perfectly harmless ghosts in her house, but her maid had confided in her son that on a few occasions there had been sudden, spontaneous fires in his mother's bedroom while she slept. The man was understandably concerned for his mother's safety, and on the offchance that there really were ghosts trying to burn down her house, who better to summon as a ghost buster than a medium?

Eileen went to the mother's house for dinner, and, after the elderly woman went to sleep, she crept quietly into her bedroom. She came away with two strong clairvoyant impressions: visions of two fires in the room, one destroying the curtains and one starting behind a bookcase; and a complete absence of ghosts in the house—she was sure the fires were being set by a living, breathing human being.

Several months later, the curtains in the elderly woman's bedroom burst into flame while the woman was supposedly alone in the room and sound asleep. The arsonist turned out to be just as human as Eileen predicted—the maid's nephew, who knew the woman had left a generous inheritance to his aunt in her will.

A particularly touching display of Eileen Garrett's clairvoyance and clairaudience took place when she was visiting a movie set in Hollywood, watching the work of the venerable and notoriously unapproachable director Cecil B. De Mille. Suddenly, in the middle of a scene, a small woman walked up to De Mille and began giving him a mild scolding about his work repeating itself and the quality of the projects themselves being second-rate and irrelevant. Eileen could hear every word the woman said and was a little in awe of the courage or insanity it took to criticize Cecil B. De Mille; and she was even more surprised that instead of ordering the woman off the set at the top of his lungs, De Mille simply ignored her and went right on with the scene as if nothing had happened.

Moments later the woman came up behind Eileen and asked her to speak to De Mille on her behalf, since she clearly couldn't make him hear her. She explained that while De Mille was very excitable, he would respect Eileen and her work. Eileen needed to pass along the message on her behalf that De Mille should concentrate on projects that would be meaningful, that would be politically helpful to those whose voices weren't being heard. With that she faded away, confirming Eileen's impression that the woman was dead.

Eileen noticed Jesse Lasky, the head of Paramount, standing

nearby. She was acquainted with him and knew he wasn't dismissive of the idea of life after death, so she pulled him aside, told him what had just happened, and asked if she should try to deliver this message to Cecil B. De Mille. Lasky was intrigued, but he assured her that there were few worse ideas than trying to give De Mille advice of any kind, from the living or the dead, and she should go out of her way to leave it, and him, alone.

She did, until two years later, when she returned to Hollywood and sensed the woman trying to reach her again. She called her friend Hamlin Garland, who'd been involved in several psychic and clairvoyant experiments with her, not to ask his advice but simply because she knew he'd be interested in her experience two years earlier, which she frankly hadn't thought about since. She was surprised when, after she'd told him what had happened, he informed her that he and Cecil B. De Mille were both neighbors and friends. He felt strongly that De Mille would be receptive to hearing what she had to say, and she managed to arrange a meeting with him.

De Mille couldn't have been more dismissive of Eileen Garrett when she arrived in his office. In fact, he turned his back on her and stared out the window as he barked at her to explain what it was she wanted. Eileen felt the woman's presence again, which was probably the only thing that kept her from leaving, and after a deep breath she started repeating the woman's words to De Mille's back exactly as she heard them. A lengthy, articulate, precise critique followed, not one bit of which De Mille reacted to or even seemed to acknowledge.

Finally, as Eileen recounts in her beautiful book *Many Voices*, the woman concluded her monologue: " . . . I would hope that you would find a great novel, an epic story, and that you, or those whom you will have trained, would present that story to the world. Then, my dear son, you will have given the world an understanding of a free country, of another people, of a people equally humble, equally shrewd, of a young people and an old people. Perhaps the last thing that you will prepare will be this film . . . an epic, a drama, a final message."

The woman fell silent, and De Mille still had yet to move. Eileen prepared to leave and was saying goodbye when he turned around, and she saw that his face was covered with tears. She was surprised and deeply moved, and she told him she was glad if she'd managed to be of some use.

"*Of some use!*" he replied. "*Some use!* I loved my mother; it is true. We didn't always understand each other, but I had a great respect for her. I have waited for this for over twenty years!"

Eileen looked back on that extraordinary meeting every time years later that she sat in awe watching Cecil B. De Mille's stunning epic *The Ten Commandments*.

Eileen Garrett was also enormously gifted at telepathy and out-of-body experiences, as she dramatically demonstrated in response to a letter from a man in Yorkshire, England, whose daughter was gravely ill with pneumonia. While being constantly aware that she physically never had left her New York apartment, Eileen astrally traveled to the girl's bedroom one night. She "saw" her outline in the bed, and she touched her and felt the perspiration on the girl's skin. She "heard" her shallow, labored breathing and began coaching her to breathe more deeply, which the girl strained to try. She then found herself "knowing" that the obstruction was in the girl's left lung, and it was simply an inflammation, something the girl could and would recover from—a fact a subsequent letter from the girl's father confirmed. Eileen felt so attached to the girl from the out-of-body healing experience that she arranged a college grant for her when the time came and her father was unable to afford it.

Probably the most highly publicized "sitting" of Eileen Garrett's career involved the crash of the R-101 airship, a British-made zeppelin, on a French hillside. Eileen had seen three separate phantom airships in the sky with smoke billowing out of them, so real that she was shocked when there was no mention of them in the press. On learning that England had just built two airships, the R-100 and the R-101, and that the R-101 was scheduled to fly to India, she managed to alert Sir Sefton Brancker, head of the Air Ministry in London, of the visions she'd had that she sensed meant disaster for the R-101.

Sir Sefton Brancker was among the forty-eight casualties of the crash of the R-101 on October 5, 1930. Two days after the disaster Eileen conducted a séance at the National Laboratory of Psychical Research, during which she unexpectedly channeled Flight Lieutenant H. Carmichael Irwin, another of the R-101 fatalities. Through Eileen he proceeded to give a detailed, extremely technical assessment of the construction of the zeppelin and what had caused the disaster. A member of the Air Ministry subsequently reviewed the information Eileen had channeled and wrote in an unofficial report that 70 percent of it was absolutely accurate, while another 20 percent was extremely likely. The séance made headlines around the world when the investigation into the crash was over and the news of Eileen Garrett's remarkable accomplishment could be made public.

These are just a few highlights of a career and life that I'm sure have been an inspiration to all of us who, as Eileen Garrett described it herself so often, "live in two worlds." She eagerly explored her gifts, she used them with great humanity, and she never compromised her integrity and her credibility, even when she was wrong—as all of us have been and will be, since no one but God is 100 percent accurate 100 percent of the time.

She was never particularly curious about that place called the Other Side, but I know she's there and that she hears me every time I thank her.

8

THE RESIDENTS OF
THE SPIRIT WORLD

Obviously, the core of spirituality, the purpose and soul of its existence, is the spirit world itself, a world that can seem so mystifying for a place from which we all came and to which we'll all return when our finite, imperfect bodies give out. We've all been part of the spirit world, and we'll all be part of it again. And the more I can demystify it for you, the more familiar and deeply personal it will feel to you, so that you can end your fear of it, embrace it, and cherish its intimate presence in your life for the soul's eternity it clearly proves.

I want you to understand the difference between spirits and ghosts. I want you to understand why none of us will ever be Angels, and why that's okay. I want you to understand who to welcome when they come to visit, what to watch for, who to send away, and how to go about it. I want you to understand God's logical perfection in the relationship between us and the Other Side. I want you to understand so clearly that you never wonder again, you *know* how surrounded you are every minute of every day by the comfort, help, clarity, and love the spirit world is already providing if you'll just be still and listen. As the beautiful saying goes, "Make time for the quiet moments, for God whispers and the world is loud."

SPIRITS

When our bodies die, we literally do go through a brilliantly lit tunnel. It doesn't descend from the heavens to retrieve us, as lovely an image as that might be. Instead—take it from a woman who had her own near-death experience and saw this with her own eyes—the tunnel rises from our own bodies at about a thirty-degree angle, more "across us" than "up."

The trip through the tunnel is a gorgeous, weightless experience of utter freedom from our confining bodies, from gravity and from the negativity of earth. We not only don't feel as if we've died, we feel thrillingly alive. All our sadness, illness, worries, frustrations, anger, resentment, and confusion fall away like the useless baggage they are, and we're filled with nothing but peaceful joy and an all-loving, all-encompassing understanding.

Waiting at the end of the tunnel is the sacred white light of God, through which we pass for an ecstatic reunion with loved ones, including our pets, from every lifetime we've ever lived both on earth and at Home. Once we've completed a rearrival process that includes a review at the Scanning Machine of the incarnation we've just left behind, we resume the busy, perfect, exquisite lives we interrupted for the spiritual education we went to earth to pursue.

One of the most surprising facts about the Other Side is also the reason that the tunnel that takes us Home rises at about a thirty-degree instead of a ninety-degree angle from our bodies: that divine, impossible beautiful paradise for which we're Home-sick from the moment we leave it until the moment we return is another dimension that's actually located only three feet above the ground level of earth. It exists at a much higher vibrational frequency than we do here, which is why we don't perceive our intimate proximity to it, any more than normal human hearing allows us to hear the extremely high-frequency pitch of a dog whistle.

So now you know why those who have visual encounters with the spirit world invariably comment on their impression that the spirits seemed to be "floating" a few feet above the ground. The truth is, they're not floating, they're simply moving on their own ground level on the Other Side, just three feet higher than ours.

You'll also hear the frequent observation that a loved one visiting from Home looked wonderful, younger, and/or like they looked in their prime. There are a couple of reasons for that. One is that there is no illness, injury, infirmity, or imperfection of any kind on the Other Side, only the most robust, exhilarating health we can possibly imagine. The other is that when we're at Home, we're all thirty years old. I once asked my Spirit Guide Francine the question you may be asking now: "Why is everyone thirty?" She answered, "Because they are." I had no idea where to go from there with the conversation, so I left it at that.

I need to add that the spirits of loved ones won't always appear to be thirty years old when they visit. Nothing is more important to them when they come to us than that we know with absolute certainty that it's really them. If we'd recognize them with ease at the age of thirty, no matter what age they were when they went Home, they might come to us in what is now their natural form. But if they went Home when they were, let's say, five years old, we'd be unlikely to recognize them as a thirty-year-old, so they'll show up as the child we remember and would know on sight.

The spirits of the Other Side live in a world unencumbered by our earthly limitations, which gives them many abilities we can look forward to when we've gone Home again. One of those is the ability to bi-locate, or be in two places at the same time. If you've had a visit from a deceased love one, you might check with family members or others who were close to them to ask if anything "unusual" happened to them as well—it's not unusual for spirits to make simultaneous appearances (in some form or other) to those who are missing them, if only to say that they're well, happy, and very much alive.

And don't be discouraged if others see a deceased loved one and you don't. Not everyone is born with the gift of clairvoyance, or the ability to see beings or objects from other dimensions, and there's nothing necessarily predictable about who has it and who doesn't. A wonderful, absolutely true story illustrates that point beautifully.

A friend named Bryan, as down-to-earth a man as you'd ever meet, had a beloved white toy poodle named Squinkley. One of Squinkley's favorite "jobs" was riding shotgun in the SUV while Bryan ran errands, and Bryan was devastated when Squinkley passed away at the ripe old age of sixteen.

Six months after Squinkley died, Bryan dropped his SUV off at the dealership to be serviced. He was walking away toward the friend's car who was driving him home when the mechanic yelled, "Hey, mister, don't forget your little white dog!" Of course Bryan stopped in his tracks, turned around, and said, "What did you say?" The mechanic, gesturing toward the front passenger seat of the SUV, repeated, "Your little white dog. You don't want to leave him here all day."

Bryan naturally walked back to look into the SUV, and saw nothing. After a moment to collect himself and try to grasp what was apparently going on, he looked at the mechanic and said, "I don't know how to break this to you, but you just saw a dog that died six months ago."

All the color drained from the mechanic's face, and he backed away from the SUV and, by all accounts, wouldn't go near it again for the rest of the day.

Needless to say, Bryan had a million questions when he'd finally recovered from the initial shock, but they essentially boiled down to just one, with a couple of variations: why had Squinkley appeared for a mechanic he had never met but not for Bryan, and why did a mechanic, who neither knew nor cared about Squinkley, get to see him when Bryan, who adored him, didn't?

The answer: clairvoyance. Squinkley didn't just appear for the benefit of the mechanic. He'd been sitting right there in his usual seat beside Bryan all along, riding shotgun and keeping him company while he ran his errands. Bryan, without the gift of clairvoyance, simply wasn't "tuned" to the higher frequency it would have taken to see Squinkley in his spirit form. The mechanic, on the other hand, was obviously very clairvoyant, and judging by his reaction to seeing a dog who'd passed away months earlier, he would gladly have muddled through life without that particular gift, thank you. In fact, I'll always wonder how many times that mechanic saw things that no one else around him saw and somehow convinced himself he was just imagining things.

Fortunately, the spirit world has a variety of ways of letting us know they're around whether we're clairvoyant or not. All it takes is an awareness of what to look for, a willingness to pay attention, and a mind that's open enough to allow for the possibility that you might not be imagining things at all.

Here are just a few of the common signs of a spirit visit:

They'll create a scent we associate with them—a favorite perfume, a favorite fragrant flower, a favorite aftershave or pipe tobacco, a favorite food they loved to cook or bake, a favorite incense or scented candle, and so on.

They'll perform a subtle sign of affection that was a habit of theirs during their lifetime, especially a light breath or touch to our hair or the back of our neck, or a gentle hand on our shoulder while we're driving.

They'll manipulate objects around you to call attention to themselves. Watch for an unusual number of coins to start showing up in illogical places. Keep an eye on framed photographs, often but not necessarily photos of your deceased loved one, that might be repeatedly moved so that they're facing a different direction than usual or lying flat on the table where they're kept. Notice rocking chairs that begin rocking when no one's near them. Pay attention to music boxes or toys that suddenly seem to self-activate. If your keys disappear from a place you're sure you put them and reappear in some highly unlikely spot, by all means allow for the possibility that you misplaced them yourself, but don't automatically disregard the equally likely possibility that some loving spirit is trying to say, "Hello, I'm right here."

Because spirits have to travel back into our dimension from theirs in order to visit us, they often attach their energy to such powerful conductors as electricity and water in order to help with their "reentry." They'll create bizarre behavior in TVs, appliances, telephones, computers, and any and all other electrical devices. And it's no coincidence that they're at their most active during lightning (electrical) storms and between the hours of 1:00 a.m. and 5:00 a.m. when the night air is at its dampest and the dew is at its heaviest. Of course, as always, be practical. Not every malfunction around your house can be attributed to the spirit world. Sometimes what you need is a good repairman. But fair is fair when it comes to practicality—when there's no reasonable, logical explanation for unexpected phenomena around you, the possibility of spirit visits can actually make just as much sense when you understand how and why they happen, don't you think?

Spirits are also capable of creating an amazing, seemingly impossible feat called an "apportation," which some of you are likely to witness if you haven't already. Apportation is the transporting of a physical object through space and through apparently impenetrable barriers. A story a client shared with me explains this far better than any simple definition ever could:

Her father passed away after a long struggle with Alzheimer's disease. She and her two brothers honored every request in his will while planning his funeral, from the music he asked for, to the suit he wanted to wear, to his mother's engraved hand-carved one-of-a-kind rosary that he wanted to be holding as he was buried. My client and her brothers each kissed the rosary and then, together, placed it in their father's hands as their last loving gesture before the casket was closed and slowly lowered to its final resting place beside his beloved wife.

They were speechless with some combination of confusion and awe when, the next morning, they gathered for breakfast in the kitchen of the family home and found that same engraved one-of-a-kind rosary in the middle of the table, glittering in a ray of sunlight that was streaming through the nearby window.

Once they regained their ability to form complete sentences again, they began ruling out every earthly explanation they could come up with. Yes, it was definitely their grandmother's rosary, right down to the subtly engraved "For Julia M." that their father had cherished so much that he'd asked to be buried with it. And no, it wasn't possible that all three of them had imagined kissing it, draping it around his hands as they said goodbye, and then watching it descend into the ground with him the day before.

That left only two ways the rosary could have found its way to the kitchen table that morning: either someone dug up their father's grave during the night, took the rosary, drove two hours to the family home, crept into the house without setting off the elaborate alarm system, left the rosary on the table, and crept out again undetected; or their father, free from his body in the spirit world, had apported the rosary to his children as proof to them that he was alive and well.

I'm as big a fan of earthly explanations as the next person, but of those two alternatives, can anyone honestly say with a straight face that the first one makes more sense than the second?

So, next time an object appears in a place that makes absolutely no sense at all no matter how hard you try to logically explain it, please stop and remember the rosary and the apportation that delivered it from a father to his children, smile, and thank the spirit who's just trying to remind you that they've never left you at all.

It won't surprise you that many of the clients who come to see me about a deceased loved one want to know if that loved one has a message for them. They seem to be hoping for news of a hidden will, or a safe deposit box full of cash, or some kind of resolution to an earthly dispute. And I admit, it never ceases to fascinate me that the inherent message when a deceased loved one comes through in some verifiable way—"It's true, the spirit survives death!"—seems to be a bit of a disappointment, as if the client would prefer a surprise pile of cash to proof of eternal life.

I promise you, ninety-nine times out of a hundred, when you sense that a deceased loved one is trying to communicate with you, the message is nothing more and nothing less than the miraculous truth that they're not dead at all, that they're right there with you, and that you never need to fear death again. And when they have more to say than that, you can count on it that it will be loving, comforting, positive, and happy, for the most logical of reasons: the perfect paradise they've transcended to is a place of emotional and spiritual bliss, unconditional love, thriving physical health, and total, peaceful understanding of everything that was and everything that will be. Any entity you encounter who seems to be sad or angry or mean or resentful or injured or negative in any way is *not* visiting from the Other Side. (We'll discuss shortly who they are and where they're visiting from.)

Just as some of you are clairvoyant, or able to see spirits and objects from other dimensions, some of you are clairaudient, or able to hear spirits and sounds from other dimensions. Because of the significantly higher frequency of the Other Side, you'll undoubtedly experience what I do—high-pitched, very rapid chirping that's often reminded me of the Chipmunks, for those of you who are old enough to recall who they were. The majority of the time, though, the spirit world will communicate with our world telepathically, silently transferring thoughts and information from their minds to yours. You might easily find yourself looking back on a wonderful conversation with a visiting spirit and realizing that neither of you said a single word out loud.

There are a few questions I'm asked by the majority of my clients when they're struggling with the loss of a loved one, and I want to answer them here, for the benefit of anyone who's grieving. These answers are utterly reliable, absolute, and from the bottom of my heart, I promise you.

Are they happy?

That is a resounding "yes!" They're living in blissful, peaceful perfection on the Other Side, in an atmosphere alive with God's love. Their health, mentally and physically, is thriving. They're surrounded by countless loving friends, busy and active with pursuits that stimulate and fascinate them, and there's not an instant of negativity, fear, or uncertainty in their world. Yes. You have my word, they're divinely happy.

Do they miss me?

Not really, but don't let that upset you. Here on earth we have perceptions that are limited by such concepts as "time" and "beginnings, middles, and ends." The moment we're Home

again, we remember all we've forgotten about God's promise
of eternity. Eternity doesn't just mean "we always will be." It
also means "we always have been." There is no such thing as
time. There are no beginnings, no middles, and no ends. Our
spirits know when they're Home where we belong that within
the blink of an eye—which in the context of eternity could be
a hundred or a thousand years in earthly terms—we'll all be
reunited on the Other Side. They'll be ecstatic to welcome us,
and in the meantime, they're busy, happy, and visiting us far
more often than we even know.

What about all those things we left unsaid?

Say them now. I promise they'll hear you. But be sure you're
aware that whatever you have to say is for your benefit, not
theirs. No matter what the circumstances, from their perspective,
there is no unfinished business between you. In the perfection in
which they're living, there is no sadness, no resentment, no disappointment, no anger, and certainly no need for goodbyes, since
you'll be seeing each other again so soon. Please, by all means,
pour your heart out if it will ease any pain in your heart, and believe with absolute certainty that they'll be right there listening
to and understanding every word you have to say.

SPIRIT GUIDES

Each of us has a Spirit Guide. We select them on the Other Side
and literally entrust them with our soul as we recruit them to be
our most constant, vigilant companion and helpmate when we
make the choice to experience another lifetime on earth. And
since our relationship with our Guide begins at Home, before
we enter our bodies, our Spirit Guide will never be someone
we've known here.

All Spirit Guides have experienced at least one incarnation. If that weren't true, they'd never be able to empathize with the mistakes, temptations, fears, and other frailties that are unavoidable on earth. In fact, most of us either have been or will be someone's Spirit Guide during our soul's eternal journey.

A Guide's job is to encourage, advise, and support us toward the goals we've set for ourselves in this incarnation. And they have several tools at hand to help them with that challenge. Not only do they study us closely and objectively on the Other Side once they've agreed to take on this responsibility, but they have intimate knowledge of our specific intentions for being here—information of which we lose conscious awareness the moment we're born. Because of that intimate knowledge, they will never interfere with the choices and decisions we make, or deprive us of our free will. At best, they'll offer possible alternatives and warnings. But our agreement with them from the beginning is that we're here on earth to learn and grow, and we can't accomplish that if our Spirit Guide is constantly shielding us from the lessons we need to learn.

They communicate with us in a variety of ways, without being credited for the information often enough. What you've probably assumed to be your instincts, or your conscience, or your premonitions, or just "something told me," is more than likely your Spirit Guide sending you messages either telepathically or through infused knowledge, both of which you read about in chapter 5. When you suddenly, "for no reason," drive a different route than usual to your job or home and find out later that you avoided an accident; "spontaneously" change travel arrangements at the last minute and, as a result, are spared a disaster; act on "an impulse" to call a friend, only to discover that he or she needed your help at that moment; or go to sleep concerned about a problem and wake up knowing the solution, rest assured that you're receiving your Spirit Guide's wisdom loud and clear.

You can and should ask for your Spirit Guide's help, advice, and reassurance as often as you want, whether or not you know their names or who they are in general. Remember, they've been human beings at least once before, so they're well aware that our conscious memories of them and the Other Side are virtually nonexistent. Make up a name. They'll respond. Again, they won't intervene to spare you lessons that could be in your best interest in the long run. But the more you acknowledge and communicate with them, the clearer the channel between the two of you will become, and the more effective they can be in their sacred promise to help you along this rough path you had the courage to take.

I once learned a fascinating detail about communicating with our Guides, by the way, thanks to my Spirit Guide Francine. My son Paul was a young child, and he was going through a serious health crisis. I prayed and prayed from the core of my soul for his dangerously high fever to break, and I felt almost betrayed that Francine was so slow to come to me when she must have heard me begging God for His help. When I finally had the opportunity to confront her about it, she explained that our conversations with God are so sacred that not even our Spirit Guides can hear them. God is part of us, she pointed out, and we are part of Him. No one can trespass or eavesdrop when we're praying to Someone with whom we're already one to begin with.

Our Spirit Guides are the last to say goodbye to us when we leave Home and come to earth, and they're the first to help us make sense of the lifetimes we've just lived when we return to the Other Side again. For that fact alone we should never let a day go by when we don't think of them and, if nothing else, say thank you.

ANGELS

One of the most common misconceptions about Angels is that if we and/or our loved ones live pure, compassionate, generous, reverent lives, we can actually become Angels when we return to the Other Side. It's a lovely thought. It's just impossible.

That fact has nothing to do with our being incapable of living lives that are pure, compassionate, generous, or reverent enough to warrant such a divine honor. God never withholds from us, or finds us unworthy. We're prevented from being Angels for the simple physiological reason that Angels and humans are two different species.

The easiest way to remember the distinction between Angels and us is that Angels never incarnate. They never live a life on earth in a human body. They're able to take human form to accomplish brief missions here on earth. You'll notice, though, that in every account of the literally millions of stories of earthly Angel encounters, the person/Angel seems to appear out of nowhere and vanish again just as quickly. They come and go for our benefit from their Home, which is exclusively on the Other Side.

Angels also never speak. Their communication is exclusively telepathic, but it's so powerful that we humans often come away from contact with them knowing that some exchange of wisdom or comfort or sanctity took place even though not a word was uttered.

It's not that Angels don't have voices. They do, and the magnificence of their voices is impossible to capture in earthly adjectives. But Angels' voices are reserved for only one purpose: to celebrate the glory of God through soaring hymns of praise that resound throughout heaven and the universe. On at least one occasion in particular, in fact, they found their way to earth, celebrating the miracle of the birth of Christ (Luke

2:13–14: "And suddenly there was with the angel a multitude of the heavenly host praising God, and saying, 'Glory to God in the highest, and on earth peace, good will toward men'").

While some Angels are given proper names in the Bible and other religious works—Michael, Gabriel, and Raphael, for example—Angels are androgynous. There are no male or female Angels. Their bodies and facial features are identically exquisite. They also transcend and encompass all races when it comes to their skin color. Everyone who sees them, both on earth and at Home, comments on how their skin seems to sparkle, as if the sun is perpetually glistening off of it. The source of this beautiful effect is actually their illumination from within, as their very essence is the sacred, perfect white light of their Creator.

There are eight levels, or "ranks," within the vast population of Angels, but it can't be stressed enough that there is no difference in importance among those ranks. There are no "more" or "less" important Angels. They earn advancement from one level to the next through their body of experience, and with each new level comes more power. They accumulate experience by protecting us from harm, saving lives, bringing us messages, performing miracles, or simply infusing us with sudden moments of love or joy or comfort or hope when we need them the most.

All eight levels of Angels are charged with being God's mightiest, most direct link between earth and the Other Side. They're physically distinguished from one another at Home by the color of their wings. In ascending order, from the least experienced to the most experienced and powerful, these are the eight levels:

- Angels—dusty gray-white wings
- Archangels—pure white wings
- Cherubim—white wings with gold tips
- Seraphim—white wings with silver tips
- Virtues—pale blue wings

- Dominions—green wings
- Thrones—deep purple wings
- Principalities—solid gold wings

The first seven levels of Angels can initiate intervening on our behalf in a crisis. They're available to us in the blink of an eye whether God sends them or they sense our need on their own. The brilliantly powerful Principalities, on the other hand, come only through God's command and/or through our very specific call for them. The Principalities can create miracles, prevent fatalities, and turn around even the most lost, misguided lives.

In addition to the countless Angels who constantly watch over us during our brief trips away from Home, we're also assigned our own Angels on the Other Side before we come here. The more difficult the goals and challenges we've chosen for ourselves for each incarnation, the greater the number or ranks of Angels who are specifically designated on our behalf to keep added divine watch over us.

And you'll be glad to know as you proceed with your own spiritual odyssey that the more spiritually open, generous, and conscious we become, the more added Angels gather around us, drawn like moths to a flame as the light of God's love inside us begins to glow so brightly that we almost sparkle like the Angels themselves.

GHOSTS

Here's an essential but commonly misunderstood fact: spirits and ghosts are *not* the same thing.

On the surface, that might seem like a "who cares?" announcement, but it's important to know if you're on the receiving end of a visit from one or the other. Spirits should be celebrated and embraced, while ghosts, also called "earthbounds," should be sent away as quickly as possible—not because they mean you any harm, nor can they actually inflict any harm, but because they're lost, confused, and need your help in getting Home where they belong.

The one tragic quality shared by all ghosts is that they don't have the slightest idea that they're dead. Unlike spirits who, when their bodies die, eagerly proceed through the tunnel to the Other Side, ghosts turn away from the tunnel, refusing to acknowledge it for reasons of their own and, as a result, remain earthbound, lonely, trapped, often angry, sometimes aggressive, trying unsuccessfully to make sense of an existence that makes no sense to them at all.

Ghosts' spirits do leave their bodies when they die. By leaving their bodies, they also leave this earthly dimension. But by not accepting their death, they don't transcend to the higher-frequency dimension of Home either, which leaves their spirits caught somewhere in between. And that creates several essential differences that set ghosts and spirits apart:

- Because they've left earth's dimension without arriving in the dimension of the Other Side, ghosts almost invariably appear in more distinct, visible forms than spirits, and their voices tend to be more earthlike as well.
- Because they haven't experienced the healing of Home, ghosts will bear visible signs of any injuries, scars, illnesses, or deformities that existed when their bodies died. You will never see a spirit who's wounded or sick or in any way physically or emotionally imperfect.
- Spirits' efforts to get our attention are motivated by their wish to comfort us and reassure us that they're continuing to love us and watch over us. Ghosts' motives, though, are much more complicated, because their reasons for refusing to accept their death are so complicated and widely varied. Some ghosts stay behind out of a confused sense of loyalty

to a loved one, a home, or a job for which they felt responsible during their lifetime. Some stay behind for sheer revenge. Some stay behind to search for or wait for a lost love.
Some stay behind to take care of a beloved child. Some stay
behind out of fear that something they did during their
lifetime was too horrible for God to forgive (which is impossible, by the way—God never turns away from us, it's only
we who sometimes turn away from Him). Whatever their
confused purpose for rejecting the fact of their death, they
remain among us with a completely distorted sense of reality. Through a ghost's eyes, locked in a time warp of their
own disturbed creation, the world remains exactly as it was
at the moment their bodies died, and the rest of us become
intruders in their frozen reality. So it's no surprise that they
can become angry, desperate, resentful, cranky, or annoying.
On occasion they can also become so relieved that someone
can see or hear them, or is willing to acknowledge them,
that they'll be appreciative and even playful, especially with
children.

- By depriving themselves of transcending to the Other Side,
ghosts forfeit the infinitely expanded abilities that spirits
enjoy. Ghosts can't bi-locate, for example, or travel freely
between dimensions. In fact, they're usually too attached to
whatever area they're frequenting to wander far away from
it.

- Their insistence on remaining in this dimension also means
that while spirits appear to be floating as they move along
the ground level of Home three feet above ours, ghosts accurately appear right here on the same ground level as ours.

- For all the reasons we discussed earlier, spirits will appear
to us in a form that will help us recognize them. Ghosts,
on the other hand, couldn't care less whether we recognize
them or not, since they're among us out of desperate confusion having nothing to do with wanting to comfort us. They

might appear as very distinct images, they might appear rather faded or without clearly defined outlines, or they might appear as half-formed shapes of heavy mist.

POLTERGEISTS

And then there are poltergeists—not, by the way, your average ghost. *Poltergeist* is a German word that translates to "noisy spirit," which is a perfect name for these mischievous, intrusive earthbounds who are intent on being as disruptive as possible. Like all ghosts, they're terribly confused and have no idea that they're dead. As far as they're concerned, one day, for no good reason, everyone around them—family, friends, co-workers, strangers, *everyone*—suddenly began treating them as if they no longer existed. Poltergeists take this bizarre turn of events much more angrily and aggressively than other ghosts. They're so disturbed, resentful, or territorial of a space they insist on believing is still theirs that they'll be as loud, ornery, and obnoxious as possible in an effort to drive perceived intruders away or simply terrify them for the sheer fun of it.

A client once shared a classic poltergeist experience:

"I was stuck for a night at Miami International Airport, waiting for a connecting flight to South America. It was deserted, around two-thirty or three o'clock in the morning, and all the seats around me were empty. I was so immersed in the book I was reading that at first I didn't notice the man who suddenly appeared and sat down next to me. When I did notice him I was immediately annoyed, wondering why he'd insisted on sitting beside me when there were hundreds of vacant chairs in plain sight. He asked me a question. I don't remember what it was, but I remember that it was personal and inappropriate, so I stood up, pointedly turned my back on him, and said sharply, 'Leave me alone.'

"He replied, 'You know, I am the devil,' and he let out a loud, menacing laugh that sent a chill up my spine. I kept my back turned and walked away, but when I was about twenty steps from him I glanced over my shoulder to make sure he wasn't following me. He was gone. I looked everywhere, but he was just gone. Vanished. That frightened me even more than what he said. Even if he'd run at superhuman speed in those few seconds when my back was turned to him, there was no place for him to disappear in those endless, empty hallways."

Thanks to my client's detailed description of the stranger's face and clothing, my psychic input, and some research, we were able to validate that that particular poltergeist was a convicted child murderer who in the late 1950s was being transported to Riker's Island when he was killed in a traffic collision less than a mile from the Miami airport. And he might easily have been one of those lost souls who refused to face the journey Home out of guilt, shame, and fear that God might turn him away. A ghost trapped in that airport might easily have kept to himself in that vast expanse, or at most just walked by to see if my client noticed him. But it's the classic mean-spirited aggression of a poltergeist to spot someone sitting alone and vulnerable in the middle of the night and insist on terrorizing him.

The bottom line is that all poltergeists are ghosts, but not all ghosts are poltergeists. And no matter which you're dealing with, I promise you that beyond seriously frightening you, they cannot and will not cause you any physical harm. At the very worst you might hurt yourself trying to run away from them. But of the hundreds of hauntings I've personally investigated and the hundreds more I've researched, *not once* have I come across a legitimate injury that was caused by a ghost or a poltergeist, and I feel confident in saying I never will.

DOPPELGÄNGERS

Doppelgänger is a German word that translates to mean "double goer," and I'm including doppelgängers in this section on ghosts not because that's what they actually are but because that seems to be what they're most commonly mistaken for. They're really an amazing, fascinating phenomenon, appearing to be the ghost of a living person whose very much alive body literally seems to be in two places at once. Some believe doppelgängers to be a shadow identity that every person has, visible only to their originator. Others believe they can be seen by their originator and also by anyone who knows their originator. Still others believe that they appear only as an omen, immediately preceding the originator's death. I'm living proof that this third belief simply isn't true.

I should mention that when I first began studying doppelgängers, I thought they were among the silliest excuses for ghost stories I'd ever heard. Then, as often happens when I'm particularly wrong about something, I was shocked into coming face to face with just exactly how wrong I was.

It was the late 1960s. The middle of the night. I was in bed, wearing the most hideous flowered nightdress in the history of nightdresses, a gift (or cruel practical joke) from my mother. I woke up in a bedroom that was so hot I was literally sweating, and there was no chance I was going to get back to sleep until I adjusted the thermostat. I assure you, I was wide awake and not happy about it as I marched down the stairs in that awful nightdress and discovered that someone, probably one of my young sons, had cranked the thermostat up to a sweltering 80 degrees. I made a mental note to kill whoever was responsible, turned the thermostat down, and started toward the stairs again.

I instantly froze in place (no pun intended) at the bottom of the stairs and gaped as I looked up to see myself, impossibly, marching down the stairs exactly as I'd done a couple of minutes earlier, wearing that same mockery of a nightdress.

I was so stunned that I felt as if my mind was short-circuiting. I couldn't even figure out which one "I" actually was, and I was wondering if somehow I was the one on the stairs, not the one who was watching, when (the only way I know to describe it) I slammed into myself at the foot of the stairway.

I was so shaken that I didn't get another wink of sleep all night, and I was circling the library the next morning when it opened. (For you younger readers, before there were computers there were these buildings called "libraries," with lots of books in them, where we used to go to research things.) I read, I studied, I talked to every colleague I could think of who might be able to shed some light on the subject.

That's how I learned about, and became a believer in, doppelgängers. That's also how I discovered, to my relief, that while they're not exactly common, they're not unheard of either. In fact, Guy de Maupassant, whose novels and short stories I'd read in college as a literature major, toward the end of his life had his doppelgänger sitting at a table with him, dictating to him. And Percy Bysshe Shelley, one of my favorite romantic poets, ran into his doppelgänger one day in Italy near the Mediterranean Sea, pointing out toward the water. And it was in the Mediterranean Sea that Shelley drowned, less than a year after his doppelgänger appeared. John Donne, the English dean and poet, was visited by his wife's doppelgänger, holding a newborn baby. He learned later that at the same moment the doppelgänger appeared, his wife had given birth to a stillborn child.

Possibly few doppelgängers appeared to more witnesses than that of a thirty-two-year-old teacher named Emilie Sagee, a French woman who in 1845 was teaching at an exclusive girls' school in what is now Latvia. One day, in front of thirteen students, Sagee was writing on the blackboard when her doppelgänger suddenly appeared beside her, copying Sagee's every movement at the blackboard but without holding chalk, in a mirror-image pantomime. The doppelgänger also appeared in front of several witnesses at dinner, standing behind Sagee, duplicating the movements of her eating but without holding utensils.

On several documented occasions Sagee would appear in one area of the school when other witnesses placed her in a whole different area at the same time. A particularly noteworthy incident took place one summer day with all forty-two students of the private school looking on. The girls were assembled for their lessons, and they could clearly see Sagee through the large window of the classroom, working in the garden. When their teacher left the room for several minutes, Sagee's doppelgänger appeared in the teacher's chair, while Sagee herself was still perfectly visible outside in the garden. A few of the girls tentatively approached the doppelgänger, and one of them passed right through it as she sidestepped between the teacher's chair and the desk. Several moments later the doppelgänger slowly disappeared again.

An interesting postscript is that Sagee never saw the doppelgänger herself, but she added that when it was said to appear, she became extremely fatigued until it had vanished.

I wish I could offer an absolutely authoritative, definitive explanation for doppelgängers, but I'm afraid the best I can do is suggest a well-educated probability:

Our spirits, when they're at Home in the spirit world, are able to bi-locate, or be in two places at once. And these relatively brief experiences of inhabiting bodies don't erase all of our spirits' memories and skills. I believe that doppelgängers are rare but real events in which the spirit gets restless, feels like stretching its muscles or simply reverting to what comes naturally for a moment, and decides to bi-locate. Then, when it either catches itself in the act and says "oops" or has satisfied its passing desire to exercise, it returns to itself again within one body, limited to uni-locating as before until it's back on the Other Side and free of all the restraints and inconveniences it tolerates here on earth.

Let me just repeat, for the benefit of any of you who might find yourself staring at your own doppelgänger someday: I saw mine in the late 1960s. If it were true that it's an indication of impending death, I'm here more than forty years later to suggest that we may have to redefine the word "impending."

HAUNTINGS AND WHAT TO DO

Hauntings, as I'm sure you know, are circumstances in which you find yourself being visited by or cohabitating with ghosts. Hauntings should *never* be confused with spirit visits. It's worth repeating: spirit visits from the Other Side should always be embraced and treasured, which is the most important reason for being able to tell the difference between a spirit and a ghost. Hauntings strictly involve visits from ghosts, and those should always be dealt with as firmly, quickly, and thoroughly as possible.

For their own sake far more than for yours, ghosts need to be sent Home. It's not easy. Again, they don't know they've died, and their reasons for remaining earthbound are widely varied and usually driven by the incredibly strong motives of either passion or fear. But I'm happy to say that thanks to a constantly growing amount of human sensitivity and awareness, a lot more ghosts than ever are being directed to the tunnel, the light, and the Other Side by people who understand that there's really great compassion in simply saying to them: "You're dead. Go Home." And sooner or later, those that we can't convince will experience interventions from the spirits on the Other Side who are far more aware of earthbound souls than we are.

So the first step in dealing with ghosts is to get past your _itial fear and shock as quickly as you can and move on to sympathizing with their desperate, understandable confusion as you stubbornly, relentlessly try to talk them toward the light of Home. Tell them that most of the loved ones they're looking for are on the Other Side waiting for them, as is the all-forgiving, all-knowing, unconditional love of God, who's holding out His arms wanting nothing more than to embrace them.

Whether or not you succeed, I can't recommend strongly enough that you take the added step of cleansing and blessing your home. It will help protect you from ghosts and all sorts of other negativity that might be lingering in your house or even in the land it's built on. The cleansing and blessing rituals take less time than *cleaning* your house, believe me, and the long-term results will be more rewarding.

All you need to cleanse and bless your home is salt (an ancient symbol of purification), a white candle (representing the white light of the Holy Spirit), and holy water.

I shudder to think how many thousands of people have paid more money than any of us can imagine to buy "genuine" holy water that was probably poured into tiny vials straight from the kitchen tap shortly before the fortune-teller opened for business earlier that morning. If you've ever paid so much as a dime for "holy water" or even been tempted, please remember this from now on: *you can make your own holy water*. And yes, I promise, it will be blessed enough to serve its purpose.

Simply let ordinary water sit in direct sunlight for three hours. Three times during those three hours, make any sign over the water that has spiritual significance to you. I make the sign of the cross, but any sign acknowledging your connection to God will work beautifully. That's all there is to it—you've made your own holy water.

Now, to cleanse and bless your house, I want you to start at night and, on the stroke of any third, or Trinity (Father, Son, and Holy Spirit), hour—at 3:00, 6:00, 9:00, or 12:00—light

You can make your own holy water

your way with the white candle and spread the purifying salt around the periphery of your house. (As I always tell my clients, when your neighbors ask you what you're doing, tell them you're killing snails.) Pause at each of the doors and windows and sprinkle them with holy water, again making the sign of your faith.

Once you've finished surrounding your house with a circle of salt and sealed its openings from negativity with holy water—or if you live in an apartment and don't have a periphery to work with—simply move throughout the inside of your home with the white candle and bless each room with holy water and the sign of your faith.

When you're finished, stand inside your front door and offer the following prayer:

> *Beloved Father, cleanse and purify this home*
> *with the white light of the Holy Spirit.*
> *Purge all negativity from within*
> *and fill it with Your loving grace. Amen.*

CLEANSE A HOME

9

PAST LIVES

Through a childhood and early adulthood of being actively involved with the spirit world, I can honestly say I gave very little thought to the question of whether or not we live more than one life on earth. My Grandmother Ada assured me that the vast majority of us incarnate many times, and while I never doubted the sincerity of her beliefs, I also maintained my relentless insistence on thinking for myself and coming to my own conclusions on any and every subject. And I had Francine chirping away in my ear about her one incarnation as an Aztec Incan at the turn of the sixteenth century and her "choice" not to incarnate again after dying at the age of nineteen. But the connection I still couldn't seem to make was this: even if past lives were a fact, what difference did it really make in the lives we're living now? If there were no impact on our current lives from lives we lived before, what was the point of exploring them? Would discovering that in 1702 I was a French courtesan and went on to an incarnation as a Chinese fisherman in 1834 make me a better mother, wife, teacher, psychic, or person in my life in the twentieth century? If not, then frankly, who cared?

By the time I reached college and began studying theology,

the concept of reincarnation naturally came up on a fairly regular basis, since most of the world's great religions embrace the truth of reincarnation and the eternal cycles of the soul between this world and the Other Side. As we discussed in chapter 3, the Buddhists believe that karma, the natural law of inevitable consequences for our actions, can be played out over more than one lifetime, and that "walking the wheel of life," or *samsara*, is the process of being born again and again until we reach Nirvana, when all karma has been resolved. Hindus follow the Bhagavad-Gita, which states: "Just as a man discards worn out clothes and puts on new clothes, the soul discards worn out bodies and wears new ones" (2:22). The soul continues to reincarnate until it reaches perfection and reunites with its Creator. In Judaism, reincarnation, called *gilgul ha'ne'shamot,* or "the recycling of souls," suggests that the soul comes to earth to make spiritual corrections, and continues to be sent to earth until all those corrections have been satisfied. While Islam in general doesn't officially accept the concept of reincarnation, there are many Muslims and Sufi sects that believe God gives us several chances, or lifetimes, rather than just one to be rewarded with an eternity in heaven or punished with an eternity in hell.

Having been raised in Catholic schools, I was especially intrigued to learn that Christianity embraced reincarnation until the emperor Constantine, who didn't happen to believe in the idea of our spirits living several lives on earth, restructured the Church in the sixth century and eliminated the concept of past lives from Christianity's stated tenets. It occurred to me that Constantine couldn't possibly have edited ideas he disagreed with from every translation of the Bible, and out of curiosity I became an avid reader of all twenty-six versions. Sure enough, there were some unmistakable references to reincarnation and our cyclical journey between here and the Other Side.

• • • John 9:1–2 tells of the disciples asking Jesus about a man who was born blind, "Master, who did sin, this man, or his parents, that he was born blind?" Now, if there was a possibility that the man's own sins caused his blindness at birth, when could he have committed those sins if not in some past life?

And then there's the seventeenth chapter of Matthew. Jesus said to Peter, James, and John, "Elijah does come, and he is to restore all things; but I tell you that Elijah has already come, and they did not know him, but did to him whatever they pleased." Verse 13 goes on, "Then the disciples understood that he was speaking to them of John the Baptist." Obviously, if a time came when "they did not know" Elijah, it must be a reference to a different incarnation, which the disciples understood to be John the Baptist. John the Baptist was ultimately beheaded by King Herod, which makes "did to him whatever they pleased" an understatement.

The bottom line was, there seemed to be more than enough theological support to further convince me that reincarnation was a distinct probability. But until I was also convinced that it had some relevance to our current lives, it wasn't going to become a source of any real fascination for me. I was much too busy completing my bachelor's degree and getting my license as a master hypnotist.

REGRESSIVE HYPNOSIS

My passionate interest in hypnosis was centered on its proven ability to heal, and my plan was to supplement my psychic readings with hypnosis sessions to help clients lose weight, overcome addictions, and get rid of phobias and other obstacles that were standing in the way of their greatest potential. And in the course of my studies, I was naturally exposed to the famous case of Bridey Murphy, which triggered unprecedented publicity about the possible blending of hypnosis and past lives.

For those of you who aren't familiar with the story, in

1952 a Pueblo, Colorado, businessman and amateur hypnotist named Morey Bernstein, curious but skeptical about accounts he'd read of past life regressions, hypnotized a twenty-eight-year-old Pueblo housewife named Virginia Tighe. By all accounts, Virginia Tighe had no interest in hypnosis or in the concept of reincarnation, but Bernstein had found her to be an excellent subject at a hypnosis demonstration party a month earlier.

With two objective witnesses present, Bernstein placed Virginia Tighe into a deep trance and led her back through time until she finally began describing lying angrily in bed, pouting over a spanking. She identified herself as "Bridey," a nickname for Bridget, and gave detailed accounts of her life in Ireland and her death in the late 1800s, all in a thick Irish brogue. She talked at length about trying to communicate with her grieving husband Brian from the spirit world to let him know she was alive, well, and still around him. She was also on the Other Side to greet Father John, a Belfast priest, and to successfully urge him to admit that he'd been wrong about Purgatory. Bridey found the spirit world to be a place where no one ate or slept, but they never became tired, and she thought she'd spent about forty "earth years" there before her next incarnation. (Virginia Tighe was born in 1923.)

A series of hypnosis sessions were taped and published, and reporters from all over the country began investigating the details of the purported life of Bridey Murphy. They were able to validate many of those details: Bridey mentioned two greengrocers in Belfast, a William Farr and a John Carrigan, whose names and occupations were verified; she talked about a place called Mourne, which indeed existed in the 1800s but had disappeared from maps of Ireland by the time Virginia was born; she referred to her father-in-law, John MacCarthy, a lawyer, whose existence was confirmed; she accurately described relatively obscure Irish customs, music, and legends of her era; and

•her colloquialisms, folk songs, and distinctively specific brogue all were found to be authentic. •

There were also some inaccuracies or unverifiable details in the Bridey Murphy regressive hypnosis sessions, and reporters from the *Chicago American* happened across the information that a woman named Bridie Murphy Corkell had lived across the street from Virginia Tighe's childhood home. So, did the long list of accurate details Bridey/Virginia revealed about nineteenth-century Ireland prove the existence of a past life, or was it simply evidence of conversations with a neighbor from her childhood years in this life? The controversy over the validity of the Morey Bernstein experiments continues to this day and will undoubtedly never be resolved. But Bernstein's book *The Search for Bridey Murphy* was a bestseller, and the recordings from the hypnosis sessions were translated into more than a dozen languages.

I was as interested in the Bridey Murphy case as everyone else in the country, although I had no opinion about whether or not I thought it was valid, and gave it no more than an occasional passing thought a few years later when I officially began seeing clients as a licensed master hypnotist. I was building a nice practice and grateful for the income that helped support my expanding work with my Nirvana Foundation for Psychic Research when one day a man I'll call Frank arrived for weight-loss hypnotherapy and changed my life.

Frank was a nice, normal, rather shy man who was obviously self-conscious about resorting to hypnosis to cure his weight problem. The session started uneventfully. Frank went "under" easily and was calm and comfortable with his responses—even when, with no warning or change of demeanor, he started talking in the present tense about his life building Pyramids in Egypt, including some detailed descriptions of anti-gravitational devices that were too technical for me to understand, let alone follow. I was then treated to a twenty-minute monologue of what I can only describe as complete gibberish. It sounded exactly like fluent Martian, with inflections and occasional moments of apparent, incomprehensible humor and gravity. I tried to affect an expression of interest while privately believing he was having a psychotic meltdown before my very eyes that it might be dangerous for me to interrupt. But finally, just as I was thinking of potential avenues of escape, he flipped right back to the normal, softspoken, slightly self-conscious man who'd walked into my office in the first place, as if the previous half hour had never happened.

Throughout my career I've taped every hypnosis session and psychic reading I've ever done, and Frank's was no exception, thank God. I needed an objective opinion on what I'd just witnessed, so without alarming Frank, who had no memory of what had gone on, I casually asked for and got his permission to send the tape to a professor friend of mine at Stanford.

Three days later my professor friend called, so excited his voice was almost trembling. "Where did you get this tape?" he asked.

I braced myself for an urgent suggestion that poor Frank be rushed to the nearest psychiatric hospital while managing a calm "Why do you ask?"

Apparently my friend had listened to the tape and then shared it with several of his colleagues, and after some expert research they'd come to an astonishing conclusion: Frank's "gibberish" was actually an obscure seventh-century-B.C. Assyrian dialect that would have been common among builders of the Egyptian Pyramids. When I hung up and regrouped from that jaw-dropping news, I made myself call Frank to tie up the only remaining loose end I could think of: as if I were taking a random poll among my clients, I asked him if by any chance he happened to speak ancient Assyrian. He didn't. And by the way, I think by the end of that brief conversation he thought I was as crazy as I'd believed he was a few days earlier.

I had a talk with Francine that night, finally asking her if maybe there was some validity and relevant point to this reincarnation thing after all.

She gave me the one-word answer that would transform my curiosity into a passionate lifelong commitment: "Healing."

The general public's interest in reincarnation was growing right along with mine, and before long several psychiatrist, psychologist, and physician friends and I were consulting one another regularly as we researched the subject. Finally we organized a panel discussion about past lives and found ourselves with a standing-room-only crowd in a large auditorium—five brilliant doctors and me, and yes, I felt "outgunned," but by then I'd accumulated several tapes of confirmed past life regressions, and I was confident enough in the validity of my work that I was eager to share it with an audience. I'd also volunteered to do a spontaneous regressive hypnosis on stage using a volunteer from the audience. My co-panelists were skittish about it, but I took my lifelong position: If it works, great. If it doesn't, oh, well. But how will we know if we don't try?

Out of the handful of brave volunteers, I deliberately picked a nice-looking young man who seemed to be the most open-minded skeptic of the group. Before I put him "under," I asked if he had any health problems or phobias he wanted to address. He mentioned a chronic pain in his right foot that his podiatrist was mystified by, and a phobia that no matter how outwardly successful he became, people would always be able to detect how inadequate he really was.

He was a good subject, easy to hypnotize. I regressed him very slowly so that the audience would understand the process and clearly see that I wasn't leading him in any way—it's essential in any regressive hypnosis that whatever information comes through originates with the client, not with me. I took him back through this life, to his birth, to his death in a life before this one, and then to that life itself.

The audience was as fascinated as I was, and you could have heard a pin drop in that auditorium, as gradually, with not a word from me, his right foot began to twist and turn in as if it were deformed. At the same time his demeanor visibly changed. His shoulders slumped, his head hung slightly, and he became a sad, apologetic shadow of the man who'd first marched onto the stage.

I asked him what year it was. He answered: "1821."

I asked him to tell me about his life. He went into great, heart-wrenching detail about his brief, unhappy life in a small town in Virginia, one of four children in a hardworking farming family. Born with a clubbed right foot, he was unable to hold up his end of the chores, for which his parents and siblings expressed constant disappointment and resentment, and during his few years in school he was lonely, bullied and ridiculed. There wasn't a dry eye in the house, including mine.

Before I eased him back to his current life I gave him a post-hypnotic suggestion and an affirmation with which I've ended every regressive hypnosis session since: "May you keep all the joy and wisdom your past lives have given you, and may all sorrow, fear, illness, and negativity from those past lives be released and resolved for all time into the white light of the Holy Spirit." And then, as I brought him into the present again and out of his trance, we all watched as his right foot resumed its normal position, and his posture straightened to that of the successful, healthy young man he was in this lifetime.

Several months later he called to report that since that night he'd never had another twinge of discomfort in his foot, and his well-deserved confidence in himself had finally begun to thrive.

In the decades since, I've had similar success with tens of thousands of regressive hypnosis clients, always using that same affirmation. But its effectiveness isn't limited to clients—you have no idea how much peace and healing it can bring to the children in your life.

By definition, no one on this earth is more conscious of past lives than children. Their memories of their lives on the Other Side from where they've just arrived are still fresh, as are their memories of past incarnations, and no one's had the opportunity to drill into them yet that sharing those memories out loud is inappropriate or downright crazy. If you listen closely and ask the right questions rather than discouraging them or accusing them of making things up, you can learn volumes about the little spirits who've come to share this lifetime with you.

I've got file cabinets full of letters and e-mails from parents reporting comments and behavior that seem completely mystifying until they understand how normal, even logical, it is for children to remember their past lives as easily as you or I remember our fifth-grade teacher or how we celebrated our most recent birthday. To name just a few examples:

- A six-year-old girl who'd been obsessed with cruise ships since she'd first seen one on a television commercial began making very specific, knowledgeable remarks about her death as a man in a uniform on the *Titanic*.
- A five-year-old boy beamed up at his mother one day and informed her that she was "the best mom of all twelve moms I've ever had."
- A couple on a hike in the woods with their four-year-old son were thoroughly confused when he came to a complete stop at a footbridge across a small stream and announced, "Oh, no, I'm not going on any bridges this time." (To the best of their knowledge, he'd never seen a bridge before, let alone had any reason to be frightened of them.)
- A five-year-old girl with a fascination for trains casually informed her father one day that she used to shovel coal on a train to feed her wife and children.

And then there was the two-year-old boy, as happy and normal a child as you'd ever meet, who would fly into a screaming, crying panic every time his mother stepped into the shower, remembering losing his mother to the showers of Dachau in his previous life in Nazi Germany.

That boy was "cured," as countless other children have been, by their parents simply talking to them while they're asleep, when their spirit minds are at their most receptive. There's no need to worry about the limited vocabulary of the child's conscious mind. Their spirit mind is as ageless as yours and will understand perfectly if, on a regular basis, you quietly reassure them with the same affirmation you read earlier:

"May you keep all the joy and wisdom your past lives have given you, and may all sorrow, fear, illness, and negativity from those past lives be released and resolved for all time into the white light of the Holy Spirit."

If you want to start a potentially fascinating conversation with your child before they're around five or six years old, when their memories of previous incarnations and lives on the Other Side are likely to start fading, casually ask them, with no implied expectations, "Who were you before this?" The answer might give you some unexpected insights into your child's personality and also help you devise a more precise version of the affirmation to offer your child while he or she sleeps if you spot a connection between a past life memory and a physical or emotional health problem they're experiencing this time around.

My son Chris was three years old when I asked him, "Who were you before this?" He told me as if he were filling me in on what he'd been doing that morning that he was a cowboy, with a horse named Cinder. He was shot in the stomach in front of "a place with swinging doors, and then my daughter ran out and held my head while I died." It was more information than I was expecting, and honestly more information than I've been given from most other children in response to that question, and thanks to my work with regressive hypnosis I remembered it in a heartbeat when Chris began having sharp pains in his stomach a couple of years later with no physiological explanation that his doctors could find. I started sitting on the edge of his bed every night after he'd fallen asleep and whispering, "Chris, I know you were shot in the stomach and it hurt you very much. But it happened in a past life, in another time. You have a healthy, painless stomach in this life, and you'll never be hurt like that again. You can let go of it now so that it can be released and resolved in the white light of the Holy Spirit." I kept it up night after night for a few weeks, and I promise you, his stomach pains went away and never came back.

Once it became seemingly inarguable that past lives could be the answer to a lot of healing in current lifetimes, the obvious question came up about how and why this was so effective. A prevalent theory among many of my colleagues was that these past life memories could just be a fantasy the mind conjures up to relieve pain, that is, imaginary realities used as a survival technique. That might be a valid possibility if it weren't for the fact that my staff and I were able to confirm the details of more than 90 percent of the information that emerged during regressive hypnosis sessions.

It was my Spirit Guide Francine, of course, who gave me the answer to why connecting with past lives holds such potential healing miracles. It has nothing to do with fantasies and fiction and everything to do with a phenomenon called "cell memory."

CELL MEMORY

I know that at some time or other you've had this experience: you unexpectedly come across some familiar fragrance, or song, or movie, or voice, or image from out of your past, and suddenly you're flooded with far more than just a fleeting memory. You feel as if the past and the present have blurred, so that you don't just remember the event you associate with that sensory "hit"; you're filled with a rush of every emotion you felt when the event happened, no matter how long ago it was. Until it passes you might as well be on your first date again, or opening gifts on a special Christmas morning, or alone in your bedroom soothing a broken heart with your record player, or dancing with your father at your wedding, or attending a loved one's funeral. Those emotional flashbacks are always powerful and intensely personal, specific to you and no one else, no matter how long or how briefly they last.

Those very same emotional flashbacks happen at the moment the spirit enters a brand-new body for another incarnation on earth, thanks to a phenomenon known as cell memory. After years or decades or centuries in the limitless, perfect freedom on the Other Side, the spirit has the sensory "hit" of finding itself occupying a human form again, and suddenly every cell of the body is inundated with the reality of other times and places when that same spirit occupied other bodies and, alive and sentient as they are, the cells begin responding to everything they perceive to be the truth.

It works like this (in the simplistic terms of someone who wasn't exactly an enthusiastic student of biology):

- Our bodies are made up of billions of interactive cells.
- Each of those cells is a living, breathing, thinking, feeling organism, receiving, retaining, and reacting very literally to the information it receives from the subconscious mind. Under hypnosis, for example, when the subconscious mind is in charge, if we're told that the hypnotist's finger is a white-hot fireplace poker and that finger lightly touches our arm, the cells of our arm will respond as they're programmed to do when they're burned and form a blister.

- Our spirit minds reside in our subconscious—safe, sound, and completely intact, no matter how healthy or unhealthy our conscious minds might be.
- Our spirit minds remember every moment our souls have experienced, in this life and every other life we've lived since we were created an eternity ago.
- The instant our spirit minds enter our physical bodies, they infuse the cells of our bodies with all the information and memories they possess, and our cells respond to that information and those memories as they're programmed to do until our spirits leave our bodies again to head Home.
- And so by accessing those *cell memories*, we can rid ourselves of long-buried illness, phobias, pain, and trauma, and also recreate the greatest emotional and physical health our spirits have ever enjoyed in any lifetime we've ever lived.

Here's one of the most common examples of cell memory I run across, that I'll bet you've run across as well, or even gone through yourself. Clients will say some version of, "I don't know what it is, but with my forty-fifth birthday coming up, I suddenly can't stop thinking about death, and I'm so afraid it's a premonition." Or a variation: "I've never been afraid of water in my life, but for no apparent reason, in my mid-thirties, I reached a point where you couldn't drag me anywhere near a swimming pool." Count on it that nine times out of ten this is neither a premonition nor all that mysterious. It's simply cell memory in action, the spirit having infused the body with the information that in its last (or most significant) incarnation, the body died at the age of forty-five, or drowned in its mid-thirties, and the cells are sending out their literal, methodical sensory warning and responses, unable to separate the consciously forgotten past life from the current one. If some form of this happens to you, I can't recommend strongly enough that you simply personalize the same affirmation I use on my clients and that I've urged you

MAYBE WHY I BECAME AFRAID OF HEIGHTS, AND I WASN'T BEFORE

to use on children while they sleep: "May I keep all the joy and wisdom my past lives have given me, and may all sorrow, fear, illness, and negativity from those past lives be released and resolved for all time into the white light of the Holy Spirit."

And in case you're wondering, the effects of cell memory aren't limited to past life experiences. I've personally been involved with several fascinating cases in which cell memory clearly affected the recipients of organ transplants. Here are two of my favorites:

A doctor friend of mine performed a successful kidney transplant on a woman named Julie, in her early fifties. He called me, concerned, to report that Julie, a longtime patient of his who had never touched tobacco or alcohol in her life, awoke from surgery with an urgent craving for a cigarette and a dry martini. Discussions with the donor's family revealed that he was an avid smoker and ended each workday with a single dry martini.

And then there was Molly, ten years old, who received a heart transplant from a seventeen-year-old stabbing victim named David. Several months after David's murder, police had few clues and no suspects, until Molly began having constant nightmares about a tall, heavyset figure in a ski mask coming toward her with a knife. Through hypnosis Molly was able to remove the figure's ski mask and identify a man named Martin—not someone she knew at all, it turned out, but a longtime acquaintance of David's. The police were given the information, Martin was brought in for questioning, and he ultimately confessed to the murder.

Amazing, but also perfectly logical when you understand the miraculous basics of cell memory, one of the most effective healing tools I've ever found when traditional medicine can't help (and *always* turn to traditional medicine first!), and still more absolute proof of the reality of our past—and eternal—lives.

THE POINTS OF ENTRY

FOR PAIN OR CELL MEMORY

Yet another thing I learned from my Spirit Guide Francine about regressive hypnosis that was never mentioned in any of the years of classes I attended is the seemingly magic term "point of entry." I truly wish that everyone who teaches and practices regressive hypnosis would learn that term and give it a try at the appropriate time, even if they're only doing it to prove me wrong. It's helpful, it's efficient, it's effective—and it's a testament to how ready and eager the spirit is to leap at an opportunity to be healed.

I was a year or so into my regressive hypnosis practice when I finally got around to learning about the point of entry myself. A client named Alain came in, wanting to address what he described as a "sheer terror" of being alone, so that he'd actually designed his life around efforts to never let that happen. He had a wife and six children, with relatives who constantly moved in and out of their house, and he'd chosen a career as a tour coordinator and guide, so he was surrounded by people virtually all the time. But inevitably there would be brief hours here and there when he was by himself, and he would immediately be overwhelmed by a sense of dread and a feeling that somehow even momentary isolation was a punishment of some kind for a wrong he couldn't identify, let alone make right. Two different psychiatrists had treated Alain with no apparent relief or improvement, and one of them referred him to me, with the usual unspoken subtext, "as a last resort."

I've rarely met clients more enthusiastic about revisiting past lives than Alain was. He virtually skipped from one life to another to another, going into painstaking detail about each of those lives, from the names of each of his ten children when he was something called a Royal Guard in Egypt to the specifics about the pioneer families he traveled with in a Conestoga wagon train as part of the California gold rush. They were all happy, healthy lives ending with consistently untraumatic deaths, and while he was having a great time telling me about them, I was getting admittedly frustrated—as glad as I was that he was enjoying himself, I also knew we weren't making any progress toward finding the root of his cell-memory-induced terror of being alone, if cell memory was actually the source of the problem to begin with.

Alain described another quick, painless death at the end of another pleasant, successful lifetime and then began telling me about the beautiful meadow now surrounding him, in the midst of majestic mountains, with peaceful animals grazing nearby. I smiled to myself, knowing how common it is for clients to experience a few moments on the Other Side between lifetimes with descriptions similar to this one. In fact, I'd been wondering when Alain was going to get around to finding himself at Home. I asked how he felt and had my pen poised above my notepad ready to jot down a reply like "Ecstatic" or "Blissful" or "Completely at peace." I nearly fell off my chair when he answered, "Desolate."

I kept the shock out of my voice as best I could as I asked, "Where are you?"

"Peru."

Okay. He'd already jumped to another incarnation. So much for anticipating my clients' responses. I asked what he was doing in Peru, and he began weeping, so distraught that he couldn't talk. It took a couple of minutes, but I finally got him to the "observant position," where he would just watch what was happening rather than experience it and understand that it was all in the past, in another life, a long time ago. It calmed him down enough to tell me the story of his lifetime in Peru that had clearly devastated him.

His wife and newborn son died in a fire that destroyed their house, he told me—a fire set by his violent, vindictive mistress in retaliation for his ending their relationship. At the time of the fire Alain was at a friend's bar in a nearby town, drinking away his self-pity and passing out for the night. He returned home the next day to the horror of discovering that his wife and child were dead, his house and everything in it was nothing but a pile of charred rubble, and his mistress had killed herself. He was overwhelmed with both grief and guilt, feeling completely responsible for every bit of this nightmare. He promptly left everything and everyone he knew behind him and disappeared to the mountains, where he tended sheep in exchange for food and lodging, silent and solitary in a self-imposed exile, until he died of exposure twelve years later.

Finally. There it was. A perfect explanation for why this poor man felt desolate when he found himself alone and considered solitude and punishment to be virtually synonymous. And between the unearthing of the source of his cell memory pain and the affirmation that all past life negativity be resolved and released into the white light of the Holy Spirit, it was as if we'd found and treated a long-hidden wound in his soul—his recovery was virtually instantaneous, and over the next several months he wrote often to say that he was continuing his healing with a peaceful, nourishing hour of meditation every day, in solitude, that he'd come to value and look forward to.

Without realizing it, Alain had inspired a positive change in my life, too. By watching him wander his way for so long toward the solution to his debilitating problem, I'd decided to ask Francine if there were a more efficient method of getting my clients to the events or lives that were creating obstacles for them without leading them there in any way. She answered, almost sighing with impatience that I was just now getting around to asking, "Tell them to go to the point of entry."

"What's the 'point of entry'?" I said.

She explained that it's the moment when the lingering pain or trauma was initially inflicted on the soul.

I've never heard of the point of entry," I told her. "So if I don't know what it is, how on earth are my clients supposed to know?"

"Their spirits will know," she said. "Just try it."

I admit it, I didn't believe her, and I didn't think it would work. I even had an apology prepared for the inevitable moment when I would tell a client under hypnosis, "Go to the point of entry," and they would reply, "What are you babbling about?" But of course that never happened. During the next regressive hypnosis session that involved a cell memory issue, I took a deep breath and told my client to go to the point of entry, and he instantly leapt to the relevant event in the relevant lifetime that allowed us to focus on the healing he was after. I even asked him once he was awake again if he knew what a "point of entry" was, and no, he didn't have a clue.

Francine was right and I was wrong, again, and I've used that valuable term in every session since. I appreciate the efficiency of it, of course. But even more than that, I appreciate the proof of the impact past lives can have on the lives we're living now, and the eagerness with which our spirits will recognize and race to an opportunity to finally release old wounds and be healed so that we can experience the challenges of each incarnation one life at a time.

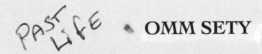

PAST LIFE • **OMM SETY**

If you'd like to read an extraordinary story of a clearly remembered past life, I strongly recommend a beautiful book called *Omm Sety's Egypt* by Hanny el Zeini and Catherine Dees. Those of you who already believe in reincarnation will find it affirming. Those of you who are still wondering will find it thought-provoking, you have my word. To give you just a glimpse of this compelling woman . . .

Omm Sety was born Dorothy Eady near London in January 1904.

She was three years old when she fell down a flight of stairs. The doctor who examined her pronounced her dead and had her body placed on her bed to be washed and prepared for burial while he drew up the death certificate. An hour later he found the child sitting up in bed, playing and completely recovered. Still swearing that Dorothy had died but unable to explain this proof to the contrary, the doctor tore up the death certificate and left.

It's thought that this event may have triggered the recurring dreams the little girl began having, of a building with giant columns near a beautiful garden. She was often found crying, explaining to her worried parents that she was homesick.

At the age of four Dorothy accompanied her parents to the British Museum, in which she was thoroughly disinterested until they came upon the Egyptian Galleries. She suddenly became ecstatic and ran uncontrollably through the displays, kissing the feet of the statues before sitting on the floor at the feet of an encased mummy and begging her parents to leave her there with "my people."

Dorothy was seven when her father happened to bring home a magazine in which there were photographs of the ruins of the Temple of Sety I, in the tiny Egyptian village of Abydos. She excitedly recognized it as her home, the columned building in her years of recurring dreams, but she was disturbed that it was crumbling and that its lovely garden was gone.

Dorothy's friendship with Sir E. A. Wallis Budge, the esteemed Keeper of Egyptian and Assyrian Antiquities at the British Museum, began when she was ten years old. Sir Ernest found the child in the Egyptian Galleries one day and asked her why she wasn't in school where she belonged. She explained that they weren't teaching her what she wanted to learn: hieroglyphs. Budge understandably took an interest in her and, over the next several years, both taught her and learned from her, and he found her easy familiarity with ancient Egyptian hieroglyphics to be uncanny.

She was twenty-nine when she married a London college student named Imam Abdel Megid, whom she followed to his native Egypt. Over her husband's strong objections, she named their son Sety, in homage to the Pharaoh who had commissioned the ancient temple she'd recognized as her home. She then adopted the name Omm Sety, which means "Mother of Sety," in keeping with the Egyptian custom of referring to women by the names of their eldest children.

The marriage only lasted a few years, but Omm Sety's life in her beloved Egypt continued, as she became the first woman employee of the Egyptian Antiquities Department in Cairo. Her amazingly accurate knowledge of ancient Egypt, from rituals and festivals to obscure facts about its geography and history, truly mystified even the most brilliant, respected Egyptologists.

One night in 1941, during the Axis air raids on Cairo, Omm Sety went to bed, locking the door to her room as usual, secure that she was in possession of the lock's only key. When she woke up the next morning she felt a small object in her closed hand and looked to find a perfect silver statue of Osiris, about five inches tall, with no logical explanation for how it got there as she slept alone in a locked room. She took it to a jeweler, who assured her it was pure silver, and she bought a silver chain to hang it from like a pendant. To guarantee that it was secure, she had the clasp of the chain soldered together, since she could slip it easily over her head, and she also had the sturdy ring that attached the statue to the necklace cast solid so that the two pieces couldn't possibly separate.

She remained mystified about where the Osiris statue had come from, simply answering that a friend gave it to her when people asked about it, and she wore it twenty-four hours a day through the rest of the war, treasuring it and whatever magic had slipped it into her hand that night.

And then one morning, a few days after the war was over, she woke to discover that her beloved silver statue had disappeared. The chain was still perfectly intact around her neck, its clasp still soldered shut. But the statue and the heavy ring to which it was cast were gone. She searched everywhere, but the silver Osiris had vanished as inexplicably as it had appeared, and she never saw it again.

(This phenomenon is called apport, or apportation, as we saw earlier. The spirit world, to get our attention, will occasionally manipulate physical objects, often transporting them through space and such seemingly impenetrable barriers as locked doors, so that they suddenly appear in "impossible" places and "impossibly" disappear again. I promise you the "good luck charm" that stayed with Omm Sety through the war was an apport from a loving, protective spirit, either from her life in the 1900s or from her life thousands of years ago.)

According to her diaries and many audio recordings, Omm Sety's ancient life, by the way, was as a young priestess called Bentreshyt, which means "Harp of Joy," who lived at the Temple of Sety I in Abydos and performed in plays that depicted the death and resurrection of Osiris, the Egyptian god of the afterlife. One day while walking in the temple gardens she encountered the reigning Pharaoh, Sety I, who fell in love with her. When she discovered that he had impregnated her, she committed suicide rather than expose him and bring shame on him.

One night in March 1956, Omm Sety climbed alone to the top of the Great Pyramid of Giza and spent the night there, preparing herself emotionally and spiritually for the new life she was about to undertake. Several hours later she descended the rough stones, gathered her few possessions, and used her one-way train ticket for her journey to the small, dusty village of Abydos, where there was no electricity and no running water. She became one of its most treasured residents and historians, often going to the nearby Sety Temple, removing her shoes, and leaving offerings at the chapel of Osiris, until her death in Abydos in 1981.

As a valued part of her legacy, many archeological discoveries—including the ruins of the temple gardens she'd dreamed of as a child, tombs, other temples, and tunnels—can be traced directly to Omm Sety's precise directions, based on knowledge that by all accounts far exceeded anything she could have learned through traditional academic studies.

This helps to explain why there are a great many of us who will always believe without a doubt that, throughout her rich, generous life, this brilliant woman wasn't learning, she was simply remembering.

PART III

WHAT'S REAL,
WHAT'S NOT,
AND HOW TO TELL
THE DIFFERENCE

10

HOW IT'S DONE: THE FRAUDS

It's sad but true that fraud is an inherent part of the history and pursuit of spirituality. And with people turning to psychics, fortune-tellers, mediums, and other spiritual "experts" in record numbers in these uncertain, scary times, it's essential that you know who and what to look for, and who and what to run screaming from, in your understandable search for help and hope to keep these times from being even scarier than they already are.

"THE COLD READING"

You call or sit down with a psychic you've never met before. He or she looks wisely into your eyes for a long, thoughtful moment and then, in a voice filled with empathy and compassion, begins:

"You've had a hard life. You've had good times, but you've also had more than your share of bad times. Dark times. But now you're starting to come from darkness into the light you've deserved for so long.

"There's been a significant woman in your life. I feel she may be older than you. It's been a difficult relationship sometimes, but you've learned a great deal from it, and from her. You might even be related to her, either in this life or a past one. I also sense someone important in your future whose initial is 'D,' or possibly 'R.'

"You're very patient when you need to be, but when your patience is exhausted, you tend to feel enormous stress. You're also an extremely loving person, which sometimes makes your life's burden heavier to bear, because you're rarely appreciated as much as you should be. In fact, no one, not even your closest friends, truly understands how much you've suffered . . ."

By now you're hanging on the psychic's every word, amazed at how well this total stranger knows you. What luck that you've found such a gifted, insightful, sensitive person to share your problems with and ask for advice.

Or, more accurately, what luck that you've found, and generously paid, a fraud, who's simply performing "the script," also known in the psychic arena as "the cold reading." There are a thousand variations on the script, but they all have one thing in common: they apply to approximately 99.9 percent of the population. They're the psychological version of, "You're a mammal, you have thumbs, and you have a tendency to walk upright on two legs, although not until several months after you were born." And delivered with enough sincerity, they can be so convincing that it won't even occur to you until later that you didn't hear a single fact that applied specifically to you.

Listen closely at your next reading or on your next call to a psychic hotline, and consider the distinct possibility that you're on the receiving end of "the script." Are any details coming up that could only be relevant to *your* life? And if so, pay close attention to who's really volunteering those details. If you're talking to a fraud who's good at following the script, the truth is, *you* are.

I believe clients are entitled to as many reasonable details as possible during a reading. I need to pause, though, to stress *reasonable* details. Those do not include your street address, or your Internet screen name, or your grandfather's birth date. There are some wonderful mind readers and mentalists out there who can probably spew those things right out, along with all sorts of other trivia you already know. I'm neither a mind reader nor a mentalist, nor are most legitimate psychics. When you come to me, I always start with the assumption that you're there for information you don't already know. You're entitled to that from me or from any other psychic you turn to.

You're also entitled to a reading that doesn't cost even one dime more than the fee you were quoted when you made the appointment or the phone call. If you're ever told during a reading that you can have added services for added money, you're being scammed. Walk out or hang up. And it's no coincidence that the practice of adding special fees for supposedly special circumstances is particularly popular among those who happen to be adept at "sensing" (read "completely making up") the dreaded specter of a curse.

THE TRUTH ABOUT CURSES

If there really were such a thing as a curse, can you imagine how many I'd have on me after all these decades of private and very public practice? Between those who think all psychics are fake, those who think I'm a spawn of the devil, and those I've busted for everything from fraud to murder, do you really believe I wouldn't be walking around twenty-four hours a day with a black cloud over my head, grimacing every few seconds at yet another pin being stuck into yet another Sylvia Browne doll?

The threat of a curse is nothing more nor less than an attempt to control you through fear and/or separate you from as much of your money as possible. All that a psychic/fortune-teller/medium needs to make you vulnerable to the suggestion that you've been cursed is (a) the fact that you've come to see them in the first place, which by definition means there's something in your life that's not going well; (b) the probability that from time to time, like everyone else on earth, you've experienced some bad luck through no fault of your own; and (c) a sincere desire to figure out what, if anything, is causing your bad luck and what can put a stop to it. Those who tell you that a curse is to blame have one very important thing in common: they're liars.

There's only one person on this earth who has the power to put a curse on you, and that person is *you*. If you believe you're on the receiving end of a curse, you are, with no one to thank but yourself. There's an old saying that goes, "We create what we fear." A fear of curses illustrates that fact beautifully. Those who think they're cursed spend their lives being suspicious, afraid, and paranoid, perceiving good luck as nothing more than a setup for a letdown and bad luck as more evidence that they're right. If living like that doesn't define a cursed life, I don't know what does.

I mean no disrespect to cultures whose belief in curses is ancient, traditional, and as alive today as ever. In fact, much of my outrage against the "curse business" is on their behalf, since in so many cases their deeply ingrained beliefs are being exploited and used against them. They're being frightened and tricked into handing over their hard-earned money to finally be rid of something that never existed in the first place.

And you can count on it that the only way to get rid of every supposed curse, no matter what it is or who's wished it on you, is money. Not God, or prayer, or more regular church attendance. Not even more active charitable work or more generous donations to help tip the karmic scales your way again. No, only money will do, payable to the psychic/fortune-teller/

medium who's broken the terrible news of this curse to you. Mind you, it might be your jewelry, or your car, or your house instead, or anything else you own that can be converted into money. The other thing you can count on is that once you're either cleaned out or starting to voice your suspicions, your money will magically disappear, right along with the psychic/fortune-teller/medium, and you'll be left with nothing more than the imaginary curse you paid to be rid of in the first place.

The vast majority of these con artists are never prosecuted because, for one thing, they're very good at knowing exactly when the time is right to change their names and locations, and for another thing, their victims are usually too embarrassed at their own gullibility to come forward and file appropriate complaints. But trust me, a whole lot of very intelligent, level-headed people have been victimized, some to the point of losing their life savings to the "curse business"; so please, don't get embarrassed, *get mad*! Remember, these frauds, most of whom are extremely good at what they do, have an advantage over you the minute you walk through the door. As I said before, they know that if things were going well for you, you wouldn't be there. And when you're going through a rough time, it's natural to be weaker and more vulnerable than usual, no matter how educated, practical, and cautious you are. When the right person with the right amount of compassion and conviction assures you, "I know what's wrong and I'm the one who can fix it," you *want* to believe them. Not to mention the very human tendency, when it appears that our usual approach to life isn't working as well as it should, to hear a supposed "expert" offer a possible alternative explanation, even if it's one we would typically scoff at, and to think, What if she's right?

To prove that she *is* right, that she knows a curse when she sees one, she'll typically treat you to an adept series of sleight-of-hand illusions that, unless you've studied an elementary book of magic tricks, might convince you once and for all. (We'll be

...scussing those a little later in this chapter so that you'll know what to look for.) The "proof" that there's a curse involved will inevitably lead to a whole new flood of added expenses, ranging from the necessity for more sessions to the sale of special curse-banishing candles (fresh from the 99¢ store, yours for only eighty dollars apiece) and a vial of "holy" tap water, just to give you a modicum of protection until your next session.

Don't be surprised if, over the course of several increasingly expensive readings in which she manages to explore the details of your finances and other assets, she comes to the shocking realization that the dreaded curse has attached itself to your car, your jewelry, and/or your life savings. But what luck, she's got the perfect solution: all you have to do is rid yourself of the afflicted assets by giving them to her and the curse will be gone. (One of many obvious questions is that if something's genuinely cursed, why on earth would she want it?) Whether or not she makes it appear that you're giving it to her is beside the point. I don't care if she pretends to set fire to it, throw it in a nearby body of water, bury it in a church yard, or make it vanish into thin air, the minute it's left your hands or your eyesight, it's hers, and you'll never see it again.

There are a lot of variations on curse scams, but three simple facts will save you both money and pain no matter what scam you might inadvertently stumble into:

- Anyone who tries to maximize your fears and vulnerabilities or use them against you to make you even more afraid and vulnerable is trying to control you, not help you. Run, don't walk, to the nearest exit.
- There is *never* a reason why a reading with a psychic, medium, fortune-teller, or spiritualist should cost you one penny more than the price you agreed to pay at the beginning, nor is there ever a reason why they should encourage you to schedule readings on a regular basis. Any effort to

make you dependent on them will be strictly for their benefit, not yours.

- The minute you hear any synonym of the word "curse," whether it's "hex" or "evil eye" or "dark cloud" or any other term implying that you've been targeted for some kind of spiritual harm or damnation, leave or hang up immediately and follow the advice you'll find at the end of this chapter for reporting frauds.

Again, please remember that countless very bright, good, well-intentioned, hard-working people have been victimized by con artists such as these, so there's no need to feel stupid or embarrassed. These cruel thieves can only stay in business if their victims remain silent, so speak up immediately if you've been scammed by anyone you've turned to for any form of psychic or spiritual help.

THE TRUTH ABOUT POSSESSION

A close relative of the curse is the "diagnosis" that you've been possessed. I don't care if it's supposedly by the devil or by a deceased loved one or by a divine entity of some kind, the bottom line remains the same: *No other spirit but your own can ever inhabit your body without your permission*. It's an impossibility. Period.

We've all read religious dogma and seen some scary movies about an evil, satanic spirit overtaking some unsuspecting soul and having to be driven from the body through a usually violent series of exorcisms by a healer, fortune-teller, or member of the clergy. And it's inarguable that exorcisms have been used for thousands of years as a euphemism for abuse, as a substitute for desperately needed psychiatric or medical help, as punishment for the disobedient parishioners of various religions, and as an obscene, lucrative scam. It bears repeating: *no spirit but yours can enter your body without your awareness and permission.* When it happens with your awareness and permission, it's called "channeling," which you read about in the first chapter of this book as part of the relationship between me and my Spirit Guide Francine.

Mind you, what I believe occasionally has to take a backseat to what a client believes if I'm going to be of genuine help, and there are times when a client's reality is so religiously or culturally ingrained that I have to work with it rather than against it, even when I'm as strongly opposed as I am to theories about possession. A very handsome, well-educated, deeply upset Jamaican gentleman came to my office a few years ago, visibly frightened and ashamed to confess what brought him there—he wanted me to "cure" his right hand, which had been possessed by Satan. The stress of keeping this shameful secret was affecting everything in his life, from his ability to concentrate on his engineering work to his avoiding his family and friends and his new love interest, so they wouldn't discover that somehow or other, evil had gained a foothold on him.

Believe me, I gave him my best, most logical, most impassioned reasons for my certainty that the loving, compassionate, perfect God who created us would never have devised a spiritual structure for us in which our souls can be hijacked against our will at the whim of any other spirit, evil or otherwise. But his religious and cultural faith in the reality of possession and the devil was so inherent, absolute, and non-negotiable that I wasn't about to add to his anxiety by disrespecting his truth.

And so, taking a deep breath to summon my upbringing in Catholic schools and my years of study of world religions, I held his "possessed" right hand in both of mine and performed the "exorcism" that I was sure would work because he believed with all his heart that it would, and because neither of us doubted for a moment that God was right there in that room with us. The nuns from my catechism classes would have been proud of how much I'd retained.

"Most glorious Prince of Heaven, St. Michael the Arch-angel," I prayed, "defend us against the rulers of this world of darkness, against the spirits of wickedness. God of Peace, crush Satan beneath our feet, bind him, and cast him into the bot-tomless pit . . ."

And this dear man, with tears streaming down his face, remembered the Catholic texts right along with me, so that we finished the prayer in unison: "From the snares of the devil, de-liver us, O Lord."

We sat in silence for several minutes, and finally his whole body slumped as if for the first time in much too long he'd released every bit of the crippling tension he'd been holding. Then he opened his eyes and smiled at me from ear to ear.

"The devil is gone," he quietly told me. "He escaped like a coward through my left hand."

He'd arrived believing he was possessed; therefore he was. He left believing the devil had been banished from him; there-fore he was. He was overjoyed, and so was I. I wasn't about to complicate the result by explaining what had really happened in our hour together, with God's help:

The right side of our brain controls our emotions. The left side controls our intellect. In his case, as it happened, the new love relationship in his life was making him behave in ways that made him feel foolish and out of control, preoccupying him to the point where he was unfocused when it came to his work and other relationships that were important to him. (And let's not pretend for a moment that we haven't all been there.) Thanks to his religious and cultural upbringing, the unfamiliar sensa-tion of his intellect being overshadowed by his emotions was most logically explained as "the devil has possessed my right hand," followed by, "He escaped like a coward through my left hand." All that really went on in my office was his intellect taking charge again, which was much more familiar to him.

And to add a psychic postscript to this story, considering what I knew that this manipulative, game-playing woman was going to put this naive, relatively inexperienced man through before she was done with him, I wondered if he might have been better off if there really were such a thing as possession.

A FEW TRICKS OF
THE FORTUNE-TELLING TRADE

To the best of my knowledge, I've never met or heard of a legitimate physical medium—as we discussed in chapter 7, those mediums and fortune-tellers who produce physical phenomena to suggest the presence of the spirit world. But I've met and heard of literally hundreds of their victims, heard descriptions of the "readings" they experienced, and become curious enough to explore how these frauds manage to fool such generally bright, often well-educated people. And thanks to such dedicated "fraud-busters" as Harry Houdini and any number of sleight-of-hand magicians, I found that it's really not that mysterious. All it takes is a client who's in some kind of despair and eager for relief from the emotional pain that despair is causing, which means they're vulnerable and their defenses are down, and which, of course, is what prompted them to seek help and hope from a fortune-teller to begin with. From that point on, it's a safe bet that any physical phenomena that occur came straight from a basic book of magic tricks. The diagnosis of a curse is particularly popular among physical mediums, in large part because curses are so simple to "prove."

Very often the client will be told to bring a fresh egg to the reading from their own refrigerator, with some explanation about how eggs tend to absorb negativity and will prove once and for all whether or not a curse is present. Because they're bringing the egg themselves, the client is already more trusting than if the fortune-teller were the one providing it. The test involves nothing more than the fortune-teller cracking open the egg right before the client's eyes. In the highly unlikely event that the egg looks normal, no curse is present. Far more often than not, though, the client looks on with horror as a clearly diseased, disgusting mess is revealed, with some nasty and often bloody mass infecting the yolk and indicating one of the worst and most expensive curses the fortune-teller has ever had the misfortune to unveil. The poor client is usually eager to throw open their wallet to rid themselves of the "proven" curse, and what luck that this particular fortune-teller happens to know exactly what to do. The fact that this particular fortune-teller also happens to be the scam artist who dropped a small piece of raw liver or other unsightly blob from the palm of their hand into the yolk as they cracked open the egg is hard to detect if the fortune-teller is even slightly skilled at this trick.

It's also not uncommon for the dreaded (and imaginary) curse to manifest itself in the client's money. To prove that money will literally diminish in the cursed client's hands, the fortune-teller will fold or roll up a small stack of five- or ten-dollar bills, slip it into the client's clenched fist, and chant or pray for a few moments for effect. When the client opens his or her fist again, the stack has either devalued itself into one-dollar bills or transformed into completely worthless cut-up newsprint. Of course, the original folded or rolled stack of fives or tens is now safely stored up the fortune-teller's sleeve or in some discreet hiding place under the table, in place of the identically folded or rolled stack of ones or newsprint for which the fortune-teller exchanged it before it went into the client's fist. But the amazing transformation right there in the client's "very own hand" can work very effectively on the trusting and vulnerable.

What I said earlier in this chapter bears repeating: any time something of value leaves your hands and/or direct eyesight when you're dealing with a physical medium or fortune-teller, *count on it* that it's been exchanged for something worthless before it's been disposed of or handed back to you. I can't encourage you enough, if you're even considering a session with a fortune-teller or physical medium, to browse through a beginner's book of sleight of hand or street magic tricks before you go. Knowledge is power, after all, and the more information you possess when you walk into the room, the less likely the odds of your being scammed out of your hard-earned money.

Physical mediums who claim an ability to contact the spirit world through the use of what can only be described as special effects can be incredibly persuasive to the bereaved, especially since many of them were and are very skilled at tricks that are likely to be more dramatic than basic sleight of hand. And the traditional dim lights of a séance only enhance the illusion.

A typical séance involves the medium sitting at a table with one or more guests, with everyone at the table holding hands and placing their feet on one another's shoes to (seemingly) guarantee that all hands and feet, including the medium's, can't move undetected. Everyone's eyes must be closed, needless to say. For a whole lot of special effects that might occur, though, the medium does nothing more than slip a foot out of a supposedly secured sturdy shoe and they're free to ring hidden bells and play hidden tambourines with their toes beneath the table. Table tipping can easily be accomplished with the undetected freed knee. Nearby furniture can be pushed over with the freed foot. "Actual" levitation, rising inches above the chair, for which everyone's eyes are allowed to be momentarily opened, can be mastered by nothing more than "pushing off" with the freed foot or feet, while the guests on either side of the medium will swear that her/his feet (shoes) never moved.

"Spirit manifestations" can be very effective tricks, particularly in a room with no windows and only one locked door. In that case, there will invariably be a hidden sliding panel in the wall, a trap door in the floor, or a false side to a piece of furniture tall enough to house a well-disguised, cosmetically eerie assistant until it's time for an entrance and subsequent "vanishing."

And then there's the amazing blank slate trick, which has been known to fool even the most skeptical of clients and audiences. This invariably involves an assistant as well, in this case one who will "casually" chat with the guests before the séance and learn just enough information for the slate trick to make a remarkable impression. The medium displays a small blank chalkboard and chalk to the guests and invites the spirit world to write something on it that will be meaningful to someone seated at the table. In the meantime, the assistant has written a message of some kind, based on something he or she learned during the earlier conversation, on a separate matching chalkboard, which will be hidden under the table or handed up through a trap door for what I promise you will be an inevitable switch of slates rather than any mysterious writing from a visiting spirit.

Oh, and the flying trumpets and other instruments that swoop through the room on cue? (I've never quite understood what trumpets have to do with the spirit world, but they seem to be very popular among physical mediums.) On close inspection, if only you were allowed such a thing, count on it that you would find a small network of invisible wire (fishing line is virtually transparent in a dimly lit room, for example) from which the instrument, suspended on matching invisible wire, can travel above the table in midair and disappear again, thanks to the manipulation of the handy assistant in the next room. Just think of the stage version of *Peter Pan*, or the famous chandelier effect in *Phantom of the Opera* and you'll have the general idea.

• • •

If you've been the victim of a fortune-telling fraud, I can't urge you strongly enough to forgive yourself for being vulnerable and promptly report the scam, with as many details as you can provide, to your local district attorney, or to my office, (408) 379–7070. You have my word that we'll notify the appropriate authorities and help put as many of these despicable thieves out of business as we possibly can.

11

HOW IT'S DONE: DEVELOPING YOUR OWN SPIRITUAL ARSENAL

There's only one way that spirituality can have a profound impact on your life, and that's for it to become truly *yours*—not just to be a lot of lovely rhetoric, but to be internalized, as natural to you as breathing, as much a part of you as your certainty in a Higher Power, a force bigger and greater than the obstacles, sorrow, and setbacks with which we humans are so often consumed. Reading and hearing about the comfort to be found in the spirit world is only the beginning, like a road map that's helpful but is of no importance at all until and unless you take the journey yourself.

This final chapter is devoted to guiding your first steps on your own, intimately personal journey, in the hope that somewhere in these pages is the spark that will reignite the fire within you. This in turn will fuel your passion to live the rest of the days of this lifetime with a whole new joy, optimism, inspiration, compassion, love, and faith in how essential you are to the Creator who promised you eternity and never, ever breaks His promises.

THE SIMPLE ART OF MEDITATION

I want to stress the word "simple," since I've heard from so many clients that they "can't" meditate, don't know how to meditate, or don't have the time to meditate. I think part of the problem is that the most common depiction of meditation involves sitting cross-legged on a mat, often wearing a special outfit of some kind, with an instruction to "clear your mind."

In fact, you don't need a mat, you don't need a special outfit, and if you're like me, your mind is never busier than when someone tells you to clear it. It reminds me of being told not to think about elephants for the next five minutes—you won't have devoted more time in years to thinking about elephants than you will for those five minutes.

All you need to do is to sit comfortably, preferably in a quiet place. *Comfortably*. If crossing your legs is comfortable for you, great. If it's not, that's fine too, just put your feet flat on the floor. Ideally your spine should be straight, with your head aligned with the top of the spinal column. Wherever you can *comfortably* accomplish that, whether it's the floor, a chair, or your bed, is perfectly acceptable. Remember, meditation isn't an endurance test, it's time you'll come to look forward to, so plan accordingly.

"Comfortable" applies to your clothing as well. As long as it's not restrictive, and you're as unaware of it as possible, anything you choose will work beautifully.

Settle in, close your eyes, and for the first minute or so, breathe normally. Rather than "clearing your mind," just relax it. A helpful image is to think of those moments when you consciously relax your shoulders, or unclench and relax your hands. Now simply apply that same concept to your mind. Unclench it. Relax it. Give it a rest. If the result is "clearing," that's a bonus, but it's not essential to meditation.

Now, gently pay attention to your breathing. Gradually slow it down and let it deepen. Think of every inhale as cherished nourishment and every exhale as cleansing. Appreciate that process and let it be your focus for as long as you want. Without any effort on your part, thoughts will begin passing through your mind. Feelings will ebb and flow. There's no need to process those thoughts and feelings, or try to control them, just observe them and be interested by what it is you think and feel at a time that you've set quietly aside for yourself and no one else. And in this quiet time, listen without trying or forcing it in any way and see if you can hear what your spirit has to say that usually gets drowned out by the noise of your conscious mind.

After about twenty minutes, gradually return to your normal state of consciousness. Don't rush "coming back." Open your eyes slowly, and don't be in a hurry to stand up. Just ease yourself back into the rest of your day or evening and look forward to next time.

Meditating every morning and every evening is *great* if you can find the time. But even if you can only manage it a few times a week, you'll still be so grateful in the long run for the conspicuous improvements in your overall well-being.

And yes, that really is all there is to meditating—nothing more, nothing less. Once you get into the habit, you'll understand what I mean when I add that it's also only the beginning of some wonderful, deeply personal surprises.

DEVELOPING YOUR PSYCHIC SKILLS

As I've said many times before, not everyone has the gifts required to be a psychic, but everyone has some psychic abilities. It's similar to the difference between being a concert pianist and simply knowing how to play the piano. You can still enjoy it and practice it, whether or not there's ever a performance at the Hollywood Bowl or Carnegie Hall in your future.

It's essential to remember in any psychic exercise that the information you have to offer doesn't and can't come from you. It's not yours to take credit for, interpret, edit, judge, or interfere with in any way. You're no more "brilliant" for whatever information you receive and transmit than a cell phone is for the information *it* receives and transmits. So, with the exception of receiving and transmitting with clarity and precision, your only responsibility is to stay out of the way. Set your ego aside, and relax your conscious mind as we discussed in the meditation section so that it doesn't get involved.

Also, don't get too analytical about how the information reaches you, any more than you spend a lot of time wondering how on earth your cell phone works without any wires attached. Once you begin practicing and discovering what your own personal gifts are and aren't, you might find that you *hear* the information (i.e., you're clairaudient); that you *see* the information (i.e., you're clairvoyant); that you *feel* the information (i.e., you're clairsentient); that you received the information as infused knowledge, which means it was transmitted directly from some other mind to yours with no conscious awareness on your part of where it came from or how you received it; or any combination of those possibilities. The only bottom line that matters is that you got it, and that it's accurate.

And let's face it, if the information isn't accurate, it's worthless. You're not going to be accurate 100 percent of the time. Only God can accomplish that. But to give you a yardstick with which to measure your effectiveness, you should know that a 70 percent accuracy rate is above average, and the most successful professional psychics test more closely to between 80 percent and 90 percent.

You can practice by yourself or with a friend, whether you've got a spare five minutes or a spare hour. The "practice" part involves developing the ability to get your own mind out of the way and the ability to recognize and receive the information as it comes to you. The more accustomed you get to simply opening the channels that are available to you, the more quickly the information will come. Alone or with a friend, though, you'll start with a question to which you can't possibly know the answer and then record your responses on paper or on tape so that you can begin tracking your accuracy.

One important note if you're practicing alone: *never* let the question you ask be about yourself. There's not a psychic in this world, including me, who's psychic about themselves, or, for that matter, about anyone they're very close to. Once you're emotionally invested in any way, it's virtually impossible to step aside enough to get valid psychic information.

Now. Bearing all that in mind, here are the three steps to practicing your psychic skills:

1. Ask a question, silently or out loud, to which your conscious mind won't know the answer.
2. Say, to yourself or out loud, in your own words, any version you want of, "Hit it, God." Use that as your reminder to step aside and be receptive to wisdom far beyond your own, however it manifests itself.
3. Commit to accepting and repeating verbatim the first response you get.

Believe it or not, once step 2 becomes second nature to you, the hard part becomes step 3, because very often the responses you receive make absolutely no sense to you at all, and it takes all the nerve you can muster to say them out loud.

Many of you are familiar with the story of the very sophisticated, articulate woman who came to me to discuss some career issues, and based on the psychic information I was given I had to make myself look her in the eye and say with some semblance of confidence, "You have a worm farm." Psychic or not, I couldn't have been more shocked when she replied, "Yes, I do." Or the time I sat there on national television and kept having to say to grieving parents about their deceased son, "He keeps talking about balloons. He's letting you know it's really him by talking about balloons. What's the connection to balloons?" Imagine my relief when the father said, a little tentatively as if he weren't quite sure this was the connection or not, "Well, I used to own a balloon factory."

See what I mean about step 3? However goofy or improbable the answer sounds to you, in the end it's really none of your business. You're only the messenger, nothing more and nothing less.

Just one more thing before you begin and continue to practice: "fishing" is strictly off limits. "Fishing" essentially means equivocating—coming out with the answer you received and then, at the first sign of confusion or uncertainty on your "client's" part, trying to turn a potentially wrong answer into a right one by resorting to guesswork. For example, if you clearly hear and repeat the word "balloon" and get nothing back but a blank stare, don't start fumbling around saying things like, "Or, uh, maybe it was . . . uh . . . 'ballroom,' or 'broom,' or maybe he, uh, ran a hot air balloon business in a past life . . ." You'll sound as if you're doing exactly what you *are* doing—making things up as you go along, which is disrespectful to the spirit(s) who gave you the information and to the person who asked for your help. If you heard "balloon," say so and stand by it. You may be wrong, or they may realize the connection later (which often happens, by the way). But as you work on your psychic skills, remember, no "fishing"!

Most of all, enjoy the experience of expanding the rest of your senses that I promise you extend far beyond the five you're most accustomed to.

A FEW MORE
EXTRASENSORY EXPERIMENTS

In chapter 5 we discussed a variety of disciplines, and there are three in particular that you can explore with no risk and very little time and effort. Whether or not you find a practical use for them, or discover that they're not among the psychic gifts you've been given, I promise you'll benefit from trying out new extrasensory "muscles" you may not have used before.

And before you begin, remember to spend a few moments doing rhythmic breathing and mind-relaxing as if you're preparing for a meditation session. It's self-defeating to experiment with any extrasensory skills when you're anxious, pressured, or trying too hard. There's no such thing as "failing." Openness to broadening your potential is success enough.

PSYCHOMETRY. Psychometry is the ability to perceive and interpret the energy that's been absorbed by inanimate objects. All you need on hand to explore this skill is an item you know nothing about and someone who knows enough about that item to tell you whether or not your perceptions are accurate.

After a few moments of deep, meditative breathing, and relaxing your mind, touch or hold the object, and if it helps you to focus on it, close your eyes. Then simply pay attention and accept your first impressions. Remember, you might perceive the object's energy in the form of visions, smells, sounds, emotions, or such physical sensations as heat, cold, or pain.

Do you have an immediate emotional reaction to holding or touching the object—happiness, sadness, loneliness, anxiety, serenity . . . ?

Do you notice any immediate physical sensations when you touch the object—are you suddenly hot, or cold, or in some kind of pain (and if so, can you pinpoint it on or in your body) . . . ?

Do any images come to you (if so, describe every detail you see)—a living room, an office, an old barn, a church sanctuary, a train station, a park . . . ?

Other than any possible aroma of the object itself that you can detect with your physical sense of smell, do you perceive any whiff of extra-sensory fragrance that might once have been prevalent in the object's environment—fresh-cut flowers, incense, aftershave, pipe tobacco, pine, newly mown grass or hay, cologne . . . ?

Can you hear any sounds other than those in your physical vicinity that might be associated with the object—music (if so, identify it if you can), a train whistle, birds, a busy diner, barking dogs, traffic, horses, crickets, a dinner bell . . . ?

Keep describing, out loud, anything and everything that comes to you about that object, without editing yourself or trying to gauge your accuracy—or lack of it—by the reactions of your "witness." Not until you've said all you have to say about your extrasensory perceptions of the object should you let your witness tell you what they know about it so that you can judge how valid your perceptions were. If the answer is "not valid at all," that's okay! There could be any number of reasons for that, ranging from this not happening to be one of your gifts to your conscious mind inadvertently getting involved, and any time your conscious mind gets involved, you can count on nothing but guesswork. If the answer is "valid about some things but not others," that's okay too! Any accuracy is better than none, and you really will get better with continued practice, just as you do with any new skill.

And if nothing came at all, but you enjoyed the experience, keep on trying with other objects and, as a result, keep on challenging your extrasensory potential.

REMOTE VIEWING. Remote viewing allows us to perceive and describe details about a specific location that we're separated from by distance, time, or a physical barrier. It's another exercise you can try to practice with ease, taking as little or as much time as you want. You can do it alone or with another person who's at the location you're planning to view, as long as you have a way to check your accuracy.

For your first few efforts, choose a place that's familiar to you—the living room of a friend, for example, who you're sure will be at home. Take a moment for deep breathing and relaxing your mind so that your conscious mind won't be leaping in with assumptions and filling in blanks instead of letting your "extra senses" take over.

Now, calmly and quietly let your mind travel to the room you've chosen. Start with a wide shot, an easy overview of that space and decor you know so well. Then begin examining the details.

Are the draperies open or closed? If they're open, what do you see through the window or glass doors?

Is the television on or off?

Are the lamps on or off?

Is there anything on the furniture or on the floor that usually isn't there—a coffee cup, a newspaper, a book, a magazine? (If so, can you identify the primary color of the cup, book, or magazine cover?)

Is anyone in the room? Where and how are they sitting? What are they wearing, in general? What are they doing?

Can you hear anything in particular? If you can hear the TV or radio or CD player, or if someone is on the phone, try to distinguish a few words, or something recognizable about the TV show or song.

Is there a particular smell in the room—something cooking

in the nearby kitchen, a vase of flowers, air freshener, a scented candle, a recently used cleaning product?

Keep studying details until you're satisfied that you've formed a clear, precise image for yourself of that particular room at that particular moment, then call your friend and check on your accuracy. If it's less than brilliant at first, don't be discouraged; just keep practicing when your curiosity suggests it or when you just want to do something potentially more interesting than daydreaming when your conscious mind feels like taking a break. This is a skill that absolutely improves with practice, and at your own pace you can start remote-viewing less and less familiar locations, as long as you're sure there's an immediate way to authenticate what you see.

In case you're wondering, it's essential that you not call to validate your perceptions until after you've finished receiving them, to rule out the possibility that you're receiving them *telepathically* . . .

TELEPATHY. Telepathy is the silent, direct, instantaneous transference of information, knowledge, or feelings from one mind to another without the use of the five physical senses. It involves a sender and a receiver, and it's another extrasensory skill you can easily practice with the help of a volunteer who'll stick to the agreement not to give any visual cues at all—no facial expressions, no nodding or head-shaking, no body language of any kind that might in any way guide you toward or away from the information they're passing from their mind to yours.

Even though telepathy can occur over great distances, sometimes involuntarily (as we saw in chapter 5), there's no need for you and your volunteer to be separate when you're first experimenting. The two of you should agree on one subject at a time for your volunteer to send. "I'm thinking of something. What is it?" is a silly, pointless way to begin. Just make sure you choose subjects that involve a wide number of possibilities—a world-famous landmark, a historical figure, a geometric shape, a playing card from a standard deck of cards, for example—but not something as complicated as a sequence of numbers or a jumble of random letters of the alphabet. Your volunteer needs to concentrate as cleanly and clearly as possible on the image they're sending, so it will be helpful for both of you to spend a few moments on deep, regular breathing and relaxing your minds. It will be especially tricky to keep your conscious mind out of these exercises—not to start thinking of all the landmarks or historical figures it can come up with, for example, which will reduce the experience to nothing but a guessing game.

Now, your part of this process involves nothing more nor less than simply receiving and accurately identifying the information being sent to you. As always, take the first information that occurs to you. The longer you take to respond, the more tempted your conscious mind will be to get involved, and your first response is the only one that counts. Your accuracy will be immediately apparent, and you're very likely to improve with practice, so don't get discouraged.

A variation, by the way, is to have your volunteer draw a picture or shape—hiding their drawing motions and the picture itself from you, obviously, so that there's an actual image for you to telepathically receive and describe.

You and your volunteer can also switch roles, so that you're the sender rather than the receiver. There's a school of thought when it comes to telepathy that some of us are gifted as senders while others are gifted receivers. To oversimplify an example, if you find yourself thinking of someone and within a short time you hear from them, you might be a stronger sender, while if you tend to know who's calling before you answer your phone, you're more likely to be a stronger receiver. I'm not at all sure it's important to be categorized as one or the other. What I am sure of is that I agree with the researcher Ingo Swann, whose position was that developing any and all of our extrasensory gifts can "expand the parameters of our perceptions," and what easier, more effortless goal than that can we possibly pursue to enhance our lives and our spiritual awareness?

UNCOVERING YOUR PAST LIVES

I would love for each of you to have the experience of a legitimate past life regression from a legitimate, reputable regressive hypnosis specialist or psychic. Unfortunately, those are few and far between. The opportunities for defrauding clients when it comes to revealing their past lives are virtually limitless. The most obvious involves simply leading them while they're "under," often in such subtle ways that the client may not even detect that it's happening, so that the client learns and pays for exactly nothing reliable about themselves at all. There's also the popular and pathetic device of the hypnotist/ psychic leading the client into the "discovery" that they're the reincarnation of someone famous—Napoleon Bonaparte, Cleopatra, and Benjamin Franklin seem to be big favorites—with, by definition, no way to prove or disprove it. More often than not the client is skeptical, and yet . . . what if it's true? They're not likely to walk out the door disappointed, even though they've just been fed a line of pure fiction. (I can't even guess how many thousands of past life regressions I've done over all these years, and the closest thing to a reincarnated celebrity I've unearthed was a nineteenth-century British economist I'd never heard of.)

The good news is, until and unless you can experience a truly legitimate regressive hypnosis session (and ideally one you can verify after the fact), there's a wonderful meditation you can do that will take you safely back to your own past lives. It's a fascinating journey I hope you'll take the time to try, with just a few simple suggestions before you do.

Ideally, you can find a trusted friend to read this meditation to you. You'll enjoy the experience so much more if you can relax and enjoy it than if you have to keep glancing at these pages to find out what to do next. And a friend can take notes as you go along, since it's not uncommon for you to forget some of what you saw, heard, and felt once you've "come back."

Be patient with yourself while you're getting comfortable with this journey. You may get stuck along the way, or run across a hurdle that for some reason you can't get past. If that happens, relax, and rest assured you'll get past it next time, or the time after that. The more familiar you become with this meditation the less self-conscious and the more confident you'll be, so enjoy the luxury of knowing that there's no hurry, no pressure, and no way to "fail."

You might occasionally find yourself not just remembering a past life event but feeling as if you're reliving it, to the point where it frightens you or causes you pain or sorrow. Should that happen, have the friend who's guiding you through these next pages remain calm and tell you to "go to the observant position" so that you can step back from whatever's upsetting you and be reminded that it all happened a long time ago, and you're simply watching a very, very old home movie.

Last but most definitely not least, you have my word that this exercise is 100 percent safe. You can end it in an instant, whenever you choose, and there's no danger whatsoever of your getting lost "back there" and having trouble finding your way back to the present again.

I want you to sit comfortably, both feet flat on the floor, in a quiet place that's free of distractions. Relax your hands and rest them on your thighs, palms upward.

Close your eyes and imagine yourself surrounded with the white light of God's Holy Spirit, its warmth embracing you and absorbing your cares and burdens into its divine healing power.

It caresses your feet, soothing every muscle . . . the soles . . . the arches . . . the toes, one by one . . . calming . . . releasing tension . . .

The sacred light slowly moves up to the ankles . . . the calves . . . the knees . . . each cell returning to its healthiest, most thriving age . . . blood circulating freely, renewing and restoring . . .

Your breathing slows and deepens . . . more rhythmic, unlabored . . . as peaceful as sleep itself . . . as God's light continues . . .

Through the thighs, the buttocks, the stomach . . . cleansing, nourishing . . . massaging the chest now, and the shoulders . . . total relaxation becoming its own essential force, surging through organs, the lifeline of the spine, inch by inch . . . erasing all pain . . . all negativity . . .

Flowing down the arms, to the wrists and the hands . . . each finger, one by one . . . you feel fluid . . . your breathing deepens even more, every exhale a healing release . . .

Up the neck, warm and soothing, to the face . . . the temples . . . the back of the head . . . unseen hands lingering . . . jaw unclenching . . . mouth relaxing . . .

Eyes still closed, look up at the bridge of your nose and count slowly to twenty . . . only to twenty so you won't fall deeply asleep . . .

Breath slow and rhythmic, eyes closed and relaxed, all tension divinely released from your body . . . I want you to travel back in your mind to the age of twenty . . . a birthday . . . your college dorm . . . a special vacation . . . Christmas . . . any event that stands out . . . If nothing becomes obvious or details are slow to come, gently remind yourself that you were twenty once and, without pressure, remember your life in general back then . . . where you were living, where you worked, who was around you, your favorite song or movie, any detail, large or small, will eventually open like a flower and reveal a whole scene hidden there . . .

Suddenly that scene comes flooding back, as if it's happening at this very moment . . . every color, every smell, every sound and voice . . . look all around you in your mind until it's present and vivid . . . what you're wearing, what you're feeling . . . If it's a happy memory, relive it . . . if it upsets you, simply step back and observe it from your safe distance . . . Stay as long as you want, reliving being twenty again . . . and, while you're there, say to yourself, "Any negativity that I'm carrying from this age, let it be resolved and released into the white light of the Holy Spirit, to the age I am now and throughout my happy, healthy, productive, innovative spiritual life . . ."

When you're ready, and not a moment sooner, move on in your journey to the age of ten . . . another birthday, another Christmas, a classroom, a day at camp, a new friend, any day at all you can easily find your way to . . . If nothing comes, find a bigger picture . . . what grade were you in, where did you live, who was your teacher? Let it come at its own pace until a vivid scene reveals itself . . . Explore it . . . Notice everything . . . Relive a happy scene, only observe the painful . . . Stay as long as you like, and say again, "Any negativity that I'm carrying from this age, let it be resolved and released into the white light of the Holy Spirit, to the age I am now and throughout my happy, healthy, productive, innovative spiritual life . . ."

Now, eyes still closed, mind wide open . . . you're returning to the moment when you were conceived . . . Don't think, just call on your sensory perceptions . . . accept whatever enters your mind . . . maybe nothing but darkness at first . . . quiet and comfortable . . . and let images emerge from it at any pace they choose to reveal themselves . . .

And then, with blissful grace, find yourself traveling through a beautiful, glowing tunnel, calming . . . soothing . . . a time tunnel . . . pages of a calendar wafting past you in a soft, lavender-scented breeze . . . back, back, back, the dates on the calendar pages in descending order . . . as you're happily propelled through the tunnel toward the divine white light ahead of you . . . arriving . . . stepping through its warmth, safe and secure . . .

You're instantly bathed in a glow of royal purple, the color of spirituality . . . Bask in it and feel it penetrate your mind, sharpening your consciousness . . .

A screen appears in front of you, and on it a brightly colored map of the world reveals itself . . . You step to it and say, "Wherever I have validly been before, through the grace of my soul's memory, let my hand be guided to that place on this map." Without thinking, or looking, or interfering at all, let your spirit direct your hand to the map . . . Now look to see where on the map you're pointing and, wherever it is, say with faithful acceptance, "My spirit remembers. My spirit will take me there, to that place, and that time . . ."

In an instant, you're there, in a place and time your soul once called Home. You feel safe, excited and curious, eager to know more, and you start taking in every detail. Look around for a way to see your reflection—a mirror . . . a store window . . . a glass door . . . a pond— and study the person you once were . . .

Are you male or female?

Are you short? Tall? Medium height?

Are you slender? Round? Muscular? Heavy?

What color is your hair? Is it long or short? Thick or thinning? What does your hairline look like as it shapes your face?

What color are your eyes? Are your lips full, or thin? How small or prominent is your nose?

What are you wearing? Every detail . . . not just colors . . . look closely and notice each item of clothing . . . from your shoes or bare feet or sandals or thick boots to your high silk neckline or rough wool military collar or starched shirt and tie . . .

Don't think before you answer. The less you edit yourself, the more easily and honestly your responses will come . . .

How old are you . . . ?

What year is this . . . ?

Where do you live . . . ?

Do you have a family . . . ? Parents? Siblings? A spouse? Children? What are their names . . . ? What are they like . . . ?

Is there anyone around you who's in the life you briefly left to take this journey . . . ? Look through their gender, their physical appearance, your relationship with them . . . Who are they in your present life . . . ?

And now it's five years later . . .

Where are you . . . ?

Do you have a job? What is it? Describe what you do at work . . .

Are you in school? Describe your classroom, and your teacher . . .

Describe where you live . . . Walk to its largest window and describe the view . . .

How do you feel in this place where you live? Are you happy . . . ? Sad . . . ? Fulfilled . . . ? Afraid . . . ?

Remember, answer without thinking . . . Nothing you say is wrong . . .

And now . . .

Take yourself to the moment of your death in that life . . .

Don't be frightened, you're just observing, not experiencing, and you know you survived it, simply relax and watch yourself go Home . . .

How did you die . . . ?

Who was around you, if anyone . . . ?

Who came for you from the Other Side . . . ?

Who was the first person you saw when you emerged from the tunnel . . . ? Do you know that person now . . . ?

Looking back on that life, what was its purpose? What were you there to work on, and what did you learn . . . ?

Accept your first answer . . . don't think . . . how many past lives have you had . . . ? Which of those lives was the one you've just visited . . . ?

Now, peacefully surround yourself again with the cleansing white light of the Holy Spirit, banded by the rich green light of healing . . . a prayer . . .

"May I embrace all the joy and wisdom with which that life blessed me, and may all pain, sorrow, and negativity from that life be released and resolved forever into this divine white light that protects me wherever I go, through the life I'm living now and all lives still to come. Amen."

Feel a peaceful sense of well-being flow throughout your body, mind, and spirit as you instantly, easily return to this life . . . Happy, rested, and refreshed, thank God for your safe journey and this glimpse of your own eternity, and then, smiling, open your eyes . . .

"THE LAB": A SELF-HEALTH
MENTAL EXERCISE

I'm an avid believer in being proactive when it comes to our health. I believe in regular checkups with our physicians, following their orders when we're sick, and taking the best possible care of ourselves between visits. And part of that best possible care is a wonderfully healing and relaxing meditation called "The Lab" that my Spirit Guide Francine gave me many years ago, assuring me that "When you create your own Lab in your mind, we on the Other Side can see it and join you there to help you." It takes as little or as much time as you choose to give it, and even if you only manage to work it into your schedule once a week, I promise you'll benefit from it, if only because it will give you a beautiful time-out from the inevitable stress every one of us goes through as a natural part of life.

If it helps at first to read the following material into a tape recorder and play it back for your first few sessions until you're accustomed to it, it's not a bad idea, and if quiet background music will help relax you even more, by all means, add that too. Remember, this time is *yours*, for *your* benefit, and you deserve to enjoy every minute of it. Other than that, all you need is a private, peaceful space where you can make yourself comfortable. Then just close your eyes, take a few long, deep breaths, and begin:

I want you to visualize a room, a rectangular room of any size you like, as long as it feels perfect to you. Leave the wall that's farthest from you wide open. As for the other three walls, let a soft, calming green wash silently over them until they look smooth and flawless.

In the middle of each wall I want you to add a large arched window, and through each window I want you to have a view of sparkling, serene water—a pond, a hushed, lazy river, a sea that extends to the horizon, whatever whispers to you of both peace and power.

Now, create a table in the center of this quiet green room. Make it large enough for you to lie on, and stay focused on it until it's carved with the most exquisite designs you've ever seen.

One piece at a time, beautifully decorate your room. Add furniture, artwork, candles, flowers, a grand piano if you want, anything and everything that will add to the perfection. The more detailed and personalized your room, the more real it will seem to you and the more you'll look forward to returning to it, so don't hurry. Keep adding and subtracting until you're sure you've never seen a room you've loved more.

Turn to the open wall across from you now, and in its center I want you to suspend a magnificent stained glass window. It's your masterpiece, a breathtaking collage of brilliant blues, golds, greens, and purples, and you marvel over every inch of its design as you create it. In the middle of those impossibly vivid colors, slowly and reverently place any symbol that connects the core of your soul with its divine essence.

One quiet step at a time, walk through the perfect Lab you've created, feeling the thick soft carpet on your bare feet as you appreciate every detail with which you've surrounded and honored yourself.

You stop in front of the stained glass window and watch as a diffused light begins glowing behind it. You feel the warmth as the rainbow of colors beam out at you, one by one, entering deep inside your mind and your body, each ray cleansing your soul.

Royal blue . . . tranquility and heightened awareness . . . filling your heart . . . your spirit . . .

Gold . . . your divine dignity . . . your mind sharpens . . . you know beyond all doubt the uncompromising love of your Creator . . .

Green . . . healing . . . pierces you to your core, empowering you, renewing the strength of your soul . . .

Purple . . . the sovereign color, your birthright as your Creator's child . . . your spirit soars with sacred nourishment . . .

Through the center of the window a pure, brilliant glow pours past *the symbol of your faith and bathes you in the healing white light of the Holy Spirit. Its blessed peace, stability, and power warm the top of your head . . . down to the contours of your face, one by one . . . your neck and shoulders, releasing the stress and tension you carry there . . . down your chest, your spine, each bone, each muscle relieved of every pain and burden . . . your stomach, your abdomen, soothing, cleansing . . . slowly down your legs, so relaxing they feel as if they might melt . . . your ankles, your feet, between your toes, your tired soles painless, cooled, refreshed . . .*

You almost float to the perfect table you gave yourself. The white light of God moves with you, surrounding you, a cloak of pure love flowing around you like silk as you lie down on the table. Its surface is smooth and firm against your back. You're safe. You're protected, and all fear leaves you, resolved in your cloak of light.

You silently ask your most beloved spirits from the Other Side to be with you. They've been waiting, watching, and they're with you in an instant, gathering around you—your Spirit Guide, your Angels, the loved ones you've grieved for and missed so much. With them are great teachers and doctors from Home, brilliant minds there to heal you. Surrounded by such perfect wisdom, perfect comfort, perfect love, you feel your mind relaxing its grip on all burdens, all sadness, all grief, all useless noise, all confusion, all chaos, and your Spirit Helpers lift them from you one by one and release them forever.

Their Hands reach out and wait above your body as you reveal the source of your greatest pain and ask for their healing. You feel the sure, skillful touch of those expert Spirit Hands, hard at work with divine certainty, calming, peaceful, taking away your pain, making you whole again. Every cell of your body lets go of all memories of illness, fear, and trauma. You're restored to the healthiest, most vital moment of your life.

Healed and comforted, while the Hands continue their work, you fall into a deep sleep. A minute, an hour . . . time doesn't matter. You know you'll awake refreshed, unafraid, renewed, and confident that there's nothing you can't handle, because you are God's child, you are blessed, and you can walk confidently into each new day, certain as never before that He'll be by your side no matter what.

You are so loved.

Cherish that joy in your soul as you open your eyes.

THE TOOLS OF PROTECTION

Among the most valuable, and easiest, skills I can share with you are a series of images I call "the Tools of Protection." I like to think of them as invisible but very real suits of armor of our own creation that we can wear wherever we go to dispel darkness and negativity while keeping ourselves cloaked in a perpetual sacred force field.

You can use any of these that appeal to you, or all of them if you like. You can devise your own, for that matter. All that's required is fixing the image firmly in your mind before you head out into the world. Whether that takes you twenty minutes of meditation or two minutes while you're in the shower is completely beside the point. Any amount of time that creates your own Tools of Protection and helps establish the habit of never leaving home without them is exactly the right amount of time to spend.

If you're skeptical that the Tools of Protection can make a difference in your life, by all means try them for a week or two, just to prove me wrong. They won't cost you a dime, and they certainly can't cause you any harm. Nor will they eliminate all the negativity in your path, since overcoming negativity is a big part of the reason we're all here to begin with. What they will do is reduce the amount of emotional and spiritual clutter around you, the irrelevant interference that undermines your self-confidence, tries to pull you off track, and makes every insidious effort to disrupt your connection to your divine birthright, your Father, your Creator, your God.

- THE BUBBLE OF WHITE LIGHT. I want you to keep yourself perpetually surrounded by the divine white light of the Holy Spirit, of course. But the bubble is just added protection in situations that are traditionally or potentially difficult, and it's an image you can create in the blink of an eye, especially if you're familiar with *The Wizard of Oz* and remember Glinda, the Good Witch of the North. She traveled from place to place in a shimmering, transparent bubble. And that's exactly what I want you to do. Simply picture yourself floating inside a glowing bubble made entirely of the white light of the Holy Spirit and enjoy the sacred confidence with which you breeze through even your most stressful moments.

- THE CIRCLE OF MIRRORS. It's an interesting fact about negative energy that it's repelled by its own image, where it can see the ugliness beneath the masks that so often fool those of us who only search for the goodness in our midst. You'll find it very productive to put that fact to use and picture yourself moving through life inside a perfect circle of mirrors, taller than you are and facing away from you. Positive energy will be drawn to you, while negativity will go out of its way to avoid the monstrous reflection that stands between itself and you.

- THE GOLDEN SWORD. Another interesting fact about negativity is that it's cowardly until and unless it perceives that it's found you at a disadvantage. And it wants no part of the Golden Sword you can summon for protection by visualizing it—ornate, sparkling with jewels, and gleaming with perfection—suspended in front of you. Let its hilt form a cross on your forehead (over your brow chakra) and its blade extend down the length of your body like a razor-sharp, impenetrable declaration of your divine, God-given strength.

- GOLD AND SILVER NETS. The image to start with is that

of a delicate version of a fisherman's net, made of spun gold and silver gossamer braided together with the white light of the Holy Spirit. The net is weightless but stronger than steel, and you drape it over yourself for glistening protection from the top of your head to the ground at your feet. As an added, proactive bonus, when any negative entities approach you, you simply drape an identical net over them as well, to contain and neutralize their effect without their ever quite knowing why their proximity to you left them feeling so depleted.

May these and your own sacred Tools of Protection be with you every minute of every day of this lifetime you designed for the growth, wisdom, and added perfection of your soul, more confident with every step you take that you're never alone; that the spirit world and its Angels are a constant, loving, powerful presence around you, offering support and comfort if you'll simply allow them into your heart; and that there will never be a moment when God isn't lighting the path that will lead you safely Home again.

ABOUT THE AUTHOR

SYLVIA BROWNE is the accomplished author of more than fifty books, including twenty-two *New York Times* bestsellers. As a highly acclaimed psychic, Browne consults with police and the FBI to help solve missing persons and other high-profile cases, in addition to her work providing private readings. Browne also founded her own church, the Society of Novus Spiritus, more than twenty years ago. She appeared regularly on the *Montel Williams Show* for seventeen years, is a frequent guest on *The Mike and Juliet Show,* and speaks regularly across North America. Her son Chris Dufresne is also a psychic. Browne and her family live in California.